GREEVES PASSING

A Novel in Fugue

RICHARD HAWLEY

*For Sue,
With all good wishes
&
highest hopes,

Richard Hawley
Autumn, 2015*

Copyright © 2015 by Richard Hawley

ISBN: 978-0-9882497-5-2
Library of Congress Control Number: 2015937913

Printed in the United States of America

Publisher: Short Story America Press
Design: Soundview Design Studio

All rights reserved. No part of this book may be transmitted in any form or by any means, electronic or mechanical, including photocopying, recording, or by any information storage or retrieval system, in part, in any form, without the permission of the publisher.

Requests for such permissions should be addressed to:

Short Story America
221 Johnson Landing Road
Beaufort, SC 29907
Visit us online at www.shortstoryamerica.com

FOREWORD

HILMA WOLITZER

I first encountered John Greeve three decades ago in *The Headmaster's Papers*, a haunting debut novel composed almost entirely of letters to members of Greeves school's staff, to his friends, his family, and the families of the boys in his charge. What Richard Hawley managed to reveal in that seemingly limiting form was nothing less than the rich, eventful trajectory of a life. John Greeve is above all a truly good man, made memorably real as much by his admitted flaws and failures as by his essential decency. I've thought about him often over the years, as you do about a friend you miss and who still influences the way you think and act long after you've lost touch.

Now here he is again, to this reader's delight, in what Hawley refers to as "a novel in fugue." That musical reference is perfect for the polyphony of voices in *Greeves Passing*. John still leads the chorus with his resonant words—in letters, a handful of modest poems, stirring remarks to the school body, and his Last Will and Testament. But his wife Meg and their son Brian, inveterate journal keepers, soon enter in written counterpoint, expanding on and illuminating the family drama. Meg, who is seriously ill, writes faithfully in her "little book," and Brian, gone missing in the process of finding himself, does the same in his diary. Like his father, he tries his hand at creative writing, too. Both mother and son record intensely private memories and thoughts they're unable to share more directly with anyone else.

John yearns toward each of them with love and a sense of dread, while attending to the demands of his role as headmaster—coping with recalcitrant students, litigious parents, and the increasingly worried administrators of the Wells School. This is a place, in John's view, that doesn't preclude fun, but is, more urgently—like family and religious practice—the training ground for a moral life. It isn't surprising to learn that Richard Hawley, like his fictional hero, has been the headmaster of a school for boys. There is a verisimilitude in his depiction of the functions and politics of that kind of institution. But Hawley knows even more about the inner and outer selves of boys during their exuberant, treacherous passage toward manhood.

Greeves Passing is filled with narrative and emotional suspense. Hawley satisfies one of the first rules of good fiction by eliciting the reader's desire for a particular outcome. In this case, one wishes for relief from what feels like impending doom and, against all odds, for the joys of reunion and reconciliation. But even God, in whom John Greeve believes, despite declining to seek divine consolation, doesn't always provide happy endings. And every serious writer is committed to the intrinsic truths of his story and the people who inhabit it. These characters are clearly cherished—will they be spared what seems like their inevitable dark fate? Things can go either way, but the reader's desire remains undiminished throughout.

In our digital age, emoticons are often substituted for emotions. Texts and emails may be expedient, but they simply can't replace the many pleasures of real letters—their literal and metaphorical unfolding, the personality of someone's handwriting, the miniature beauty of postage stamps. Even my postman regrets the reduction of his old burden. Lord Byron noted that "Letter writing is the only device for combining solitude with good company." The same could be said about reading an epistolary novel as expressive and vibrant as this one.

For Tony Jarvis, again

*Margaret, are you grieving
Over Goldengrove unleaving*

– Gerard Manley Hopkins

John:

        Wells, Connecticut
        27 August

Mr. Hugh Greeve
Pembroke House
St. Edward's School
Framingham, Massachusetts

Dear Hugh,

I arrived home from the Cape in the dead of night, and it wasn't until this morning that I found your wonderful letter.

Of course you flatter your old—well, seasoned—uncle by deferring so graciously to his years of experience, as if, in school life, that added up to something reliable. I am not always sure that is so. Every day of school, at least once, I am aware that what I am doing is completely new, baffling, and that I am empowered with no special skill or insight or strength to deal with it. Remember this admission some time when your own headmaster seems hopelessly pompous or officious. All of us are really, at the nub, timid and desperate, new boys at school, compensating.

But quite frankly, I am flattered that you wrote me. Mainly, however, I am excited about the prospect of your appointment at St. Edward's. For what my opinion is worth, I think the school is just right—small and humane and standing for something. From what I've been able to see of him, Ted Phillips looks like a promising headmaster to work for. He's so young and earnest he terrifies me. You could do worse than to begin with a young and growing school. But I hope as you become grand and important there you see to it that the school doesn't get too big. The limit should be the size at which easy personal acquaintance of everybody in the school is still possible. When a school grows beyond this point, it no longer has a coherent personality, but instead becomes a complex of factions. One experiences big schools as "institutions" and behaves towards them with less than his best intimacy. I think old Endicott Peabody who founded Groton had it right when he said a school should maintain itself as a family (he kept Groton under two hundred boys). But now Groton has gotten bigger than that, and so, I'm afraid, has my shop, although I curse that economically sensible development. A digression—pardon.

Your load is of course overwhelming, but that's as it should be your first year. All of it—the dormitory, the soccer, and the classroom preparation—is essential for getting school life into your bones. This way you will know by the end of a year or two whether School is for you. You will see as the year wears on—often to your horror—that it is futile to try to divide your inner "personal" time from school time. It won't work. The harder you try, the more you will see your (limitless) school duties as an infringement on your "real life." Now everybody feels this strain sometimes, to some extent, but my advice is to give in to school life—plunge in and ride the currents, then climb out for refreshment during vacations. (No one has vacations like school people; we may be broke, but we are granted heavenly stretches of idleness.) The most empty I have ever felt in my schoolmastering days is when I felt I was holding back, saving myself for something. Someday I will tell you about my closet-poet period.

I wish I had some useful insider's tips on starting out, but I'm not sure I do. Something inside is urging me to say "keep out of faculty intrigues," but I know that is impossible. Schools very shortly become close, at times suffocatingly so, but that's part of their value. I think human communities were made to be as intense as school communities actually are. I don't think the culture at large is suffering from too much community but from far too little. In schools we do have to live and work with each other intensely. If we are liars, we live through the consequences of our lies. If we are loafers, we experience the reactions of whoever picks up the slack. Everything marvelous and everything petty about each member soul comes through in a small residential community. The result is often terrifying, and for this reason, especially in the affluent and empty now, the "outside world" often seems a beckoning escape for school people. But you can hardly be interested in escaping, having just volunteered.

Those St. Edward's boys are lucky to be squaring off opposite you. Young faculty are always, in the adolescent mind, bridges to adulthood. Even dreadful young teachers, in whose number I would never include you, serve as plausible models of attainable adulthood, while settled and middle aged types, no matter how effective, are no help in this regard. Physical youthfulness, apprehension, doubt, impulsiveness—qualities young teachers try so hard to suppress—are wonderfully sympathetic to adolescents. They relate easily to disorder, desperate effort and posing—these things are, you might say, their life.

How I ramble. What I really have to say is that the prospect of your first year at St. Edward's and your letter to me make me very happy. Although continually humbling, teaching is a wonderful calling. No matter how badly any aspect of it goes, you will never doubt the worthiness of the task. It will always be noble to pass on the best of what we know. Perhaps we two might even combine to convince your skeptical father of this before too long. I wonder, really, if my brother didn't throw up those barriers to taking the St. Ed's job just to test your commitment—I wouldn't put it past him. Fathers and sons seem to have a way of confounding each other, don't they? My own most painful doubts and second guesses revolve around the way I modeled work and adulthood for Brian—apparently quite unattractively. The last we heard he is still living the beach life in Portugal and Spain. Meg and I both pray that he either finds or doesn't find himself soon. We miss him.

Meg of course joins me in sending her love and best wishes. She would add a few lines herself, but she is staying on the Cape to get over some coldy aches and pains and to check out the latest of her wonder doctors in Falmouth. So in the rather dusty solitude of my study, I will now get on to cranking out the tidal wave of memos and agendas which will set our own school year in motion.

I'll have to admit I am looking forward to taking it all on again—all that life!

Love from both of us,

Uncle John

Meg:

Little House

I don't know.

And that's the truth, little book. Here you are, your gorgeous marbly covers spread wide like some ripe and ready girl, all your creamy white pages spilling out to me waiting for—what? For me to scratch and ink you into fullness, to finish you, to make you heavy with old Meg Greeve. Like all your book-y sisters, quiet but maybe not dead on their dedicated shelves. In the end you will be me. All the me there was.

Gloomy greeting to a sweet-smelling new Little Book. What are you—109? I've just checked. You are. Hello! Welcome, 109. Forgive my scribbling you up.

Inventory. Late August, still at Little House, East Sandwich. John's packed up and left the Cape to stoke up Wells into a school year. So sad for me, but all right. Blessed lovey, he wants me to have this sun-blanched quiet time. He knows the train's pulling away, chugging and puffing toward June and prize days and commencement on the commons. No stops on that train for the craggy old engineer.

He did and didn't want to leave me here. He knew I'd love the time and the sweet quiet, but he was rattled by Dr. Karipides' report. "Tests" to be done. *Tests!* How artlessly forbidding can medicine get? "Blood work." *Work?* What a way to talk about blood. I am pretty sure John is terrified. Poor baby has seen too much to believe people always get past their nasty bugs and fevers and lumps and sweats. Dangerous quality in a headmaster. Better to be an idiot optimist, hale-fellowing through everything, all smiles and granite handshakes, dumb as a post, strong as an ox.

Old Meg's not strong as an ox today. She's maybe strong as a gerbil. Funny, annoying way to wake up to the world: a weight, like grainy liquid behind my eyes, strange sour mouth, dodgy cramped lowers. Stomach shut tight, no appetite. I get up, shuffle around, bathe and brush, and—no forward motion. The sun makes ripply white and yellow fire on the cove, and I can just hear the seaside flaps and bangs beyond the screens, but all that light is too oppressive and strong for me today (again!), and I move leadenly in the direction of a chair. No fever this a.m., 100 degrees when I went to bed. Just *proceed*, leadenness, proceed, proceed. Make your point, get on with it. Nothing hurts. Everything works. So why don't the wheels go when I clunk her into gear? "I'm concerned," says handsome and unleaden Dr. Karipides under his fascinating skull-wide black brow. And tests to boot. Indignities in every orifice, in the tender crook of my arm, hot punctures and those horrible little plastic boxes of blood, clipped together like children's toys, each darkly and sickeningly full of me, for the tests. How much more healing if the angular and unibrowed Dr. Karipides had placed his great brown hands on my shoulders and said: Mrs. Greeve, I find you the most fascinating woman I have ever examined. Forgive me for falling in love with you. But no. Blood work.

Back again. Some tea and tuna fish toast are now sitting meaninglessly within. What a curious thing to have no appetite. An affront to living. Appetite drives the whole green world, and here is the solitary and ever bonier and beakier Meg G. sitting *indoors*, a peculiar figure, should anyone peer through the screens. But apparently appetite is unnecessary to percolate my tiny neurons into thoughts, words, memories. Scratch, scratch, scratch.

Bad moment at the mirror. No light on, so the murk spared me the usual outrage at alien puffs and creases and pallor. But the hair! John's beloved girlish bob gone straight as a string. What's happened to the reliable seaside air? Why is my hair hanging close to my temples like straw? Not like straw, like dead hair. Come on, hair, be a good feature again. The woman in the mirror looked like one of those TV puppet creations—bloopers? puppettes? No—Muppets. A bird with a comical beak wearing a wig of dead straight hair, bangs down to the glasses. Maybe it's the glasses. Surely when I remember to take them off I will be alluring again, and Dr. Karipides' "concern" will dissolve into the first glimmer of desire.

Two weeks past 55, no need to be an old bird. Contemporaries of mine are still movie stars (in careful lighting) and make exercise videos in spandex.

Two weeks past 55, a bespectacled Muppet with bad lady's hair, not blood but something like dirty dishwater slopping through her system, I am still in my true heart a girl. A girl, Dr. Karipides, not a concern.

The trick is to locate the girl. And today I find her in Maine, on the point of sun-baked boulders at the tip of Blue Hill. The little dirt path behind the boat house through the pines is almost grown over with blueberries and poison ivy, and only Siri and I with a giddy knowing disguised as foolishness dare this path, and we emerge into a thrilling wash of loud white sunlight on the rock heaps. The water is stingingly, numbingly icy and so clear the pebbly sea bottom is all honey and emerald. There is every way to hide from view among these radiant rocks. From? From Stinky and Freddy, the crusty old lobstermen who set their pots along the shallows? From the low sleek hulls of yachts small as toys on the horizon? From the planing gulls? No, I welcomed the gulls, the gulls, and the pressing sun on my cheeks and belly and thighs. We browned and browned ourselves, in a week the color of honey, in two, chocolate. And some secret, blood-loving quality of northeast sunshine always brought up reds and peach through the leathery brown. There is no complexion more affirmingly healthy. Skin glowing that way would disengage the reflex, even in my mother, to say don't overdo it, dear. The point was to overdo it, to offer my body like prayer to the radiance. To say yes and yes and yes in chorus with the gulls. When we baked so long our beaded bellies were hot to the palm, we would inch, daring ourselves, off the rocks into water so cold that for an instant it blocked all sensation, then, whether at ankle or thigh or hip, it left a delicious ache that made us squeal in amazement at the possibility of such cold. Back on the hot stone, my skin would tingle electrically for shivering minutes as breezes skidded over goosebumps and the water pooled cold and clean on the umber of my belly.

Oh girl! And your sweet, flat, perfect, untried belly. Yes, and now it is clear (again) why I return to my girl bathing on the rocks. No accident, I suppose, that the stalled and unstirrable old Muppet lady locates the girl in her first ecstatic stirring. The good sweet rush of it, neither itch nor burn, but like them, beginning in the depths of my belly, or in a breeze across my midriff, anywhere really, then connecting all my parts, lips, breasts, palms, the tips of my toes, wherever sun met skin. I stretch, I arch, I arch my girl's hips to meet the unseen sun. Then all of it is drawn together deep inside, and I can feel the glowing mass of it in my sex. There were no words for it. How I wanted to move with it, to touch it, stroke it, hold it.

Siri, bless her heart, felt everything. In memory—could it have been true?—we were one flesh. I was certain her skin felt what my skin felt. She was bigger, blonder. The more of her was extra me. We came to the rocks knowing the same thing, for the same unstated, rapt communion. This was, if there were words, why we were so deliciously hiding. It was too bright, too sacred for the family dock or for boats. My eyes were sealed shut against the sun when Siri said, Meg, have you ever stripped? *Stripped.* Bless you, bless you, Siri, for that wrong right word. The dangerous, vulgar word was supposed to be about alluring others to forbidden feeling. Stripper. Striptease. Strip poker. We knew—I knew it was about releasing a personal secret. Strip. It was about returning to something overwhelmingly prior and rich, a green bright world where I had been naked forever. We laughed. Looked at each other wide-eyed, laughed and laughed. I propped myself up on my elbows and scanned the rim of the sea and the far shore. Only white tips of sail on the horizon. When I turned back to Siri, she had unhooked her top and it fell to her lap. Her smile was a surrender. The soft little buds of her breasts were milky white in the sunlight. She threw her head back and hummed up into the sun. Bless her. What a simple perfect pleasure: to strip. I pulled my own top over my head and lay back in wonder. Now the clothed world, the racket of our cottage, the crunch of doors closing, the clink and tinkling of the boats' rigging down the dock were banished from memory. This is it, this is me, this is all I want. I glanced back at Siri and saw, as I knew I would, that she had peeled out of her suit bottom. Her thighs from my angle of view now seemed strangely full, and the sun made delicate threads of fire among the pale hairs over her mound. Again I thank you, Siri. I squeezed my suit bottom down over me feet, lay back, and made angel arcs with my arms and legs. Then I lay still and let the bright day in.

I suppose it was sex. But sex seems to me always involved with the other. Siri and I, summer friends, were only extended selves. We tickled and touched, held each other's faces in our hands, played looking into each other's eyes to see who would break into laughter first. It was important in our charged and thrilling nakedness to look only into her eyes. Everything beyond the fixed shaft of our dumb mutual staring was pulsing with sun and promise. The whole crisp sea-washed world had stripped. Once, not that day but that summer, the pulsing was too much for me, and I edged off the roasting rock into the stunning freeze of the water, crouched so my belly and bottom were submerged. Stealthily, I touched myself and worked to bring the tickle to flower. The water was so cold it felt like toothache along my boney shins. The impulse to sex under ice water—the story of my life? God forbid. Sneaked a look back at Siri who, troubled by no such modesty, lay splayed open to her strumming fingers. Her eyes were squeezed shut in a terrific grimace, and as she raised her round bottom from the rock, I erupted with pleasure, sharp as a knife in the scalding cold, where pleasure meets pain. Neither of us felt we had to explain. The perfect summer friend.

Greeves Passing

This, Little Book, is how I began to feel all right about the ultimate, or if not all right, too much in its thrall to be bothered by recriminations. Always have been. Still am—or would be, if this curse of leadenness would lift. What's it been now, weeks? No, months, really. Since May. Oh dear, Meg. No wonder you fly back to Maine.

May I fly back again. Maine is the beginning of goodness, the beginning of deep knowing. I wanted a Maine for Brian. *Brian!* Where are you? Come home, come, come, come home. Little House, the boat, the Cape, the iron boundary around these summer weeks—this was supposed to be Brian's Maine. Maddening cipher, beloved boy, I hope you had a secret Maine that would take your mother's breath away. Or is that what you're up to, looking for your own sort of Maine? I suppose. I suppose that's what we all do. Why Portugal? Why a Maine beyond my dim imagining? Why is this love of mine, this wide open, oceanic, *ask nothing* love of mine so resistible to you, boy? How can love repel? Am I kidding myself? Is it just need? I know neediness repels. But I would promise not to need, only to love, only to know. Surely it's a mother's right to behold the son from time to time. *Ecce puer.* Brian, you are so cunning, so subtle. You know what breaks your mother's heart. And your father's. Is that what you need? To break his heart and win? Are you perhaps breaking mine inadvertently, in addition? Why break hearts? Why flee? Why win?

See how I go from Maine to misery—or is it from misery to Maine to misery, which is essentially from misery to misery. Is that the story of my life, or perhaps a preview? Should be kind to little book and put away my pen. Supper time—hah!—in Little House, and what has Mrs. Greeve achieved on this lovely, blowy August day? She saw patches of cerulean blue beyond the screens and cumulus clouds billow into majestic and no doubt portentous shapes. She saw the pines shiver and the maples sway. She eyed grossbeaks at the feeder, and they eyed the gross beak inside. She grew objective. She remembered the erotic but could not feel it. She grieved for her little Greeve, her little grief. God—stop it. Scratch, scratch, scratch. Now on to non-supper. Still no temperature.

Brian:

San Rafael, Portugal

Dear Diary. Here we go again. I've never been able to keep this up even though I must have started a dozen times in school and college. It's weird that I want to. Is it a good thing or a sick thing to want there to be a record? I'm not sure if this is real writing or playing around. I sit down to do it with a little extra tension. I can feel myself resisting, even being kind of afraid of it. I was very fussy about the process. I spent a lot of time "preparing"—poking around the stationers for just the right kind of writing book. The one I liked turns out to be a business ledger. If I knew anything about business, I probably would have figured out that all those grid lines had to be there for a reason. But the cover is terrific. It's stiff, textured black leather with smooth red leather around the corners and down the spine, and it weighs a ton. The clerk at the San Rafael stationers gave me a suspicious look as he took my escudos. What does this scraggly Yank from the beach want with an account book? The working people of San Rafael don't seem to be crazy about Americans, at least American kids.

Come to think of it, they may not see me as a kid. I'm twenty-three. I doubt that they think of their own twenty-three-year-olds as kids. Insight: I think of myself as a kid. Maybe that's an American thing. Insight: The working people of San Rafael don't resent me because I'm an American, they resent me because I don't do any work.

I'm uncomfortable. The idea of sitting on the beach of a Portuguese fishing village and "writing" is very appealing. The reality is pretty lame. I've never been able to do anything in the sun, not even read. It always kind of clouts me in the eyes whenever I look up. And though it sounds strange to say it, it's noisy on the beach, and I'm talking about an empty beach. The surf comes sloshing and hissing in an irregular rhythm you don't get used to, and today there is a steady damp wind coming from off shore. It actually has a sound, somewhere between a shushing noise and a hum, and every now and then there is a thumping, as if someone is shaking out heavy blankets.

It is uncomfortable sitting on the windy beach of San Rafael, squinting against the bright haze and writing in your fifty pound ledger. Even though I took off my shirt and wedged it behind me, the granite slab I'm leaning on is gouging into my back, and my butt now feels like two boney knives trying to get through my skin into the sand.

So what is this all about, this bitching into the new diary? Is it about San Rafael? About my vagabond life? About "writing?" None of those things. It's about the letter and money order I got from Dad this morning, general delivery. It's about how I almost couldn't stand to open it, about how, when I did and started reading, I was so tense I was sweating. There was nothing unfriendly in the letter. He's becoming completely hands-off. There was a little about his and mum's summer stuff at the Cape, the news that cousin Hugh is going to teach at a prep school. Trying not to sound firm or demanding, he asked me to make contact, just so they would know if I'm ok. The money order was for $200. The last one, in Avignon, was for $300. I probably missed some. Maybe I'm falling in dad's esteem. He would hate it if he thought I believed that—he would hate it if *he* believed that. I doubt my mother and father are mad. That's not the style. The style is to wonder and to speculate and to worry. Can they be good parents if I'm a bad son? If they're not good parents, are they good people? John and Margaret Greeve must, above all things, be good people.

How to be good to Brian? A difficult boy. Good, loving, modern parents know they cannot *control* a twenty-three-year-old son. A boy has to find himself. That's Dad's life theme. He's built his school on it. He says it in chapel. So in my case, the job is obviously not to lose touch altogether, maybe toss a little cash sweetener in from time to time. That says: I'm still your parent, and I'm being pretty terrific and unselfish about your weirdness, but feel free to do whatever you want.

Feel free. Guess how free I feel. I get the equivalent of a fever even opening an envelope with my father's initials on the envelope. I would get that fever whether I was living in Hartford or San Rafael or Mars.

I'm working on my freedom, though. The $200 helps a little. That leaves me $1600, not counting the $600 I am setting aside for if and when I ever chicken out and decide to go home, $2200 total. Living like this, that's a pretty long time. Maybe I'll get to freedom.

I am not going to write back, which makes for guilt, which makes for an actual loss of freedom. But in the long run I'm going to break out of this. Sorry, Dad, but only a little sorry. I wish he didn't know I was here—probably the card I sent to Hugh.

Now I have to see if my knees and butt still work. Not a very inspiring first day, diary.

Just remembered—my *first* diary came from Woolworth's when I was about eleven. It was dark green leather, actually leather-looking plastic over cardboard, about the size of a paperback, and it had a little key. I bought it with my own money and I was very serious about it. I walked into my room and saw Mom sitting on my bed and reading my diary. It was an electric shock. I had just been writing about the daughter of one of the dorm masters. She was older than me and her name was Jeanette.

I remember that there was a page in the diary where I had written, "I think I'm starting to love Jeanette"—and other things to do with "love." Mom was not at all embarrassed or guilty about reading the diary. She may really have thought I had no secrets. If anything, she seemed overjoyed to see me. "This is so sweet,

Brian," she said, "and you're such a good writer!" I was so tense I couldn't say a word.

That was it for that diary. Better luck this time. Time to fold up the ledger and pull my ass out of the sand.

John:

29 August

Mrs. Margaret Greeve
Little House
Ticonsett Lane
East Sandwich, Massachusetts

Dear Meg,

I called periodically yesterday, but you were out, so I'll write this note in the interest of adding something besides seed catalogs to your waning summer mail.

Arrived late Tuesday p.m. to find the empty house just as bleak and indifferent as I expected. I would like to know what generates dust in a tightly closed-up house. The grounds crew may have cut our lawn once or twice, certainly not recently, and despite our pleas, the flower beds have, I am afraid, been ignored. Arnold tells me the crew has been preoccupied with a water-main break under the athletic fields. Whether or not related to this, our tap water is now the color of tea. It's been raining in sheets all day, and there is a pervasive sense of Wuthering Heights about the place—that is, of Wuthering Heights if Heathcliffe had let it to Mr. Chips.

I trust you are well, free of aches and full energy restored. Was that Greek-sounding physician everything you had hoped? Was he expensive—speaking of which: before you close up, could you try a hand at getting some sort of estimate from Jenkins about what the yard costs are going to be for the boat? Brother Frank, being steeped in wealth, doesn't seem to mind paying staggering sums—in fact, seems somehow honored by it, as if they, like yachting itself, were part of being included among

Greeves Passing

the truly established. Anyway, please try with Jenkins. I know I could never do it. One has to admire Jenkins' control.

Rest up. I envy your being there. There is too much going on here for my taste. I finally—and luckily—got a replacement for Frankel in math, a nice woman named Florence something who has gone back to school to awaken her dormant college math major. She is awfully eager and a fast, nervous talker. I hope the boys don't annihilate her. For my part, I am waiting like a crouched panther for Frankel or for some future Frankel employer to ask me for a letter of recommendation.

The faculty look refreshed, and I'll have to say it, the boys already here for practices look great. Part of it is normal back-to-school-optimism, but part of it is the style of the day. It seems OK now to wear clean clothes and hair looks less ratty. It is so obvious that the way one turns oneself out bears directly on how one speaks and behaves—how could we have been so dense and timid over the years? (The curmudgeon raises his scaly head...)

I wish the transition were not so direct, but I am afraid there has been nothing from Brian, here or at school. It's maddening not to be able to get in touch—even to be mad at him, even to send him money! Maybe I am not acknowledging my repressed envy of his approach to life. I suppose he has committed himself to systematic truancy as completely as I have committed myself to school. But he is not subtle enough. I too am a closet truant. I too long for the beach. The difference is that I want to play for the other side, too. I crave the release of flight and leisure, but, just a little more, I want to know what everybody else is doing and to be in on it up to my ears. Which, like it or not, I am. New faculty arrive for "tea" (I have already opted in favor of beer and wine) in a half hour.

Adios, love. Longing to speed to the airport when you give the word.

J.

Meg:

Little House

Grey and soupy day, both outside and in. I was 99.5 degrees this a.m., if I read the new thermometer right. Not a very impressive temperature, but sufficient to describe this head-full of-soot feeling. Amazing. I find myself longing to erupt into some spectacular symptoms. Perfect phrase: under the weather. I am under the weather as a potato bug is under a damp log. I am shunning the mirror for the time being, because I don't want to look at a potato bug. Thought I might renew my resolve to flush out the lead with preposterous doses of water and fruit juice. So far this has only resulted in leadenness with constant peeing. Being "proactive" — horrible neologism—doesn't show me much. Bugger off, malaise.

Letter from John left me sad. No word from Brian. I could sense John not wanting to tell me this. Departed children. No ache, no clasping void like this. Why are we made to hurt like this when, in some more or less socially acceptable way, children leave us. Why do we have them? To have them and lose them. God, teach me why having implies losing. Must everything negate? Why negate one's own body food, a baby, a boy, my Brian, my Brian. John's not wanting me to feel this only succeeds in dissolving me. I know he is sick with it, numb with it. He tries to absent himself, to isolate the Brian hurt as one kind of hurt among the world's knowable hurts. Poor dear wants to figure it out. He doesn't know, doesn't want to know that this loss is pre-word, pre-name. Only a man would cry out Absalom, Absalom. A woman just cries, cries in. Having implies losing. Know this, you apple-cheeked, sun-bleached beauties toting your sausage-limbed treasures through the East Sandwich general store. They detach, they go away.

John talks of opening up, de-musting the house, the bright cycle of pre-season workouts and cook-outs and orientations. I can somehow hear the clamor, the thud of cleats on the hard summer turf. Who is it, the coaches, who turned the impulse to play into such ferocious work? Who knows, to them it may be play. Even picturing it makes me so tired. Poor John, I think it makes him tired, too, but he can't possibly acknowledge such a thing. He's a headmaster. He is obliged to see and feel that it all matters. The big game must be big. Maybe it is big, and I am too diminished to see it. That's what's wrong with me, little book, no big game on my schedule. Just tests.

John misses me. He's never quite right when he's by himself. But he's right to be there, me here. He may crash around a bit, fidget around the house, but in the office he'll be blessedly, savingly on task. He will phone and scribble, meet and plan. People will present wonderful and vexing knots for him to untie. Until he's home again, with his drink in his study, he'll be fine. Poor John, sweet love, sweet lover.

If I weren't an ailing, pallid old coot behind the screens, I would get out on the dock and empty the dinghy of last night's rain, paddle out to the Valmar and pump out her bilge, so that Frank and Valerie will know we've done Our Part when they come up this weekend to cruise. Fact is the very thought of padding down the hill to the dock and trying to turn the nine-ton dory on its side makes me shuffle toward the bed. For one thing that's no kind of dinghy to have. Why couldn't we have one of those weightless little white ones with the optional sailing gear for the putative grandchildren? Frank, however, insisted on a hulk of a craft rivaling the Valmar itself for size and heaviness. Possibly he was motivated by boyhood visions of himself in *Captains Courageous*. The dory in fairness would be a good vessel from which to harpoon blue whales, but as a dinghy to ferry us (ferry to dinghy us?) fifty yards between mooring and dock it is a mistaken choice. Nobody is comfortable plying its great oaken oars. Personally, I get almost no purchase on the water line when, even seated on a cushion, the oar handles meet me at the level of my forehead. Under the legitimate cover of ill health, I will let the dory become a bathtub of rainwater. Perhaps all of the horrible pincher bugs will abandon ship. Over to you, Frank.

Afternoon, a long one. The day refuses to improve. Maybe a little fire will roast away the damp. Later. Tea, toast, and jam, which I thought might make a needed break from tinned tuna poached in water. Didn't do the trick, although perhaps not the jam's fault. So, so strange to will a mouthful of food along its dry descent. I must return to broth. Good old salty broth still seems to belong in my mouth.

Some nice busy Handel things on the little black Sony will liven things up a bit. Why does music sound so good in this cottage and so muted and ordinary on our sleek and reputedly excellent stereo in the school house? Also, how can such a pure and finely differentiated sound come from the three little tiers of this Sony? John says it cost about a hundred dollars. It plays discs, it plays our old cassettes, it makes a radio, and its mysterious little ruby light is always on. In the dark it's like an ancient eye, and I feel in those hours that the Sony knows me.

A perfect afternoon you would think (*do* you think, little book? If so, for god's sake, speak up!) for an x-word puzzle, but once again the *NY Times* lets me down. The only undone puzzles are Tuesday's and Sunday's which I'm saving for the unbearable, semi-naked intervals between Dr. K's tests. Even with plodding deliberation and exquisite penmanship, today's puzzle went down in fifteen minutes. I am saddened anew remembering the gifted, purer puzzlers of yore. Those were the days, when a puzzle was a puzzle. Now airplane magazine puzzles are cleverer. And who needs all the brand names and pop group references? What's wrong with freezing topical awareness at the point where the name of FDR's dog and "Only a Paper____" come ready to a puzzlist's lips? So sad to have to pen in (again) "Pop singer John—always Elton. I wouldn't mind so much if I hadn't seen Elton John once on some kind of television celebration. Very disturbing—a kind of sad and beefy accountant, uncomfortable at the piano bench, wearing peculiar glasses with lenses framed in heart-shaped plastic. Very, very off-putting. I believe there is something deeply wrong with pop singer John. But worse, today's clue, "Lexicographer's bane," yielded "neologism." Why? Why would a neologism be a lexicographer's bane? If I were a lexicographer, a neologism would be my delight, my lexographic reason for being. I suppose I could write a letter to Mr. Shortz at the *Times*, since, after just fifteen minutes, I have plenty of time, but I am sure his desk is spilling over with such letters. As Flower the skunk said to Bambi (or was it, I think, to Thumper), if you don't have anything nice to say, don't say anything at all. Good advice, little book, but if I took it, then where would you and I be? Maybe both of us still virgins.

Darkness coming and, if I can stir, a fire. So long, b. You know I love you.

Brian:

San Rafael, Portugal

We drink too much wine. This is probably because it's the only thing we can afford a lot of. It costs three times as much to buy Cokes, and twice as much to get that horrible orange powder that Deirdre mixes with water to serve with meals. But extreme cheapness is not the only reason we drink too much wine. Insight: we drink wine because it structures time whenever we're clueless about what to do, which is quite a bit of the time.

Sitting for two hours with coffee or wine in a café feels like something, like a nameable part of the day, and you can get the illusion of doing something vaguely social when you're sitting around with wine, filling and refilling the glasses, learning how to shape the little buzz you get, how to keep the tart, grapey coating on your tongue from making you feel too acidic. You sip a little, throw something minor into the conversation. The sipping and monitoring the buzz make you less desperate to talk. You don't feel you have to fill in all the silences. Which is fine, but it leads to drinking too much wine. When you get up in the morning and start thinking about filling the day, it's the thing you remember you know you can do.

A big problem is that Ryan and Deirdre and I don't have too much new to tell each other. We've been together four months now, since Amsterdam, and there don't seem to be many secrets or surprises left. But it's still a pretty good arrangement. Senor Carrera lets us have this little house (well, shack) for amazingly little, and shared three ways, we could probably live here for over a year. The can is a little crude and we have to ask Senor Carrera to use the shower in the house, but basically we're in good shape. We're practically on the beach, we can see the ocean, and there's a room for Deirdre to set up her chalks and paints.

We spent a lot of time talking about how weird it could be being a threesome. Triangles are supposed to be unstable, but we're doing OK. My position is evolving into the permanent brother, and they're the couple, the lovers. The lovers part seems to be flattening out the longer we're together. They're still making it, but unless they've learned to be amazingly quiet, they're making it a lot less often. There are also a lot fewer of those moody fights they used to have. Maybe we're moving closer to two brothers and a sister arrangement. Being an only child, I'm not sure I'd know if we had it.

I still like Ryan and Deirdre. They were nice to me from the first time I met them in a beery rock club in Amsterdam. Even though they were fairly new together and just getting it on, they were already homesick, and I helped. I think they felt they were adopting me, which after about six just about solo weeks was fine with me. Except to get a little irritated now and then, we've done pretty well together. Deirdre's pretty nice to me and very affectionate, without being a tease. We can horse around a little, and I can put my arm around her when we're walking or sitting in a film, and she gives me unexpected, very nice kisses sometimes before she goes to bed or sometimes just out of the blue, like when we're washing up after a meal. I've been pretty careful about not putting on any moves myself, and this has been good, because Ryan doesn't seem to be uptight at all about Deidre and me. I think he's pretty alert though.

In a way living in such close quarters de-sexes things a little. You kind of build up a protective screen hearing Deirdre and Ryan in bed, catching glimpses of Deirdre undressed or half undressed, aware that when she comes back after a shower, she isn't wearing underwear, because she's washing it. I think I actually notice more details about Deirdre's looks and her little habits than I did when I first met them, but I'm less likely to get turned on than I was then. Maybe pretty soon I'll be oblivious to the fact that she's a woman. She'll turn into a sister completely.

I used to be more on the lookout for other girls. That was the original plan—that I'd find somebody like Deirdre and we'd be a foursome. But the two girls I spent any time with since Amsterdam were both disasters. The last one, Sissy, who told me two different last names, actually robbed us in Lisbon. She took Deirdre's best earrings and her watch. Ryan and Deirdre were tremendously pissed off about that, and some of that feeling, rational or not, got passed on to me for a while.

You get into a bad syndrome being girl-less. You get worked up and kind of hyper-interested in women (even more hyper if you're concentrating on behaving yourself with Deirdre), and then maybe you move too fast when anybody gives you any kind of positive signal. That was Sissy, and I'll have to admit she was very sexy, but she was also weird. You could barely get her attention. Maybe she was speeding.

So now I kind of doubt my instincts. And I haven't felt too sex-crazed for a while. Which is another reason to believe that maybe we're drinking too much wine.

John:

3 September

OPENING REMARKS TO THE SCHOOL

To the boys and to the ladies and gentlemen of the faculty and staff of the Wells School—a warm and joyful welcome into our one hundred and sixth year. And to those of you—more than a quarter of you—who are new to Wells this fall, a special welcome. We count on our older boys and staff for keeping tradition, but we rely on our new boys to bring us to life.

I suspect there will be plenty of vigor from this new third form, who are ninety strong and who are possibly the most able and talented class to have been admitted since I have been at the school. Have I said that before? Pardon me. I really do hope that all of you old-timers will extend yourselves a bit and make not only the third form but the new upper formers feel at home. It shouldn't take much for most of you—perhaps just a brief recollection of your arrival here. Let's also give a special welcome aboard to our new boys from overseas: Helmut Fuerst, our ASSIST student from Cologne, Germany—will you stand, please, Helmut?—and Paul Conniston, from the Westminster School in London. Paul is our English-Speaking Union Exchange Scholar. Will you stand, please, Paul? Both Helmut and Paul are playing football, or soccer as we for some reason call it, and I understand they are doing us no harm. Welcome to Wells, both of you. I hope your year with us is rich and full.

For that matter, I hope this year is rich and full for all of us. I am confident, at least, that it will be full. That is school as usual, although, honestly, I am not sure that school is ever usual. In fact, at its best school is the opposite of usual. It's a planned disequilibrium, all obstacles, all challenges. You know a little algebra after last year, so now we'll see if you can know geometry, and if you think you've got that down, trig—and so on. If you thought you could handle third form English, how about a term paper, a twenty-page term paper with footnotes and a bibliography, an honest bibliography? So you finally moved up the tennis ladder and were playing varsity third singles last spring; how will you fare among the three—or is it four?—nationally ranked new boys? You did all right in introductory French; are you ready to speak it, and nothing else, in class this year? Will you make it into the Group? Will you stay in the Group? Will your room mate work out?

Will you be able to face your friends when they come up against you in Student Court? Will the girl you met and liked so much in July remember you when she is back in the lively coed company of her local high school or at Middlesex? Are you ever going to reach six feet or five feet eight or five feet six? You are on academic probation; are you going to make it? You are third in your class and captain of everything; are you going to make it? Into Harvard or Duke or Stanford or Williams?

As I said, all challenges, all obstacles. But I think it would be a great mistake to try to make school any other way. Except for the challenges and obstacles, how could we find out what sort of persons we are? How could we ever learn which prizes are worth having and which don't matter? School—at least Wells School—insists that you measure up to things: to mathematics, to composition, to dramatic or musical or athletic challenges, to getting along in an intense, changeable, rather small world of adolescent boys and their teachers. School—at least Wells School—insists that there are worthy things, true things, to measure up to. In a way, the school measures you by assigning you this or that grade or by placing you on a first or second team, but more importantly you measure yourselves against past performance, against your more gifted, less gifted, equally gifted fellows, against the system, against the odds.

Greeves Passing

School can be very intense, and as many of you know, it can make you feel tense. But it also makes you feel alive, sometimes—when you are trying your hardest, when you are most engaged—almost supernaturally alive. This feeling, rare as it is, is worth pursuing. I think you'll find it is most likely to occur when you are pursuing or "measuring up to" what is good in its own right: for example, excellence, rather than an 'A' or a victory, but it is a fatal mistake to confuse the two. They are not the same thing.

At any rate, I hope each of you will take on the challenges and obstacles of this school with enthusiasm. Each of you is different and will quite rightly take on school in a different way. But in one important respect you are exactly alike, perfect equals. And in this respect we will expect the same thing from each of you. I am speaking of course about the moral side of things. Besides all those other particular challenges, this school is going to insist that you measure up to basic honesty and decency. As we have explained to all of you before, new and old boys alike, we are going to insist on your telling the truth and your treating each other and us teachers as you yourself would like to be treated. These challenges are obvious, ancient, and very often tough. None of us is worth a damn without them. They are not, however, very hard to understand. The quality of this school depends on them, and so does the maintenance of civilization. There is no way to avoid these challenges, either. They will commence as soon as you leave this hall, if they have not commenced already.

As I was putting these remarks together last night, it dawned on me with some irony that they were not, really, very original. I'll bet their equivalent were said, certainly more eloquently, by Athenian schoolmasters on opening days 2500 years ago. The descendants of those Greek schoolmasters without question told aristocratic Roman boys the same thing five hundred years later when Rome's empire was in the ascendant. And I happen to know that such words were spoken by headmasters Guarino and Vittorino to their Italian pupils fifteen hundred years later still, during the Renaissance. The same things were said, perhaps more forcefully than ever, by Thomas Arnold and other great English schoolmasters in the last century. So my remarks this morning have been terribly unoriginal, but perhaps for that reason terribly important, too.

The idea that there are eternally worthy and true standards which people can understand and which they ought to measure up to, while very ancient and at times thought to be the very foundation of civilization, is not in style at the moment and has not been in style for a good part of this century. The opposite view—that there are no provable standards and therefore no obligations to them—takes thousands of forms and is very much among us. If there are no true standards to measure up to, it would follow that the self is free to do what it pleases. The self, after all, is supplied with a mixed bag of feelings, some of them marvelously pleasurable, and with standards out of the way, these may be pursued without interference. But, maddeningly, without interference, the pursuit of pleasurable feelings leads to unutterably bad feelings. People get impatient, jaded, careless, bored, alcoholic, and gross. They seek remedies from the bottle that caused the sickness. People overdose themselves with liquor or drugs or with sex or with power or with things—even when there is clear evidence that these pursuits are the cause of their dissatisfaction in the first place.

Not long ago certain pundits labeled our age the "Me Decade," but for more than a decade I have been waiting for it to pass. I say this not because I am a puritan who hates to see a self out having a good time, but because of a certainty—maybe my only certainty—that in the long run a self can't have a good time in pursuit of its own satisfaction. Few of us with the perspective of several decades' time have observed any net increase in energy, productivity or happiness during the Me Decade. It's been, frankly, a flat and anxious era. Even the anti-war and ecological sentiments expressed at the outset have quieted, mainly, I think, because they were movements aimed at measuring up to standards, like justice, and world peace and a sustainable environment. The pursuit of standards and the pursuit of immediate satisfactions are incompatible.

If we're honest, we admit to feeling driven both ways. If we're honest, most of us will admit the selfish drives are usually stronger; we might know better, but it's easier to do what we feel like doing. Without help, we always do just that.

The help is training. Training. We get it in good families, we get it in enduring religions, and, if we stick to business, we get it in school. It's not always fun, but it really isn't supposed to be. Nevertheless, I think that if you can commit yourself to business, to "measuring up," you will be surprised, at least if the history of Wells is anything to go by, at how often fun tends to crop up, often when you least expect it.

Well, I've gotten rather near a sermon, haven't I? But I risked doing it because I wanted so badly to say that I hope you measure up—and that you want to measure up—this school year. Incidentally, I hope that I measure up. The fun, I am sure, will look after itself. It always does.

At this point Mr. Upjohn has a few instructions about this morning's meetings, about schedules, and about books. The real business of the day.

Have a very good morning.

Meg:

Little House

Awoke to pure azure behind the dark pines. Felt a little leap of hope, raised my head. But nope. Soot behind the eyes, the awful tense little hum behind my breast bone. Pee seems thick or not quite right, unless I'm imagining things. Temperature 100. I am wrong, all wrong. Not the way I feel, but knowing the wrongness, left a hard ball of dread in my guts. Juice, water, tea with honey. By mid-morning fear begins to dissolve.

Called Dr. K. to report my flat, unacceptable condition. He is concerned—sweet—and says he will try to get my tests moved up. Now, for some reason, this sounds like a good idea. Yes, let's *do* something to this malaise. Let's poke it, suck out samples, fry it with x-rays. Let's hurt the bugger back.

Called John today about the tests change and to ask him, breezily, not to come down. Dear love, his anxious witness only amplifies my own. I tell him I'm fine. I joke about my diet of canned tuna. I blather on about putative days on boats, the bird feeder, convey the impression I'm actually out in the weather. It's my good luck that J. is actually distracted. Frankel, the young and very goofy-looking math teacher has broken his contract and, on the brink of term starting, bolted. This kind of thing always amazes J. I understand it perfectly. J, believing that all human beings are endowed at birth with a capacity for empathy and a working forebrain, cannot understand how someone can Let Down the Side, knowing the trouble it causes others. Yet I understand. That very fact, the reality of a world, Wells School, where one must never Let Down the Side, feels stifling, feels an intolerable prison to a certain kind of soul. Of course they bolt. It could be a matter of spiritual life or death. What a world. We have to negate things in order to live; passionate affirmation blinds and ultimately kills us. But poor J.

Where in late August do you find a mathematician who can keep the rascals of Wells in line? What such person is idling around, open to an invitation to descend into the den of a boys' boarding school in nether Connecticut? Oddly, this is the kind of pebble J seems to like in his shoe. He actually finds such people.

I should not be mean about Wells. Wells has been sweet to me. The whole socio-economic complex has been sweet to me, provided me with houses full of rooms, things to eat, periodically sent me careering around the globe. Great libraries amass books for me to read. I am squired to heartbreakingly beautiful plays and concerts. I have been asked to do virtually no work. No one infringes on my liberties. I have never felt compelled to answer a phone. No one makes me entertain deadening people in my home simply because they insisted on once entertaining me. I have been free. I can go outside, or not, or could until my maker threw this gray and raspy blanket of flu over my head.

I must take pains to remember, little book, that I have been dealt a fabulous hand. Inwardly and outwardly I have probed and sometimes flown off where no one ever could have imagined. For no good reason, some people have loved me. I have loved them back. J, Brian. I awake from first memory into a great, cosmic conversation, still going, even through the static and gloom of this bug.

Chicken broth, toast, and a sent-from-heaven, deeper-than-deep nap. Awoke in a light, pleasant sweat. Temperature a shade under 99. Ta-dah!

This music, Brahms again, is just about perfect. Sun's down, the sky still glass-blue. A chill in the house, but there are fixings for at least a few more fires. It's time to clean up this joint. Night-night.

Brian:

San Rafael

Thank God for books. That's maybe the best thing I got from being a Greeve—the idea that time with books was prime time, not something to do while you're on the can or to bring on sleep. I'm halfway through Hesse's *Narcissus and Goldmund*, and it's one of those times when I just want the book to open up and go slow. Somebody ought to do a study on how you can feel more alive, much happier, in the situation of a book than you do in real life. That is actually true. I'm feeling more in the book's Middle Ages, although it's a pretty magical Middle Ages, than I feel I am on the beach in San Rafael, Portugal. I dare any writer to make this era magical.

I think that's what the sixties were trying to prove—that there was a way out of the twentieth century, a way into the magical feeling of newness and surprise that great stories give you. I came pretty close to saying that in a big paper for de Werte's Culture of the Sixties course at Amherst, but he sort of shot me down. He said I was ignoring the political and economic realities underlying the changes in styles and attitudes. He said I was looking at the sixties the way Life Magazine looked at the sixties—like a big photo spread of Woodstock, with lots of long-haired people wearing gypsy clothes, smoking dope, and listening to the Beatles and the Dead. I've never seen a Life Magazine in my life, but maybe he was right.

But it was de Werte's history class that got me started on Hesse. He had us read Siddhartha and write a paper on why this elderly German's tale of the Buddha written in the '40s was picked up as a cult book by American kids in the sixties. I think we all wrote the same paper—that American kids were looking for new ways of thinking and feeling—but we were way off. Siddhartha is good the way *Narcissus and Goldmund* is good. Hesse knew how to get out of this world, how to do it seriously, not farting around like Tom Robbins, Ken Kesey, and the druggies.

I love the sixties, at least my "incorrect" view of the sixties. All the history I had to study is in black and white except for three periods, ancient Greece (and that's I'm sure because of Mr. Coates at Wells), the Middle Ages, and the sixties. De Werte would probably tell me I have a Life Magazine view of the Middle Ages, too—all Robin Hood and Joan of Arc and Round Table adventures. Right again, de Werte, but it's in COLOR, colors like jewels. It's alive, and you in your bow ties and your office piled high with journals, and Amherst and Rte. 9's creeping hell of McDonald's and malls aren't. All of that is dead and dull as a magazine no one would ever want to read.

Got a little lost there. The sixties I love is the Beatles sixties. I can still remember the class when de Werte played us Sergeant Pepper. I can't remember anything about the lecture that came first, only his putting the needle into the groove of Sergeant Pepper and all those surprising, jingle-jangling, just-right songs filling the lecture hall. That's what I mean about colors. I hear those songs in color, especially the melodic ones—"She's Leaving Home," "Lucy in the Sky"—and it has nothing to do with drugs. I bought all the Beatles tapes and CDs I could find and listened to them a thousand times. The surprising thing to me is that those songs aren't about the sixties at all. If anything current is mentioned—like "Lovely Rita Meter Maid—it's treated in a stylized, old-fashioned way. There's a lot of wonderful, old-fashioned stuff in Sergeant Pepper, like "When I'm Sixty-Four," and they're not just spoofing old forms and sentimental ideas. I always got the feeling that when the Beatles told compressed little stories like "Eleanor Rigby" and "Norwegian Wood" it was more like theater than rock music. They always took you out of the present, to maybe earlier in the century, to some working-class world, to old music halls or pubs. To me they were always tightest and best when they played at a tick-tock, vaudeville kind of tempo, songs like "Maxwell's Silver Hammer," "Penny Lane," "For the Benefit of Mr.Kite."

Now I'm crazed to listen to the Beatles. It's great to be able to love what people did. But I still can't understand the big appeal of the rest of it. The Stones, the Byrds, the Who. They must have something that appeals, some message that moves people the way the Beatles moved me, but how come I hear none of it? They all sound so thin and predictable. Could it just be the bad-boy, spacey posing? The look of someone like Mick Jagger. There must be something there, but to me it's all in black and white, people too self-consciously working at it, part of the moment, not out of time.

The great thing is the freshness, the terrific refusal, the feeling that you can start living the way you want right now. You can feel it in those Beatles colors. You can feel it in Hesse and those films. The next best thing de Werte did, after playing Sergeant Pepper, was to show us *The Graduate* and *Butch Cassidy and the Sundance Kid*.

I guess it was a sixties movie, but *The Graduate* didn't feel that far off from now. What worked, what clicked was that the kid—for no reason his college or his parents or his country club California could have taught him—knew how to refuse everything that wasn't alive and beautiful. Maybe the most frustrating time I ever had was arguing against every single person in de Werte's section about Mrs. Robinson. They all wanted to see her as the bad witch, as the obstacle to Benjamin's winning her daughter. I remember almost shouting out, "Did you guys WATCH the film?" Mrs. Robinson was part of the solution. Of course a married friend of his parents, somebody his mother's age was an inappropriate sex partner, but Mrs. Robinson woke the kid up. She seduced him not only out of the Dominant Paradigm (de Werte), but she put him in touch with what he wanted. And she was unbelievably sexy. I can't be the only person who saw her that way. Next to Mrs. Robinson, her daughter was definitely half-cooked, merely cute. I've probably seen *The Graduate* six times, and I'm positive that the audience—at least the boys—project their sexual interest in Mrs. Robinson, which she provokes and earns, onto her daughter, who is socially safer.

Greeves Passing

Anyway, I loved it. I loved it when he was up against everybody, but absolutely set on getting what he wanted. There were those terrific shots of his driving his little red car and then running uphill—total hero—to save the day, and the Simon and Garfunkel sound track, acoustic guitars, making the colors glow like stained glass. When it was over de Werte tried to bring everybody down by asking: "Did that young couple have a future?" I wish I had been smart enough to answer him on the spot. I wish I had said: you missed the whole point of the story. By breaking all the rules of decorum and common sense, the lovers were denying the whole future-oriented way of life. Working for safe and practical futures is deadening. It wrecks the present. Not just ignoring the future, but REFUSING it, that's the only way to break out of the Dominant Paradigm, the only way to save your life. I don't know what I actually said. I probably didn't say anything.

I'm not only out of time at the moment, I'm nearly out of light. A long day in the sand.

Meg:

Little House

Abandoned you, book. You were there yesterday, shut fast in my bag, but you can't know. I thought, I hoped there would be long stretches of sitting/waiting during which I could scrawl my stories and jokes about the Tests, but the hospital folks had other things in mind for me. Medical idiot that I am, I was expecting the terrors and indignities to be lightened by the physical presence and simian charms of Dr. Karipides, but he wasn't even there. It had not even dawned on me that he wouldn't do the tests. Specialists do the tests—actually not. Sad-looking, beaten men in late middle years—the specialists—talk to you for about a minute and a half. With amazing, depressing economy, they tell you what's going to happen to you and why and express a clear but unstated hope that you won't ask them any questions. The tests themselves are performed by Amazonian young women with lesser, different kinds of medical credentials. The unvarying manic cheerfulness of the girl technicians strikes me as a sustained, largely unconscious apology for everything that is happening. Thank God Dr. K. didn't give me a clue about what they were going to do.

Best line of the day was from the technician preparing me for the colonoscopy. "Mrs. Greeve, I should tell you that some patients find this procedure unpleasant." *Unpleasant.* This from a profession that calls the excruciating pains of child birth "contractions." And yes, Miss, I must now count myself among the list of patients who found the colonoscopic procedure unpleasant. Moreover, I would be fascinated to meet someone who found the insertion of what feels like pinking sheers up one's bum and the subsequent snipping away "pleasant," or even ho-hum. Poor bum, already lewdly insulted by an early a.m. enema, followed by inquiries by more than a few rubber-gloved fingers.

Greeves Passing

No more tests for me, little book. I'll take the fever and the tuna. The blood-letting now frightens me less, since they've done so much of it, but it still makes me mad. The damn needle burns, burns the whole time it's in there, as box after plastic box is filled up—so much of it! I've never liked thinking of myself as a pump and conduits of purple-black blood. I know God wants it to stay inside us. A nice person hates to see it.

Another lulu: "You might get a funny taste in your mouth."

This before I was scaldingly injected with some kind of dye that the MRI scanners are supposed to watch as it seeps through your bloodstream. They inject you in the crook of your arm, and suddenly, as if spewing out of your tonsils, there is a mouthful of something like powdered aluminum and Pepto Bismol. I can still taste it. I can now not imagine not tasting it. My tea, my chicken broth pass over a tongue saturated with metallic chalk.

Meg—you silly old crone, carping and complaining. Here modern, high-tech medicine has gathered you into itself for the better part of a whole day. Modern insurers have treated you to thousands of dollars worth of advances. All you had to do was point your Toyota in the direction of the facility. Think how smiley and clean those women technicians were on their bouncy-soled athletic shoes. And what about the x-rays? You can't complain about x-rays. Quiet, quick, not a single intrusion up your bum or into a tired old vein. For that matter, the scanning machine, after the shock of my aluminum frappe, was kind of an adventure. Very solicitously, the technical assistant seemed to assume a claustrophobic response on my part—maybe most people are. But not at all. I was actually in the mood to lie for awhile perfectly still in a dark steel drawer. I believe I rather pulled myself together in there.

No, in the future I will approach these outings with a policy intact. Except maybe to prick my finger tip, they may take no more of my blood. Nor will buggery of any kind, in any sanitized guise be permitted. By compensation, because I am reasonable and modern, they can scan and x-ray the hell out of me.

It is strange what happens to you when you are being done one way or another in a hospital. It is all so finally and overwhelmingly about your body, about the biology and mechanics of your body, that your soul doesn't know what to do. The soul is utterly unaddressed by the tests. It detaches from the body and is temporarily dumb. Maybe for this reason I honestly did not know, while I was being dyed and jabbed and zapped, how I felt. I forgot if I was sick, suspended the ability to tell. Also, in a way I am still trying to sort out, I felt entirely gathered up into the medical process. It's not just that in their clinically vampirish way they extracted my essences—blood, urine, stool, tissues from my deep interior—I feel as if in giving myself up to them all day yesterday, however timidly, I had worshipped at their altars. I think the Latin *religare* in religion means *to bind*. I don't know if I like it, and I'm sure I never wanted it, but medicine and I are now bound. By Friday, I should know what medicine makes of me. It will be nice to get the verdict through the animal warmth of Dr. K. But whatever it is, little book, don't let me forget the rest of me. Don't let me shrink into my diagnosis. My soul. Let's remember there's me in there.

J. helps. He loves me. His worry and smart questions were like a warm bath last night. Bless that good man's heart. He doesn't hear a beaky old bag of bones with limp hair. He hears Meg Greeve, a woman he loves, a whole, well woman, a woman in any case beyond her diagnosis. I love this man.

So here's how it is. I have to give myself up to this now. I didn't will it to begin with, and I won't waste a second trying to will it away. Let's get past systems and my testy, squeamish concerns about them. What do you say, book—you and me?

John:

4 September

Mrs. Margaret Greeve
Little House
Ticonsett Lane
East Sandwich, Massachusetts

Dear Meg,

Lousy news about the tests. The only thing worse than being in a hospital overnight—even one with a view of Buzzard's Bay—is being in a hospital overnight far from home. I wish I could believe their marvelous instruments could actually isolate the cause of your feeling fluey. My own dark intuition is that it's the equivocal tap water of Little House. I don't even trust it with tooth paste and have, as you know, come to treat it cautiously with bourbon before swallowing it. But what do I know? You have probably been fighting some new inscrutable flu from Asia, and they have just the thing for it.

I wish my concern for your health was less selfish, but at the heart of the matter, I want you to come back here for my own delight. I want your company. I've grown accustomed to your face. It almost makes the day begin. I want you to cook my breakfast, etc.

My good-hearted colleagues have had me to dinner practically every night, in itself a problem, as each supper is rather a big deal: drinks, fancy things to nibble, an enormous roast, more fancy things, etc. I come home bloated and tired and in an unwilling frame of mind to prepare a balanced budget for the Finance Committee. So I write a letter or two, read a bit of something improving, and doze.

The house is very neat, but dusty. The kitchen is spanking clean except for the one tumbler and the one tea cup I use. The lawn is cut, the gardens horrendous, but with the falling leaves, we can easily conceal them from public view. I have not had a faculty reception yet, because I am afraid our recent appointment in mathematics, Florence Armbruster or Armature or Armchair, will make a pass at me in my apparent eligibility.

I'll call you Thursday at the hospital, around six. Decide before then what I can send you besides your mail. Write me, love.

J.

P.S. Around noon today I drove into town to go to the bank, and what should I spy on the jct. of rte 9 just past the bridge but a tiny, dark-suited hitchhiker wearing a bold, not-yet-spotted Wells tie. Two and a half days, and he was headed home for Hartford. He quite naturally assumed I was out on a daily roundup of escaped third formers and dejectedly hauled two mammoth suitcases into the back seat of the wagon. He told me there was no dissuading him. He had "tried it" and it was no good. It seemed to me there was nothing for it but to go to McDonald's, which turned out to be a stroke of genius, a faint but sure strand of continuity with his hearth and home, such as it must be these days in Hartford. Hardly a scene from Mr. Chips, but the lad is staying on. Really a very nice boy, almost garrulous with me now. His name is Marc Slavin, and he is the first in his family to try a private school. Never got to the bank.

Brian:

San Rafael

Ryan's taking off. He's going to grad school, a Ph.D. program at Johns Hopkins. I'm finding that this bothers me. It's not so much that I need his company—but his leaving feels somehow like a criticism of me and what I'm doing. That is, what I'm not doing, which is making something useful out of myself. I guess that's really it.

His clearing out also leaves Deirdre to me, not that we're an item or anything. It would probably be trickier to work something out with Deirdre now, as a lover, than it would to have started fooling around while Ryan was here. There are subtle little shame and honor and control issues. She's feeling out of control now because of Ryan's leaving, and so that kind of takes care of any feelings for me, at least for a while. Deirdre's got a proud, ornery side to her. She's pretty tough.

But the fact is we are living alone together now, with wide open prospects ahead. I like that, I'll have to admit. It'll be good to get out of my brother mode, which was feeling pretty eunuchy. The harmless brother thing wasn't all bad, though, and it kind of gives me a head start. If I just came across Deirdre for the first time, in a café, that would be work. It would take months to get to the comfort level we've got now. So I'll be honest. I want to be closer to Deirdre, for us to be a couple. I want to sleep with her, talk with her all night, move on with her when the time is right and try a new place.

* * *

Amazing night. About two years' worth of contact in ten hours. I'm now obsessed, turned on, agitated, but it's overall pretty great.

I had already made up my mind to buy some roasted chickens and some good wine to take home to Deirdre for a cheer-up dinner, when she came out to the beach to see me. She never does that. It suddenly dawned on me that I don't know any of her routines, or Ryan's, very well. A lot of my clearing out of the house every day was feeling I should be out of their hair a good part of the time. It's going to be nice not having to do that.

Deirdre was in a better mood. She was obviously ready for company. When she came up, I was writing in the ledger, and she asked me what I was doing. I told her it was a journal. She asked me if she could read it. I told her maybe sometime, when I put it in shape. Minor panic. Am I going to have to hide this thing?

We got our chickens, some red wine, pastries and a basket of fresh cherries. We hadn't done this before, either, and the mood was terrific. I hadn't eaten lunch, and the wine went straight to my brain. The day had been clear and bright, and I could still feel the sun on my skin and a kind of glowing in my gut. Then I realized the main effect of Ryan's being gone: there was more time. I had been living around the edges of both of their routines even more than I realized.

We put a tape of Greek music on the cassette player, and Deirdre said, "Come on, Greeve, dance." So we danced around, making it up, very uninhibited.

We ate everything and drank both bottles of wine. I wanted to keep it going, maybe go out to the taverna before it closed, maybe even spring for the village cab to take us to Cape St. Vincent where we might get real music and dance some more. At the very least I wanted to get some more wine.

I asked Deirdre if she was sad about Ryan. That stopped her for a minute. Then she said, "I'll live." I pressed a little. I asked her, if she didn't mind telling me, what she had thought her relationship with him was going to be—something long-term, maybe permanent. As usual, she was completely honest. She said she had considered everything—living with him for a long time, even marrying him. She said they had never talked about it in specifics. She said Ryan was always pretty hazy about his future plans but that she thought he had a getaway in the works from the start but wasn't going to tell her until he had to.

I didn't want to fall out of our good mood, so I said, without thinking, "Fuck him."

She said, "How can I?" and we laughed. We danced some more, then sat down and didn't say anything for quite a while. At exactly the same moment we put our arms around each other, held each other, and rocked. I kissed the top of her head, and she turned up to look at me, and I kissed her fully on the mouth for the first time. Her face and neck gave off a faint baby smell, and her skin felt wonderful underneath her shirt.

"Can you believe it," she said to me, "but I feel like I'm cheating." I knew what she meant. I told her I felt like I was cheating, too, but that I was happy I was. That seemed to make both of us more comfortable, and in a little while we started making love.

We did our teeth and went to my room. Deirdre undressed and put on one of her big painting tee shirts. When we were lying down together, she asked me if I could stand it just to hold her. I told her that was fine, and I meant it. It actually felt wonderful to hold her, to lie there with our arms and legs around one another, as if we were dancing on our sides. Deirdre said it would feel too jarring to see Ryan out of the house that morning and to have sex right away with somebody else. She didn't want to hurt my feelings, but I knew exactly what she meant. She said she didn't know what their status was supposed to be when he came back from Lisbon to get the rest of his stuff. I asked her what she wanted it to be, and she told me to please keep holding her.

It was wonderful to spend a whole night just holding and touching Deirdre, but it also drove me crazy. Neither of us slept much, and at one point I woke up more powerfully aroused than I have ever been in my life. Whether she was completely awake or not, Deirdre started to respond to me, and I thought: this is it, here we go. But then she sat straight up and said, "We can't." There was another reason besides Ryan. I tried to get ready for the worst, but Deirdre surprised me. It wasn't about Ryan or me—or anybody. She said she was having a problem with her crotch, a yeast infection. I've never heard of a yeast infection—all I could think of was loaves of bread rising in an oven. She said it wasn't a huge deal, but it was not fun, itchy and burny.

Then she lay back down. We wrapped ourselves back together, held each other and rocked.

Meg:

Little House

Little continuous sleep. Arose feeling dry, weak, no energy. Then the terrible call.

Dr, Karipides, himself no less, rang up to say most of the tests were ready and that I should come to see him tomorrow a.m. at his office in Falmouth. I had already determined his voice was funny before he added the awful "and it would be a good idea if your husband could join us." Then of course I was obliged to ask why, to which Dr. K. was predictably and professionally maddening. "The tests raise some concerns," he said. "We may have to begin thinking about some decisions." Oh for God's sake, I told him, tell me what I've got. Her couldn't, or wouldn't. "Not everything is clear" was the polite evasion. Does Dr. K. have any idea the kind of day he has created for me? Could he possibly believe that we who ail are comforted by the language of Tests revealing Concerns which require Decisions—when Tests mean snipping off bits of you, sucking out your blood, dying it blue, Concerns are malignant indications of your death, and Decisions are which grim bus to the Terminal? "You're not going to tell me the bad news, are you?" I said, not very generously to Dr. K. He told me it would be better to wait and he would know more tomorrow. Then he asked me how I was feeling.

Brian:

San Rafael

Last night we forgot about the yeast—Deirdre calls it her rot. Sex is so good, but it's too good. You can't write about it. The idea that all that surging and feeling can even happen is one thing, but realizing it's actually another person you're feeling it with—I will never get used to it, never take it for granted. Deirdre. Whatever hopes anyone had for my making my way in the world (pretty slender hopes) are shot now. I want to spend the rest of my life making love to Deirdre. I want to die of sex. Starvation is a small price to pay. Bring it on. But first bring on sex.

I remember thinking, when I was a Wells school boy, that males had sexual desire and females had sexual defenses. If you could make a girl care for you, she might permit some intimacy out of affection, but not out of desire. When a girl I was making out with at Amherst suddenly got hot and started getting wild, I froze. What was wrong with her, I wondered. How did I manage to seek out probably the only girl in Amherst with something sexually wrong with her? So much for my facts of life. The mystery I've been working on since is: if girls feel sex as urgently as boys do, why don't they get to it sooner and more directly? Maybe they do. Maybe the girls of the prep school world and Amherst are an exceptional population.

Deirdre is happy in her sex, lost in it. Deirdre is beautiful.

John:

6 September

Mr. Brian Greeve
General Delivery
Cape St. Vincent
PORTUGAL

Dear Brian,

I am writing to Cape St. Vincent on the slim chance that you have returned or possibly never left. At any rate, it's the last post office at which we made definite contact. You know, it's hard to write when you really don't believe your letter will reach its intended receiver. For this reason, too, I am enclosing only a modest money order, but good enough I hope for a few square meals. If you ever let us know where you are, I'll be glad to send along a more substantial one. It's not that I'm getting soft or generous in my old age, only that it's hard for me to shake the habit of thinking I have an expensive dependent.

As you can imagine, school has begun, Wells' one hundred and sixth year, and now we are in motion irrevocably toward June. Hugh has taken a teaching post at St. Edward's, a struggling sort of school, but with a good young head named Ted Phillips. Perhaps you are in touch with Hugh and know this already.

Your mother has been feeling achy and run-down since the end of summer and is still on the Cape in Little House. She went into the hospital for tests, which should drive any flu away. When she gets the results this week, she's coming home. Needless to say, champ, she'd kill for a word from you. I'd be a liar to deny we worry and wonder about you a great deal. Not that we resent your freedom, but invisibility?

Richard Hawley

Please write.

Much love from both of us,

Pop

Meg:

                              Little House

As we thought, little book, as we thought.

It appears I am rotten through and through. But haven't we, at moments, in our heart of hearts, known this all along? The new—perfect—killer word is "involved," as in lungs are involved, esophagus and stomach are involved. So many parts of me are involved. Treacherous, shameful parts. Damn them for their infidelity, their slovenly willingness to become involved. Are you happy now, ileum? Lung? You will soon see it doesn't pay to get involved.

"Let me show you what we're dealing with," says Dr. K. uncomfortably. Ghostly x-rays and scans are illuminated from behind to show fuzzy little blurs along the margins of, or deep within, what I must accept on faith are my internal organs. So that's what kills you—vagueness, poor definition. I am blanking on the exact name of my culprit—melanoma, carcinoma, Pamplona—they all sound to me like Caribbean fruits or ranges of the Sierras. I will get it tomorrow—if that's possible on a Saturday. I want to know my *–noma*, involver of my organs, look the bugger in the eye. I am now experiencing the fondest feelings for my immune system or whatever uninvolved part of me is registering the weak, achy, insulted reaction to my pathology. It's amazing that at the brute biological level, the level of virus and antibody, the body can report wrongness in such a nuanced, darkly elegant way. If we're not careful we get angry at and want to annihilate the faithful messengers, the "symptoms," poor babies.

As for my deadly *–noma*, Dr. K. suggested I take my bundle of hopeless involvements to Mass. General in Boston for treatment. Slightly more in range of Wells. I almost wrote "home." It sounds like a few punishing rounds of chemotherapy. Even though it's

Mass. General's job to tell me in full detail, Dr. K. pretty much assured me the treatment will nauseate, desiccate, and depilate me within an inch of my waning life. The idea is to undergo a week's "course" of the chemicals, suffer, then, if and when one is able to resume an upright position, step up for another course. Looks like two or three courses for me. I guess the superficial good news is that there will be no surgical invasions and mutilations—I'm too involved. Not wanting to make Dr. K. uncomfortable, I nevertheless had to ask him whether someone in my condition ever got better. It would depend on my response to the chemicals, Dr. K. said very evenly. Then: "It happens." Good enough for me. My return to health is at least as likely as the parting of the Red Sea, the virgin birth, stigmata, winning the lotto.

Probably a delayed reaction, but I didn't feel frightened or overwhelmed getting the verdict from Dr. K., or even on the ride home. Bless John's heart. His first words to me: "so what do we think?" We didn't think much. It was such a relief. I did fall apart a bit when we got home to Little House. It was on the deck while John was unlocking the door. I happened to look out over the harbor and I caught sight of a wind-surfer, and the words were already out of my mouth: *we have to find Brian*. It was a strange, outraged feeling. What have I been *doing*, forgetting him, eclipsing him? Have I become more involved in my deadly *–nomas* than with my living son? Truth is, I haven't thought about Brian for days, not even as a great, deep absence. I don't think I have ever done that before. I forgot him.

Remembering undid me, that horrible, almost peristaltic cramping and convulsing, a braying, animal grief forced up and out into the audible air. Poor J. I couldn't stop the flow of images: Brian hunched over the breakfast counter, his beautiful, beautiful shoulders straining the tattered ruins of a sweater, his thoughtful, sleepy eyes. I could see him hoisting his own bean pole length onto that sail board, stepping windward of the sail, arching back from the billowing sheet and taking soundless flight. Dark stick against electric blue sail; soon an iridescent feather flickering far across the bay. Where are you, Brian Greeve, my brooding heart? I see you ambling down an ancient beach, ambling away from me. I see you alone, alone in a café, alone in a rail carriage. All alone. I hope you think of us sometimes, even if they are flat and loveless thoughts. I hope I am a *presence* in you, just as you are forever a presence in me.

Brian! Come here. I need you to know this new dark thing, this change, this difference. You must not read it in a letter. You must not open this creaking door some day or, God forbid, reenter the drills and bells of Wells, and learn that I have gone. You must not be startled by that particular silence. There has been too much silence with us, boy-o. Come up, come out, come here. I want to see your slow smile. I want to see that clown spot of high color that glows into being when you are about to laugh. You know you could break through this time. If you were a presence at my passing, you could see and possibly even grieve for the finitude of me, and thus of us, after all. Maybe it would be like Dorothy watching the wicked Witch of the West melt into harmlessness at last. I will melt for you, boy-o. I will drink my chemo elixir with a full heart if you come home to me this once. Please God, please. I have believed in the efficacy of prayer. I have believed and actually felt my desire changing every infinitesimal particle between myself and the object of my desire. This day, this night, and for as long as I can transmit, I will beam this appeal out over the sea and into the all. Switch on your receiver, beloved boy.

Brian:

San Rafael

Ryan came back for his stuff today, just long enough to screw things up. He had to pack up his books and clothes into boxes and practically gift wrap everything in order for the San Rafael post office to send the packages home. It took hours. Meanwhile, Deirdre got madder and quieter by the hour. I asked if she wanted to go somewhere with me, maybe Cape St. Vincent, until Ryan was gone, but she said no. She was no warmer to me than she was to Ryan.

I hoped things would improve when he finally left—no hugs, no handshakes, no exchange of addresses—but that didn't happen. Deirdre is still down. Maybe this will be the symbolic closure she said she needed before we first made love. I guess what bothers me is knowing that Deirdre obviously cares about Ryan. She was rejected, and rejection is always absolutely terrible. It's always there, eating away. I don't want to be an aspirin or an escape for her. I want to be the person she wants. Even writing that down makes me doubt it will ever happen. Where did I get this total loser attitude?

Fact is, she'll either come around or she won't. I've got to get down to something I can stand doing. Among other things I need some books to read. I'm dry. I hope there's some place nearer than Lisbon to get some decent English titles. At Wells I used to ignore good books on principle. This afternoon I'd sell half my blood for *The Mayor of Casterbridge* or *Tess* or *Great Expectations*.

I could also try writing something decent, I suppose. Maybe my deathless personal confessions. Maybe I'll go suicidal and write hysterical poems like Sylvia Plath.

Greeves Passing

Dad, you wretch, you fucking fool,
Why did you have to run a school?
All the tedious talks
On our long preppy walks
Were insufferably, wrenchingly cruel.

Did you know that I wished I was dead
When you told me the board named you Head?
O vomit! O bile!
And a hearty seig heil!
How I bled and I bled and I bled.

Not to worry, Sylvia.

John:

19 September

Mr. and Mrs. Frank Greeve
14 Bingham Drive
Tarrytown, New York

Dear Val and Frank,

It was a great relief and solace to talk to you two last night. Without family I would be lost, literally.

We are now ensconced in our respective Boston settings, Meg in a private room (a term bearing no relation to reality) in Mass. General and I—I'll explain later—at the Copley Plaza. If medical science were less benighted by half, Meg would be at the Copley Plaza and I in the bleak cell. At any rate, Meg is doing beautifully. Her attitude is all shrewdness, attention, and dry humor. Braver than brave—and it is so damned attractive. Dr. Dietrich, the specialist doing the tests and giving the "other opinion," is a thoughtful, likable sort of person—gives the impression of having lots of time and explains things, both to Meg and me. He won't even venture estimates about treatment, remission, percentages of cure, etc. until his own tests are in. No false optimism either. Meg is sick, and it's cancer. I wonder if you can imagine the kind of fear and emptiness that statement arouses in me. I know Meg will endure whatever is required with strength and grace, but I feel like collapsing right now. I keep thinking I've got to help, I've got to be strong, but I feel like collapsing. Waiting is worst. I'll keep you posted.

Thank you, Val, for your generous offer to close up Little House and to look after the boat. I left the less equivocal food in the fridge and there is some meat in the freezer you might want to take home with you, if that is technically possible. When you are

Greeves Passing

ready to leave, just call the Jenkins number and say, "Come. Close up Little House." He knows what to do about the pipes, and he'll haul the float off to the boathouse.

This is all really very strange. Nothing is routine. There is a heavy overlay of irony and foreboding about every practical concern. The *Valmar*, for instance—will Meg and I ever sail in her again? If not, what an odd role that boat has played in our lives: a symbol of possibility, a means to never-quite-worked-out whims. Our plan was always to spend weeks and weeks sailing in and out of quiet Maine harbors, working our way slowly, maybe infinitely, down east. The school would of course give us an open leave to do this, and we would be thrillingly incognito, out of touch. But as we well know, such is never the case with boats. The head has always got to be replaced to meet the requirements of somebody's Clean Harbor Commission, the engine is never right, there is always a leak between the engine and the centerboard, unreachable by human hands—not an important leak, just enough to raise the possibility of mortal danger if cruising in cold water anywhere NE of the Cape. But could any actual cruise measure up to our hypothetical one? Probably not. Yard bills buy dreams, not voyages. Or Little House? What does Little House mean without Meg? This is pitiful stuff, I know, but it's the kind of thing I'm actually thinking.

Frank, there is one more thing I want to ask which I forgot to mention over the phone. Could you brainstorm a bit with your attorney friends about how I might locate Brian overseas? I've bombarded the post office at Cape St. Vincent where we last made contact, and I've written to acquaintances he may have been traveling with for a time, but I've heard nothing yet. I think it is very important that he be aware of what is happening with Meg as soon as possible. Are there people-finding services abroad? Do you think our embassies might help? Any tips, hunches, or advice on the matter would be deeply appreciated.

Again, thanks to both of you. Our very best to Hugh.

J.

Brian:

San Rafael

Deirdre took off this a.m. We loaded her stuff in the village cab. She'll get a train in Cape St. Vincent to Lisbon, then fly home. Big hugs, and I have her address. She cried a little, I think for the end of her Europe, her time with Ryan, maybe for my part, too. She gave me two rolled up pictures. One is a pencil drawing of me asleep. I look goofy and out of it, but she got me. The other is a self-portrait, very quick sketch. She looks too elongated and gaunt, almost freaky, but there's something there too.

So long, Deirdre. God damn it.

Meg:

School House

Back to Wells and School House. Drive not good. Felt shaky when we got in the car, then got worse. Sick-sour taste from my mouth all the way down. Very panicky. Tried lying down but made it worse. Tried separating enormity of feeling, especially as we left the Cape and I could sense the sea receding behind us, from my miserable soma, but it was no good. Malaise embraces everything.

No lunch on the road—once a pleasure. Poor J. Made Wells by 3 p.m., and I went straight up to make up the bed and got in. Dozing and waking since. J. sweetly brought up tea on a tray (bad cup) and sat with me.

House is feeling very sturdy in its stones, and I feel very far inside it, so weak in its midst. Not fit company, little book, sorry.

Up and down all night. Depositing, replenishing fluids. Took some aspirin—forgot about aspirin—and possibly in consequence slept and sweated a bit, woke up feeling a little restored. Fever down.

J. off to school early. The house again feels vast, substantial, cavernous. We've lived here for more than twenty years and still, after a week or two away, I forget the rooms. Very strange, big houses. This morning still in my wrapper I padded along the upstairs hallway peering into the guest bedrooms. Like museum exhibits, they are rather perfect in a sad, subtle, New England way: austere of course, old but not really antique spindled bed posts, the beds themselves high and hard. Faded, vaguely oriental patterns on the bulbous night table lamps. A knocked about but newly upholstered wing chair in each room, a dark bureau filched from the dormitories, perhaps a milky ceramic basin and pitcher on top, suggesting, feebly, morning ablutions of a prior century. Stacks of clean white (school) towels and face cloths in the bathrooms, heaps of blankets and sheets in the linen closet. Four of these chambers, not counting Brian's, and ours. It seems we have about three guests a year these days, yet something faintly human manages to animate the rooms as I pass by. I think it's the carpets, the warm reds and oranges and indigo of the "Persian" rugs that seemed suitably venerable and threadbare when John and I fetched them out of garage sales during our starving schoolmaster days.

Even without a light on, the walls of the upstairs hallway are astringently white. The glass and gold-leaf frames of John's Cambridge college prints give off an impersonal glimmer. The effect this morning, I decide, is really not very nice. It is certainly not an esthetic statement or domestic greeting from John and Margaret Greeve. It says instead: these are established and traditional spaces. Never mind that the tradition is finally unidentifiable and rather alien to the sensibilities of your hosts. In truth, when we first came to Wells, I took some care to appoint these rooms—set out those vestigial basins, re-shaded those ancient lamps, hung those etchings of ruined abbeys I would collect from the odd Vermont flea market. I thought at the time that I had done a pretty good imitation of what headmaster's house guest quarters ought to look like. Even then we rarely had a guest. Bad of me not to have considered the matter from a guest's perspective—which could only have been: neat, clean, slightly of another era, not really comfortable. And (I hope only subliminally) *don't stay*. Terrible really. But the carpets do say something nice to me as I pass all those open doors.

Downstairs is better. But I am so small in this house! Have I always been? There is at least color here—and big good pictures. How pleased with themselves the New England fathers must have been to have marked off these spacious, high-ceilinged rooms. The effect is really created by the light, by the high windows. Down here the carpets are rather good and the wing chairs are deep burgundy and forest green. There are pictures (all reproductions) you want to look at, a sexy pre-Raphaelite girl doleful at her escritoire, Ophelia about to submerge under lily pads. There are polished boxes on polished tables. There are so many gilt-framed photos of Greeves in every conceivable attitude that a casual observer would get the impression that we are a family of thirteen. And as with the upstairs, this downstairs illusion bears some analysis. Whence all this seeming opulence, these alcoves of cushy chairs and sofas snuggled arm to arm, this dark, jeweled den, this sleek sweep of futuristic kitchen appliances? Of course the protocols and pride and periodic state occasions of Wells School require a degree of comfort and taste. But we might be a touch grand in that department. Why? For whom? This morning it's merely making me tired on behalf of the maintenance and housekeeping staffs. But I will admit also that the colors are picking me up. I love the Cape, and Little House is a treasure, but I realize there is no color there. We left out the color.

Liv Upjohn called to welcome me home. Very sweet, but in a minute and a half I was drenched in sweat and wobbly in my knees. Yes, I told her, the Cape was wonderful, but a bothersome bug... Liv said she understood—"everybody here had the bug this summer." Anarchically, wickedly, I made a mental x-ray of everybody at Wells riddled with blurry little *–nomas*. A three minute conversation and I needed to lie down for an hour.

Dozed and wakened by the unearthly hooting of Arnold Leiber downstairs. He was seeking permission to snoop around after electrical problems her feared may have resulted from a bad storm over the weekend. He said there had been "surges" in Wells village and people suffered the devastation of televisions and other appliances. I didn't tell Arnold that I was impressed that nature still had the ingenuity to do such things inside people's houses. So I followed old Arnold from room to room while we checked things, finding only flashing digital clocks in the stove and stereo and radios, which he blessedly put right. Such very basic operations have always undone me, convincing me each time that if the little clock is flashing, a new appliance displaying the right time must be purchased as soon as possible. J., pretending to know better, retrieves the owner's manual from one of his chaotic files, then in an attitude of great sadness crouches down uncomfortably and begins to try things. Arnold, although he grows stranger every minute, is a godsend.

J. home at five. We go tomorrow, no less, back to Boston. Dr. Dietrich will have posted my pictures and findings to a reputedly excellent oncologist, Dr. Felice. Could this be felicitous? J. has already told Val and Frank the probable gist. We agree that the Wells story should be that I have had a "scare" and that I need to be tested and watched for a while. J. also asked me, so sweetly, if he thought I was still up to editing the *Wells Quarterly*. Somehow I had put that right out of my mind. But I don't see why not. That kind of focused tedium might be very good for me—the fact that the work actually has to be done and the magazine has to come out. Could be a salvation. I noted ominously this a.m. that, feeling weak and ashy, I could not engage in the NY Times crossword. It was not hard, but I could not finish.

Salad, broth, a little stir fry, wine with dinner. J. then back to school for some desk work. Before bed we watch a video episode of *Jewel in the Crown*. Deep, total immersion. Perfect. Maybe Paul Scott—and all those beautiful actors—are the cure. Somebody involved in the production must know all about *-nomas*.

Too tired to read. Medicine tomorrow. God help me.

John:

25 September

Mr. Jake Levin
R.D. 3
Petersboro, New Hampshire

Dear Jake,

I am finding this a very hard letter to write because of the weight it bears, but then you are my friend, and what are friends for?

Meg is ill, very ill. She felt feverish and achy practically all summer on the Cape, but the symptoms—no appetite, swollen glands, lumps, aches—were somehow so ordinary, except for their duration, that we couldn't bring ourselves to get serious about them. At the end of the summer she had a series of tests and then a more serious one at Mass. General, and the diagnosis is cancer. It is apparently widespread and virulent, although there have been no visibly dramatic signs of this yet. There are tumors and other irregular growths on her cervix, abdomen and breast, and probably elsewhere. The cancer has "metastasized."

We have only known something was seriously wrong for a week. The prospect could not be less promising. Neither of us knows really how to respond. It hurts in a new way. It puts you on edge. I wake up to a weak papery feeling which permeates every thought and action. The effect is to make everything feel like an anxious present. Nothing in the past seems substantial, the future unthinkable. In this present I keep telling myself the news: cancer. I can't get the off-white sickly smell of the hospital out of my system. In spite of all the routines and the gadgetry, there is an aura of personal unease generated by the staff. I don't think I'm imagining it. A sense of too many people with too much to do.

Doctors and nurses seem reticent and haggard. They are reasonable and objective in the manner of my students when they are not telling the whole story. Not that they necessarily know the whole story, at least in their heads.

The word for it is cancer, but it is much more than an irregular replication of cells and tissue. At least it's much more than that in a person, in Meg. Describing the course of a cancer in terms of what studies show, in terms of treatments, in terms of the grizzly symptoms and inevitabilities, is not it. No more than childbirth is the dilation of the cervix, rapid contractions, expulsion of a fetus and placenta. Like childbirth, cancer comes freighted with feeling and it has a theme. For Meg, her "rot," as she calls it, is a summary comment on her adulthood, a consequence in her personal theology she would like to accept, or at least understand. As you know, Meg has always been an expansive, self-effacing person, a thinker. Being sick has made her think about herself and her body. She now has to think about alternative "therapies": nauseating radiation vs. nauseating medicines, etc. She will have to decide on terrifying, humiliating surgeries. Such inescapable preoccupation with her physical self is utterly abhorrent to her. The worst thing about this cancer for her is that it is trivializing what experience she has left.

Right now we don't know how much time she has. Again, we've only known for certain for about a week. Neither of us has a feeling for this cancer's rhythm or velocity. Our most hopeful plan is to get her home and settled as soon as possible, or if that is not possible, to get her to a comfortable hospital as close to Wells as we can arrange.

Meg will do fine. Cancer could never diminish her. This morning she said her diagnosis places a damper on some of her plans for a second career. "I've always wanted to start a world-wide mission to save the rich and powerful from themselves."

It is I who may not do fine. Without distraction, I think I could do all right by Meg in her illness. The serving and tending are

Greeves Passing

easy—are a relief—when you love someone so thoroughly. What scares me is the rest: school. I haven't let myself think about it, but we're just moving into full swing, and I can't imagine holding the reins in a convincing manner. Frankly school—even just teaching school—has always been daunting to me. I still have bad dreams about it. But now, since we've been in Boston, it just feels like noise, a swarming, irritating buzz just outside the sphere of what I can, with effort, manage to think about clearly. You can't know what school is like, Jake.

So that's my news. I'm lost.

Write Meg and make her laugh. Send her a poem.

Love, J.

Brian:

San Rafael

I probably shouldn't have done it, but I checked in at the central post office for general delivery mail and, sure enough, another letter from my father. This was a fairly long one, newsy. School's starting again, and he's gearing up the old rituals and routines. The new kids are going to feel scared. They're not going to know how to say good-bye to their parents. Most of the old kids are going to have a sinking stomach as they think about starting it all up again.

Wells. The smell of those no-taste eggs in the morning. The haze in the refectory at that hour, the clinking dishes and mumbling, all of it when you're still underwater-tired. How do institutions make eggs like that? Slabs of pale rubber, almost like meat. I've never had an egg like that in a house or in a restaurant. One of life's mysteries.

Morning chapel at Wells. Up and down. It's probably due to being Episcopal, but there's something about the service that seems suspiciously designed for schools. Lots of reciting, no relaxing. Up and down. Choir was always amazing. Boys can sing. And almost all of the hymns are fine. Episcopalians know their hymns for life. Chaplain Chuck didn't have much to say, but he didn't put me off. It was Dad who always made my stomach small. Whether he read the lessons or whether he preached, I wanted to fly up through the roof. Not his fault. He's actually a good speaker. He's basically a good thinker. But it is embarrassingly personal to have your father up in a pulpit in front of everyone you know, talking—and believe me, talking from the heart—about the most personal things in the world—telling the truth, being jealous of people, coveting things, not trying hard enough, dying, sex, your friends, families. My father could not have begun to talk about those things that way with my mother and me at home. That was way too personal for us, and especially him. But to talk about it in front of the multitudes, to preach as an authority—I wanted to disappear. Fathers have to be fathers, but fathers who are headmasters are a problem, because they're no longer just your private, personal father. In a way they're everybody's father. Even the wisest, kindest fathers miss the mark when they're trying to communicate with their sons. You feel it, feel his failure to get what is really the matter with you or what you really care about, and that's understandable. You grow up and learn to live with that. But your headmaster father is missing the mark, by a little or a lot, with four hundred boys, and you feel the weight of all that missing, all the resentment, and all the sarcasm. When your headmaster father steps up into the pulpit and starts talking about the hopelessness of being cool—one of his favorite themes—you want to die.

For four years of Wells chapel I felt physically tense—ringing in my ears, acid in my gut—every minute of the service. In fact, I felt it every time the school assembled, whether in chapel or Hall or in the refectory. The only school rule I regularly broke was walking off grounds. I walked off the grounds in order to breathe.

In some ways I didn't have a home, at least a private personal home, when I was at Wells—especially after I started going there. I had a room of my own, thank God, but the rest of the house could be invaded at any moment. And was. Students, even sometimes my friends, would come over for a heart to heart with Dad, sometimes Mom. He wasn't my father to them, he was their teacher or advisor or the great headmaster, or maybe just a nice man. I could have been a little jealous of that. I was a fairly mean-spirited little guy. It wasn't that I wanted to have my father all to myself for deep counseling and inspiration. That's the last thing I wanted. I just didn't want other people to be dependent on my father, or for that matter to idolize him. I wanted him to keep his distance like other fathers.

It wasn't great, but it wasn't the worst thing either, that kids would get down on him and complain about something he said or a discipline decision he made. It was easier to go into the lounge or the locker room and hear somebody say "Greeve's such an asshole" (provided it wasn't me) than it was for some kid to come up to me and say "Your father is the most completely good man I have ever met." A lot of times those guys were the nerdiest, most pitiful people in the school. They meant it. He did reach out to those guys.

It used to hurt him when the kids got sour about school and about him—not because he couldn't take being unpopular, but because I think he really did fear that he had done something hurtful or wrong to somebody. Thirty years in a boarding school and he never got the message that boys raise hell for the hell of it, they get mad for no special reason. They need to see their teachers as charlatans sometimes. They need to hate their coaches. They need to think the people in charge are schemers or hypocrites. It's like the way people feel about the president. Who knows what presidents are really like? You just need to vent your strong, know-it-all gut feelings. Sometimes a kid would really square off against Dad in a *Wellsian* article or, if the kid was brave, to his face. Dad always took it. He was really devastated, but he wouldn't show it and he certainly wouldn't fight back. What devastated him was that he almost always liked the kid who was giving him shit. He really isn't an enemy-maker. He doesn't stand on his headmaster authority much. He just believes that there's a reason the seniors get ornery and wild every spring. He probably even thinks it's a good reason, and when he figures it out, he'll be able to do something helpful and sensible, and everybody will get happily down to business again. He really doesn't have a clue about the sheer hell in people.

That's enough about Wells. I can get back into it so fast. That was every year of my life. Years start in September and go till June. You get some time on the Cape or in the mountains, but everybody's living September to June in their heads. Coming back in cars, some booze, maybe some pot smuggled in kids' trunks. The opening convocation, setting up your room again, your room that was going to smell like stale laundry, your room with the bad plaster, the indestructible bathroom down the hall. From outside the Wells gates, the dorms and chapel and recitation hall sit on the Connecticut hillside like a Christmas card. Everything looks settled and sure of itself. Inside it's close and tense and edgy — definitely not the best days of anybody's life. Except maybe in dad's head. People buy it, though. Even the kids buy it — most of the time. They grind for grades. Beat each other's brains out for honors and prizes. The unstated secret, the main principle of the school — all schools maybe — is to keep you moving. Start up early, off to class, off to chapel, off to meals, off to sports, off to choir, off to community service. No stopping, no long, deep thinking, no rest, no surprises, no sex. I've been five years out of that airless fucking place and I'm still not out.

John:

30 September

Mr. and Mrs. Frank Greeve
14 Bingham Drive
Tarrytown, New York

Dear Val and Frank,

Sorry for the tardy response to your note and flowers, but school has been proceeding just as if my life were not in disarray. It is my considered conclusion as a schoolmaster that over the centuries during which schools have been established to pass on the culture to adolescents, the cumulative gains have been exactly zero. Every single boy seems to have to try being a laggard, thief, cheat, lunatic, etc., for himself. That you and I and millions of others have already learned these lessons matters not to these hell-bent *tabulae rasae*.

This evening as I was walking from my tidy school study to my untidy home study, a dorm master presented me with a badly shaken third former who had escalated some dorm room rivalry by urinating copiously into a balloon and then chucking this dreadful missile through the open door of his enemies. Are there appropriate words of rebuke for such an infraction? What, if anything, should I write to the parents without their losing all hope? The boy won my heart, though, by offering absolutely nothing in his own defense. Sometimes I think about my Prize Day speeches and addresses to new parents on the beautiful mission of youth and my own beautiful mission to youth, and then I think of things like flying balloons full of urine.

Meg greatly appreciates the flowers and the books. She is for the moment reasonably comfortable at Mass. General. She has made the decision to have no surgeries, and this has been hard for her. I agree with her completely, although the decision carries with it the certainty that she will have less time and probably more pain. One thing we had not thought of was that given the nature of this particular kind of cancer and its medications, she has virtually no immunity or resistance to anything else. This means, among other things, that coming home permanently is a chancy venture. This is vexing, as coming home is the thing Meg most wants. She says she can't imagine being scared of anything at home in her own bed. We shall have to see. For the time being she seems to be managing well. She has little interest in food, but she reads voraciously between jabs and intrusions from the nurses, and her conversation is still in top form. She asks after you without cease. For my sake, too, I hope your projected New England toot works out. It would be good for you to see her while she is relatively strong.

Thanks, Frank, for helping me contend with the Brian problem. It's maddening when there is no promising starting point. I have no idea what country he's in—or even what continent. I find this makes me so irrationally angry at him I can't sleep. Then I start to dredge up all the sad and vile things, including the worst, that might have happened to him. Nevertheless, if he should cruise in casually six months hence all hairy and rumpled with another incomprehensible companion in tow and learn his mother is dead, that would be a guilt and a sadness I would like very much to lighten. We shall see.

I think I'm glad school keeps me preoccupied. It feels different this year: running powerfully downwind with a wobbly, undersized tiller and no other point of sail possible.

Hope to see you soon.

Love, J.

Meg:

                                    Mass. General Hospital

Reprieve! Today just talk and preparation. Dr. Felice is an imposing presence. Not at all soulful, like Dr. K., which at this point is quite OK, as Dr. K., once he got word of my "involvement," could not begin to hide his hopelessness. Dr. F. is another story altogether. Big man, massive, bony brow, not quite Neanderthal. I'm told oncologists, like internal medical people, are extra smart because they have to do so much analysis. I want Dr. F. to be very, very smart.

His first words: How are you feeling right now? Then: I don't think I have to tell you that your condition is very serious. He didn't, but his way of laying it all out made everything firm and official. I felt almost reassured as he summarized my involvements. No longer am I a cruelly targeted anomaly, but a legitimate member of an earnest legion of multiply involved somebody-or-other's sarcoma patients. Amazingly, he wanted to examine me further, as if my file wasn't impressive enough. Mostly probes and peeps, but they also took two more little boxlets of my blood, along with a few x-rays. Mass. General's not too bad, I think, the parts I saw rather shiny and speedy, although the whole place seems inhumanly big. Before we go home, J. and Dr. F. and I are supposed to sit down and discuss my treatment. But basically, three things will happen to me. Certain of my bad patches are going to be irradiated, but that will be later, after the chemotherapy. Tomorrow I go in for my first course. There are two groups of medicines, one to poison the cancer, then another round to detoxify the poisons. Nothing experimental here, I am assured, but "new and improved," in Dr. F.'s estimation.

One rotten bit of news, however. I had somehow got it into my head that the chemotherapy would take the form of pills or another sulfuric frappe. No such luck—injected right in the tender crook of my arm. Wish he hadn't told me. I can only think of the shots the vet gave sweet old Chester when he had to be put down. Poor baby knew what was up, I think. Couldn't move his hind legs anymore and I could feel his little hum against my chest as he sat on my lap. The vet had to give a first shot so the final shot wouldn't "burn." Clearly worked. Chester just went quiet and was gone. He never stirred. It was very, very final. I wouldn't mind one of those first shots. Might even consider the second one day...

What to expect: "Everyone responds differently," Dr. F. begins, and I am at once unsettled. I can expect, however, nausea and some vomiting, dry mouth, dry throat, loss of appetite (appetite???), possibly diarrhea, then constipation, dizziness, general weakness. There was more, but I let it wash over me. Somehow I already know. Toward the end of the session, seemingly out of a fog, I heard Dr. F. saying that some women like to go out and find a wig at the outset, since that's not much fun to think about and awkward to do when the chemo is underway. I guess that's considerate on his part. I try to imagine diverting our drive back to Wells to find a wig shop. How is it that I've never in my life seen a wig shop? There are sometimes wigs on plastic heads at the hair dressers, but I have always thought they were a kind of totemic expression of the spirit of the place. I picture walking up and down aisle after aisle of wigs with J. Would this be playful? Funny? Ghastly? I laugh out loud, and Dr. F. is startled. I explain I just had a funny thought about wigs. Now I can't clear my head of loony images: looking intently into J.'s eyes as I try on the platinum blonde, the bouffant, the dreadlocks. "It's just a concern some women have," Dr. F. says warily. We leave it that I will begin my first course tomorrow morning. Imagine the entrée.

Meg:

School House

Driving back to Wells I feel lightheaded, bereft. Why wait a day? J. breaks the silence: "Should we get a wig?" *We.* Meg is funny: "You look all right for now, John, and as for me, I think I'll wait to see if I look cute like a baby." I don't want to think about a wig. (So why do I keep conjuring up these crazy pictures?) And in a gruesome way I *do* want to see my bald head.

Back home and a nap, a good, moist nap. Will there be sleep after chemo? A little chicken, salad, broth for dinner. Decide to save a glass of wine for before bed. I don't really have an appetite for it and don't know how it will pass over the tongue post-chemo.

Sat myself down in the den after supper and called Val. She went literally wordless for a minute, then was wonderful. She wanted to know how I was feeling *that moment,* then: was I afraid? I told her both things and realized as I did that it was a terrific relief to let it out, more accurately a terrific relief to have a soul mate like Val. She offered to come up and I think meant it, but I don't know. It might be awful to have anyone around if I am retching and spewing from the chemo. It might be nice to have her at the bedside later, if I am granted a kind of convalescent plateau.

Bless Val's heart. She called me back ten minutes after we hung up to recommend, of all things, an approach to cure. It's apparently the work of a husband and wife team called the Chelseas or the Kelseys, both M.D.s, who, Val says, do a lot of "non-invasive" work with cancer patients, including ones like me with poorish report cards. I can't remember whether she said some of her Tarrytown friends were big boosters of the Chelseas/Kelseys or had actually been treated by them. Val, at any rate, could not have been more fervent. It's all done by eating fruit and vegetables, making—actually training yourself to make—positive inner pictures of what your body should be doing, and having a positive, can-do attitude generally. I told Val it's probably too close to D-Day here for a purely non-invasive alternative. But by all means send the books. Who knows? Val says there is a kind of Chelseas/Kelseys sanitarium—although I'm sure I heard the word "ashram"—up in Vancouver where they live. Val made it sound like Lourdes. Can I see myself as a peach-headed, positive thinking new initiate to the compound in Vancouver? Will my chemo disqualify me? After weeks of what felt depressingly like no development, the most consequential developments are now looming, sweeping me away before I can even deliberate properly.

Val has no scientific or medical acumen whatsoever, but what she had to say, sweet intentions aside, sounds appealing, although not the idea of removing myself to Vancouver. I'm not too proud to be cancer-involved, but I really don't think I want to dwell among a cancerous sisterhood. This is no doubt small of me. But good old Val. She's been on the money before. Aren't I the kind of soul who should be in dialog, not chemical warfare, with her nemesis? Why has that approach never been part of my discussions with my doctors? Maybe it is now. Maybe the Kelseys/Chelseas are the dawn of soulful healing. A little mental note is flickering: find Mary Baker Eddy's big book and figure out if Christian Science wasn't right all along. I hope I've got enough brain cells after this treatment to follow through. This evening it seems perfectly reasonable to think Mary Baker Eddy knew as much or more than beefy Dr. Felice. Meg, you old wing nut. You flush yourself out with violent chemicals, then with the faintest sign of returned strength, you plan to read books and watch videos explaining why you have done precisely the wrong thing. Still, it's nice thinking of Val speed-mailing me promises of hope and cure.

Nice glass of wine with J. in the den. Suddenly very sleepy, almost giddy. I wasn't a baby about the chemo injections. Dream about wigs.

John:

1 October

ANNOUNCEMENT
For Chapel and both lunches
Then to be posted on dormitory landings

It has come to Mr. Greeve's attention that the field house at St. Francis's was spray painted and their sign removed from its footings Thursday night, some time between 10 p.m. and midnight. There is good reason to believe Wells boys to have been involved. This missing sign is one of a kind, valuable and an important tradition of St. Francis Priory.

If any Wells boys were involved in this vandalism, they are invited to make themselves known to Mr. Greeve today or tomorrow. Whoever does so will be placed on disciplinary probation for the rest of the term, will be responsible for cleaning the field house, and will be required to return or replace the sign. If Mr. Greeve, through his own efforts, identifies a Wells boy or boys as the offenders, that boy or those boys will be dismissed from the school.

Meg:

School House

No good, little book. Wretched, hateful chemo, wretched night, wretched day. Alone in my room, feeling small, pitiful, abandoned by science and medicine. Everything is wrong, my poor ravaged body in revolt. A white roar inside my head. Sour chalky taste in my mouth and all the way down. Stomach seizing up in sickening, sometimes unendurable cramps. No let up, nothing helps.

So this is what medicine thinks of cancer. If I were the cancer and survived this chemical assault, I would seek deadly revenge. This isn't me. This is the way technology, or maybe just men, go after illness. They want to scorch it, cut it out, beat the hell out of it. And I was all compliance. Please stop this, end this.

John:

2 October

Separate copies to the parents of:
Toby Witherington (6th)
Tom Foster (6th)
Charles DeMas (5th)

Dear Mr. and Mrs._____,

By now _____ has possibly told you that he has, along with two companions, been placed on disciplinary probation for the remainder of the term for a Major Infraction: spray-painting a wall of the St. Francis Priory field house and removing the school sign. This foray behind St. Francis's lines also entailed signing out falsely, thereby violating the school's honor code—an infraction every bit as serious as the vandalism.

"Vandalism" may sound harsh, but I am going to retain the term. What the boys had in mind, frankly, was something of a lark. And that, in our opinion, is what it mainly was, although I don't think I'll tell them that. For your information, no harm was finally done. The boys will experience the decidedly appropriate humiliation of two long weekend afternoons scouring and repainting a large field house wall, and they have already returned the undamaged sign from its place of concealment.

You can be proud of the forthright manner in which they confessed—albeit under a fairly stern ultimatum from me. They are good boys who have each put together a creditable record of achievement and service here. Please be assured that this stunt, provided its like does not recur, will do nothing to mar that record.

Greeves Passing

If you have any further questions or concerns, please call or write, and I will respond at once.

All Good wishes,

John Oberon Greeve
Headmaster

Meg:

School House

Cramps are either easing or I am used to them. Sat down to pee this a.m., and nothing came, just a searing heat. I've apparently dried up. Water. I drink and drink, but it goes down like cotton. Now it won't come out. Where does it go? J. is calling Dr. F. in Boston.

J. is very upset. Said he can't get a helpful response from Dr. F. or anybody else there. I tell him I'm not right, and in that instant we both realize we don't know what to do. I tell J. I think I belong back in the hospital, and then I'm too tired to talk, to help make the arrangements. This is terrible, and I can see J. is beleaguered with Wells snarls, has been all week. Hate drawing him into this abyss. Let me disappear.

John:

6 October

Mr. William Truax
President, the Fiduciary Trust Co.
P.O. Box 121
New Haven, Connecticut

Dear Bill,

Thanks for your note.

Three things:

(1) I will prepare for Friday's finance meeting several potential budgets for next year, showing implications for greater and smaller enrollments, also showing the implications of reducing staff. Capital and maintenance figures have to assume estimated inflation rates, so I can't see trimming there. Agree?

(2) I am afraid that in the opening-of-school crush, the Wells: Ten Years and After study has been placed on the back burner. We have collected some data from faculty, though, and I hope to have something concrete to show by the fall board meeting in November.

(3) You may or may not have heard about the ruckus surrounding our football opener with St. Ives. A very bad show: dirty playing, punches flying, coaches losing it (which provoked an unattractive, anarchic crowd response). We benched some players. St. I's didn't. The officials penalized St. I's mightily but lost control over the game. And we got thrashed.

I wrote to Fred Maitland, head of St. I's, asking for support in addressing the problem—and was surprised not to get it. The subsequent correspondence you have seen. Unable to get even an acknowledgement from Fred that the game was a sorry spectacle, we've dropped them from our program, at least for next year. There is already some stink about this. And I suspect you'll hear some, too, mostly from older Wellsians who like the frontier approach to sport and remember when...

So be forewarned.

Meg and I both appreciate your family's concern and the gorgeous flowers. She is doing remarkably well, feisty, funny, and tired of being sick.

Best,

John

Meg:

School House

Cramps just a steady ache now, like heartburn. Dry and sour all through, can't eat, can't go. Out the window brilliant blue, leaves nearly in peak color. No relation to me.

J. is taking me back to Mass. General to stay for a while. He has lined up another specialist to have a look. Highly recommended, J. says. Val's book and video await me on the night stand. Fruits and vegetables, happy thoughts, imagining my sarcoma breaking into bits and benignly washing away — road not taken.

Worried about J. Wells is no fun right now. Brian and I are raising, I know, unspeakable possibilities. There *is* malevolence at work in the world. We are nothing before it. God help me.

John:

8 October

Memo to Tim Shire
Master, Hallowell House
<u>PERSONAL AND CONFIDENTIAL</u>

Tim—So it's really drugs? LSD, no less…

See no reason to be cautious here. Even if we overreact we will do ourselves a service, especially considering the time of year. The early indications, if true, sound horrendous.

Remember to interview the boys separately and keep them separate, until you have finished. Each has no idea of what the other has said—and thus may more easily imagine he is cooked and come clean sooner.

Meanwhile I'll be in touch with the police and see what they suggest and what our obligations are.

Meg:

> Massachusetts
> General Hospital

All tucked in and wired up to my sentinel apparatus. Here since morning. A cell to myself, which is pretty cushy as the world reckons. I'm on I.V. now, my new best friend, and there is fluid once again in this sere carcass. So much better. My head is clear again. Bodily complaints seem laughably endurable. I feel oddly safe.

J's back at the Copley Plaza. Strange to think of him moving up and down those plush corridors.

In a day or two, I'll be scanned again, and Dr. F. and the new man, Dietrich, can see if the *–nomas* survived the chemo any better than I did.

So strange, I've been an officially pitiful invalid for only a week or so, but my perceptions of the Healthy World are already altered forever. Now anybody actually walking about and purposeful seems enviably powerful. Doctors, nurses, aides are godlike in the ease with which they move through the room, the hospital, the now barely imaginable world beyond. Why, I wonder, do I so quickly attribute a moral superiority to the physically able? Actually it's obvious: the physically well are able to act, to contribute, to help make the world work. Invalids are, regarded without sentiment, a drain on community resources and energy. Even in tip-top shape, I may have been a bit of a drain on the community. If I recover, I'll make it up.

So tired now. Maybe I can sleep a bit without fouling my wires.

John:

9 October

REMARKS TO THE SCHOOL

By now some of you have heard that there is an important disciplinary inquiry afoot. To stifle rumors and hurtful speculation, I want to tell you this morning that, yes, we have a problem. As the situation stands, we have learned the following:

A sixth former in Hallowell, Steve Pennington, apparently made arrangements this summer to have his brother mail him a sizable quantity of LSD to be passed on, at a price, to interested Wells boys. The shipment seemed to have arrived in Monday's mail, and Steve sold some LSD to two other sixth formers, Charles Stone and Terry Wilcox; to a fifth former, Ed Hruska; and to a third former, Marc Slavin. Over a long afternoon yesterday and a good part of last night, the five boys just named were questioned by Mr. Shire and by me, and each has admitted to as much as I have told you. Some remaining LSD and the money collected for it have been collected by Mr. Shire. The boys have been in touch with their parents by telephone, as have I. Student Court proceedings will begin when this assembly adjourns.

Brian:

Algeciras, Spain

Nothing was doing finally in Lisbon. More than a week there, hoping to maybe meet someone, get over the no-energy, almost sick syndrome, but it wasn't working.

Cities aren't great places for health. Lisbon was pleasant I guess, cheap for a city, but not cheap enough. I went through more $ than I should have, including a $200 money order from Dad which I had no reason to expect. It was nice being around the university, although it was a good hike from my hotel. I didn't manage to hang out with anybody, but people seemed pretty much like me, so it was comfortable. University life is all right, kind of a limbo. But I am down under $1700, and felt like a change, so I got a train ticket to Algeciras where there are regular boats across to Africa.

Plan is to go to Morocco. Ferry over to Tangier for a few days, get my bearings, then maybe head for some place really cheap, but on the ocean. My health theory is to go to some place dry, hot, and sunny. I'm going to bake this crud out of my system. I hear Tangier is cheap, and cities with no tourism are unbelievably cheap. Even without any new income, I could be there for a while.

John:

11 October

Mr. and Mrs. Samuel Slavin
1300 Chafee Circle
West Hartford, Connecticut

Dear Mr. and Mrs. Slavin,

I am writing to confirm officially what I told you over the phone last night: that I have accepted the Student Court and Faculty Discipline Committee's recommendation to ask you to withdraw Marc from Wells immediately.

I know this is devastating news, and it is truly unpleasant news to bear. For what the admission is worth, Marc's was the only recommendation concerning the five boys involved in this incident that I considered reversing. On his side is his newness to the school, the obvious temptation to play up to big, influential upper formers, and of course his extraordinary intellectual promise. Overriding these considerations, however, is the impact of "pardoning" him on the eighty-nine other boys in the third form. I don't want to lose any more boys here to drugs. In order not to, I need to create a climate of opinion in which drug use is consequential. We have evolved the drug policy we now have because we learned, painfully, that the use of psychoactive drugs by adolescents is dangerous to their development, although not always in ways boys can see and accept.

I am not sure how deeply Marc is involved with drugs. I was interested to learn that he is no novice. I honestly hope that this incident is sufficiently dramatic for him to reconsider what he is doing and to free himself from drugs and their social props. If he is able to do this and if he is so inclined, I invite him to come see me in June and convince me that he should have another shot at Wells. I would gladly be convinced — and will save his place in his class, at least through June.

Please address correspondence about Marc's transcripts and records to the attention of Marge Pearse, my secretary.

I am sorry things have taken this turn. May brighter things lie ahead.

Sincerely,

John Greeve

Brian:

Algeciras, Spain

Today I had enough of Brothers Karamazov. Went down the hall and had a long bath, washed my hair, and showered. And then the time seemed right for the blazer, striped shirt and tie. In the mirror I was a man of the world, no doubt about it. Color wasn't so hot after all the time in bed. Tan goes out of my face so fast.

I headed out to the Royal Scotland Hotel, which I spotted the day I got here. Instinct was perfect. Big lobby with Persian rugs, high ceilings, mainly British and German customers. I went into a dark, cool, fairly formal room called the Carvery and ordered a pot of tea. I forgot to bring a book, so there was nothing to do but look around. Not too many people. A German family with kids, everybody in shorts and tee shirts and running shoes, having tea and sandwiches. There were four or five other people scattered around drinking wine and cocktails. It occurred to me this is exactly what I wanted, sitting there doing exactly nothing.

Meg:

School House

Liberated from Mass. General this a.m. It felt so good to be disconnected from my tubes, to get free of that lobster-like bed, all of the adjustments to which bent me in ways I didn't want to bend. Wrong, wrong—all of it, the charts, the checks, the jabs, the probes, the outrageous suggestion to pee at odd hours, the meaningless food. Only one more Course. God help me. The whole business makes me feel unworthy of the Kelseys/Chelseas.

J. planned a sweet thing on the way home—but it turned sad. Not his fault. It was such a deliciously bright alpine day, he suggested we detour our trip back to Wells and call in at Little House. He wanted to settle a few things with Jenkins about shutting off the water and hauling in the Valmar anyway. At first it felt nice to shed Boston like a fussy, trafficky skin, but I forgot how forlorn the Cape can feel after Labor Day, the car-less drive-in theaters by the dazzling light of midday, the desolate Dairy Queens and lobster roll joints. The shimmer and sparkle of sky and water as we drove high over the Bourne Bridge was diamond bright—but nothing like summer. Even the gusts swishing past the windshield seemed to be saying "later," "over," "gone."

I wished I'd never reentered the house. Dark and still, just—of course—as we left it, so utterly vacated that its emptiness was an insistent presence. I couldn't bear the familiar must in the air, the aggravated hum of the refrigerator. Jenkins was nowhere to be found. From a great label-less jug we left on top of the fridge J. poured us two glasses of not-quite-gone-to-acid white zinfandel, which we drank on the blowy deck looking out over the choppy, almost empty harbor, rigging clanking somewhere, gulls. It was not restful. Felt as though we were waiting someplace unfamiliar in the wind. J. looked up and said, for some reason, "Good-bye, Little House."

Very melancholy driving off the Cape toward Wells. Neither of us said much, nor did music seem right on the car radio. As we cleared New Bedford and headed toward Providence, it recurred to me with a sudden clarity haw really poor these little not-quite-seaside towns are. Shoreham nearly broke my heart, the whole main drag a sequence of store fronts unimaginable to enter. Impromptu hair salons, nail care, used children's clothes, a closed-down carpet and tile store, closed-down bed and bath shop, more hair and nail care, closed pizzeria, uneatable Chinese take-out place, auto parts, for rent, for rent, for rent. The only life a tumble of patrons and matrons moving in and out of the 24 Hour Deli. On the roof is a listing white plywood sign with black painted letters: XEROXING, FAX. Poor Shoreham. No more fishing, no more canning, no more mill work. No one wants a summer place in Shoreham. No one wants to put a boat in at the oily, littered, faintly foul town slip. Nothing to do in Shoreham. A squeamish local paper reports cocaine has come to Shoreham. Who buys it? What are the rituals of its use? How are the sweat-shirted, tattooed young men of Shoreham transformed by cocaine? We buy a paper and J. uses the men's at the 24 Hour Deli/XEROXING, FAX.

Behind a tired shelf or two of long unwatched action videos, I spot the luridly colorful cartons containing the pornography selections. Unlike anything else in Shoreham on this blanchingly bright October afternoon, these come-ons are pulsing, livid, sure of themselves. We drive out of Shoreham, and I form the dismal equation: Shoreham is to town as my condition is to me. I want to cry.

Once again School House, when we arrive in Wells, seems monumental, cavernous, also where I belong. J. brings me broth, chicken snips, and salad in bed. Read, got lost in Edna St. Vincent Millay's poems, confide in little book and, spent, surrender. Bless J. for his hopes for this day.

John:

19 October

Mrs. Philip Stone
Honey Hill
R.R. 2
Bedford, New York

Dear Mrs. Stone,

I suppose there is no way to soften the hurt and bad feelings that follow the dismissal of a student from school, especially a sixth former. I feel, however, in Charles's case, those bad feelings may have distorted some important matters of fact. Whatever the source of the confusion, let me make the following matters clear.

(1) I made no disciplinary distinction between the boys who purchased the drugs and the boy who sold them, because both acts violate the very core of the school's drug policy. I simply don't believe the buying/selling distinction is important. Without one, there would not be the other. I am aware that state and federal laws do draw such a distinction, and I am also aware that according to every published measure of the phenomenon, the state and federal laws have done nothing to curb rising drug use among the young.

(2) I am sorry if anything I wrote or said over the phone gave you the impression that Charles did "nothing good" here. By saying his experience wasn't "entirely happy," I meant only that. I am glad that you and he feel there was so much that was positive in his career at Wells.

(3) I made no mention of reapplication for a later term or a post-graduate year because I don't think either course would be

desirable, either for Charles or for Wells. For Charles to return at a later time after a stop-gap spell at another school would suggest that our policy for senior boys who break major rules is to "rusticate" them temporarily. This is not our policy. We rarely take post-graduate students, and when we do they are generally promising scholars who are either chronologically or physically young and who want another year's preparation and maturity before college. I don't think Charles needs such a year, here or elsewhere.

(4) I did not "humiliate" Charles and the other boys involved before the whole student body. I did state briefly what happened and that Charles was involved. The boys admitted as much to the Student Court, to the Faculty Discipline Committee, and to their friends. Not to have announced to the assembled school what had happened would without question have given rise to speculation and rumor that would have been far more hurtful than the truth.

(5) I did not say, nor did I mean to imply, that "I wanted nothing further to do" with you or with Charles. I suggested that you deal with Mrs. Pearse directly only with respect to Charles's transcript. Mrs. Pearse serves as our registrar, and dealing directly with her saves a step, especially when I am out of town.

You mention that you are considering litigation. Of course this disappoints me, but you have every right to do it. It is hard for me to see the point of doing so. Charles not only had the due process of Wells school, he had it at its most deliberate and caring. I for one would be pleased to stand by our policy and our treatment of Charles in court.

Respectfully,

John Greeve

John:

19 October

Mr. William Truax
President, Fiduciary Trust Company
New Haven, Connecticut

Dear Bill,

I have this morning received a letter from a mother who says she might be interested in suing us in order to restore the dignity of her sixth form son who was recently dismissed for purchasing LSD from another boy in Hallowell. My experience of such mothers and such letters is that the ominous hints rarely come to writs. Nevertheless you might want to bounce her letter off Seymour to see what, as counsel, he makes of it. Just in case it comes to something, I am preparing a file of disciplinary memos, housemaster's notes, my address to the school, and all correspondence on the matter. I will make myself available to Seymour at his convenience, should he want more information.

Best,

John

John:

20 October

REMARKS TO THE SCHOOL

Since you are subjected, from time to time, to warnings, reprisals, and headmasterly criticism from this stage, I thought it would be nice—and also appropriate—this morning to praise you. What in particular I would like to praise is your exceptionally courteous reception of Mr. Ambioto yesterday in Long Assembly.

I will concede that his observations were rather specialized. Perhaps some general points should have been established before he plunged into the intricacies of East African partisan politics. His accent, too, made stretches of the talk hard to follow. The length of the talk was not, however, Mr. Ambioto's fault. He asked me how long he should speak, and I told him until he heard the carillon. Mrs. Pearse, however, was called away from her desk late yesterday morning, and the awaited signal never sounded. Thus Mr. Ambioto unwittingly gave us the longest continuous address ever delivered in Perry Chapel—perhaps the longest in the history of Wells. Entirely our fault, of course.

Anyway, from my perspective gazing out into all your faces, you looked a perfect sea of attentiveness and restraint. There was talk afterwards of growling stomachs, but none of this reached the pulpit.

So three cheers for you, perhaps one or two for Mr. Ambioto, and none for Greeve. I suppose one should simply expect exquisite manners from Wells boys and say nothing about it, but I can't help it. You were easy to be proud of yesterday. My compliments and apologies for the discomfort.

Good morning.

Meg:

School House

Another lazy day. Night sleep has been so strangely light. I become a hummingbird just below the surface of consciousness, to which I arise every few hours. I crave something deep and dark, the full descent, not this anxious hovering.

This a.m. I silently beheld my J. as he rose, showered, dressed and otherwise girded himself for the world. Poor baby, he tells me only a little and with wise good humor, but I know when school is hurting him. There is a flash—yes—of outrage in his eyes, a set of the mouth, a rigidity between collar and belt. The "issues" don't seem to matter anymore; that is, they certainly don't matter to me. J., who has certainly seen every variety of bad schoolboy behavior, cannot be knocked off center by what happens, but he is still too mortally vulnerable to everybody's meanness. He can't rest, literally, if one or another of his privately unhappy colleagues projects bad will or deviousness onto him or a decision he has made, invariably with great patience. Why aren't my prayers for him answered? Why hasn't he come to know, now and forever, that he is all right, sound, valued, loved, imperfect, but very, very fine? How come any spotty fifteen-year-old who has pinched an illicit hookah from his spotty friend's closet can call up such depthless disappointment and worry in my J.? How can boys who behave like thugs in the course of their football games—as if football itself were not an invitation to assault and battery—unsettle J., at fifty-six, to the point he cannot take up a forkful of food? And when the heads of school and coaches of teams who play foul decide not to notice, why does this surprise him? He is not inclined to nostalgia; he does not claim to have seen a better day. Is this perhaps his best quality, this inability not to feel precisely as bad as others want him to feel? Folly, malevolence, ignorant surmises hurt him. What dark, sad, prior part of him lets him absorb and store up the sins of the world as his own? Is this why I love him so? Is this why I, so deceptively and eggheadedly unflappable, hate, I mean HATE the self-absorbed and mean-spirited colleagues who bring him down, the effete weasels who let Wells School feed them three hot meals a day, furnish, heat, clean and improve charming flats and houses for them, pay them a livable salary to teach 150 minutes a day for eight and a half months a year? I have learned—but why hasn't J.—that awful people are shrewdly good at awfulness. They are not clumsy and superficial in their slights and affronts. They know, for instance, that they don't even have to question J.'s integrity and ability to devastate him; they need only to perform badly themselves. John will suffer on their account. He will take himself to task and let others take him to task for anything wrong, mean, or shabby at school, as if his capacity for hurt were infinite. And is this how Wells thrives? By allowing every awful person to escape the deadening burden of his or her awfulness by letting John take it on? For he will. He always will. And aren't I a big help? A dried up, sour-mouthed bag of bones, toxic fluids pulsing fitfully through her vessels in search of still more toxic intruders. After bad days and dark hours, J. will look at me and say, "So Wells comes to this?" Poor sweet baby will never say, but he doesn't have to say, so wife comes to this? So just what is his capacity for deadly empathy? I hope it is vaster than I can fathom, but it cannot be infinite. God help us.

Stop. This day did not begin in such gloom. It began with a vision of J. standing at his bureau. He had just stepped into his shorts, his hair still wet and tousled from the shower. His hands were placed lightly on the bureau top, creating an impression that he might be posing some grave silent question to the mirror. I believe he was just resting, one of those morning pauses before the will sets one in terrible motion.

Very nice to take a long anonymous measure of the man I have loved so much. Morning sun somehow irradiated the drawn shades to create a pearly grey light in the room, perfect atmosphere for not-yet-day. Such a man, standing so still beyond the foot of the bed. Still a very beautiful man. I'm so lucky to have a tall, rangy J., that great vulnerable stretch of back, the good nubs of his spine, the sharp symmetry of shoulder blades. For the longest time he didn't move. What must he have been thinking? Was it thought? I hope it was pure feeling. Oh, the beautiful back, the beloved milky skin. J., I thought, you are so exposed. Behind that precious wonderful back, the worst could happen, no doubt will.

I remember that back burnt brown, color of coffee and cream, glistening with cold salt water. J. had gotten hold of Geoff Dusenberry's old yawl for the honeymoon, and it somehow seemed due to us that there would be a week of unbroken July sunshine, light but steady air, and plenty of room to put in at every cove. I can see us, feel us at anchor off Cuttyhunk. Five o'clock and the late sun still a needling presence on face and neck, back and sides. It occurred to J., most modest of men, that we should be naked every possible second. Or was that empathy, too? If so, bless him, bless that insistent sun, the caressing puffs, the creaking, rocking hull of that sweet old boat. Below decks, nuzzling in the cockpit, standing brazenly at the bow, thigh to thigh, cock to belly, nipple to rib, J.'s great warm brown hand clasping the back of my neck. That week, little book, there was no beginning or end to it. No one had to tell us a thing. We would row the dinghy to shore, cadge some yacht club shower and emerge to find each other irresistible to the touch. Any dockside bar was hilarious. Nobody ever knew as much as we did. But at Pocasset we didn't know enough to get out of the rain when, eating our lobster under what we thought were the stars, it started to rain like stink, and we were soaked to the skin before we could rise from the table. We were insane, but also inspired, to board our dinghy in the deluge. As it filled up to the point of swamping, we paddled around hysterically from mooring to mooring, looking without aid of flashlight for our yawl. Of course we found it. We were in the great grip. We were in thrall. There is no getting dry from salt water, but we made dry, silky skin. There is no getting warm, even in summer, on a stormy night on the water, but we were snug as babies. I remember a buttery kerosene lantern hanging over the sink below, all night ripples of dull gold washing back and forth over our gold-rosy skin as the boat rose and fell, rocked and creaked. Oh that was sex. How beautiful to fall back into that oceanic knowing while moving with the ocean itself. It did not start or stop, there was only the holding fast, rocking together, the greedy blindness, the swimming over and into each other, saying yes to it all, yes to everything. I was so powerfully blessed to have learned then that the depth of sex is not in any act—I forget our acts—but in the realization that in all of it we were, I was, held fast in the larger dance. J. and I were there, then, tuned to that surely cosmic, surely eternal frequency. THAT, readers of manuals, swallowers of hopper-uppers, is the truth. That is the point. Did we come together? Beside the point. We were rapt together, held fast in the bigger thing. He came, I came, came and came. Only in the misty morning, by no means first light, did I awake in my salt water-chafed and rather chilly flesh, lying atop bed clothes seemingly as damp as I was. At the foot of our berth, J.'s white little-boy's bum and long brown back. Making coffee for us. There could be no plan for such a morning. The three or four days ahead of us were incalculably vast, brighter than the spangling horizon. In a minute there would be hot coffee and all of J.'s long brown delicious self. "Meg," he said, "do you know how much I love Pocasset?"

Broth, salad, one of those paper thin ribbons of steak. Not disagreeable. I will be strong like bull. J. at a meeting till late—then maybe a glass of wine with him. It's been a nice, nice day with you, little book. Maybe there is life after chemo.

Brian:

Algeciras, Spain

Booked my ticket for Tangier today. I didn't realize it only takes an hour or so—you can see it from the pier.

I was thinking about getting a cabin or something. When I get there it's going to be hot sun, lots of sparkling water, light food, and sleep until I'm healthy. I may have to blow some money. But even in the worst case, which is going home, I'm not showing up sick. That would probably confirm the worst thing the Wells folks have ever thought about me. Nobody is getting that satisfaction. I'd rather be dead than pitiful.

Met a bizarre guy at the booking office. I thought he was British, but he turned out to be some kind of South American. He says he has relatives in the states, but he also says he has relatives everyplace else we talked about. He must be about my age, and he looks like something out of a movie. He wears a wrinkled tropical suit and a striped tie. He has a lot of red hair on top but short around the sides. The hair in front almost covers one of his eyes, and he keeps tossing it back. He's very affected, but pretty funny. He was also all over me. He wanted to know where I was staying, what I had for money, who I knew in and around Tangier. I found myself backing off and lying like crazy. I didn't know what he was into, and talking to him felt like a lot of work. When I left him, I had sweated completely through my shirt. Too bad, he was a person I might have hung out with, at least had a meal with, when I was a hundred per cent. I really haven't had any kind of conversation since Lisbon. His name was Avery Fish, and I wasn't up to an evening with him.

John:

25 October

REMARKS TO THE SCHOOL

First let me thank you for saving me this important spot in your rally. I'm not sure I can rival Ted Frank or Carl Maslow for passion or Coaches Shire and Kreble for determination, but I can serve you in two capacities: as a historian and as a prophet.

The historian in me insists that in order to make sense of these final contests with Haverhill, we must take a longer view than just this season. For this season has revealed a very young, very plucky, and rather unlucky Wells football team which has won only two games, while suffering six defeats. Two of those defeats were by less than a touchdown, and four games in all were lost in the last quarter of play. In contrast Haverhill, my sources tell me, is riding a crest of the Seven Schools wave. They are undefeated. They have played only one close game this season, and they are, according to an inside source who cannot be named for reasons of his personal safety, complacent in the extreme about Saturday afternoon. In other words, we have got them where we want them. History would bear this out. In the forty-six years we have met Haverhill in football, we have beaten them thirty-one times. They have returned the favor thirteen times. There have been two ties. Of those forty six contests, only twenty were played when Wells had a losing record. Of those twenty games, Wells won thirteen, lost five and tied two. This bears out an old and almost forgotten Wells proverb which goes something like, "A strong Haverhill squad does not a Wells defeat assure." Words to that effect.

But as all you Western Studies scholars know, history is not the only source of knowledge. There is also direct revelation. Here too I have had access to well-placed sources. Last night I was unable

Greeves Passing

to sleep and was nodding off fitfully at dawn when I detected a lightening on the horizon. Too early for the sun, I told myself and sat bolt upright. Suddenly the room was aglow with light, and everywhere about me I heard the whooshing and flapping of wings. Then lo, dark and quiet were restored, and all was as it had been, with the exception of a rectilinear luminescence glowing faintly on the pillow case. This was a sealed envelope which I picked up gingerly and which I will share with you this afternoon.

Please bear with me…

It seems to be a card, a blank card….no, there are some figures here…it says…it says….Haverhill 20, Wells 26. Extraordinary.

One more thing, boys, before we head out to fulfill this prophecy. It's trite—but still important—to remind you that how we do it is what matters, not what the scoreboard says. Many of you recall that this year's football season got off to a sour start at St. I's. That was a game I would like to forget, and my regret has nothing to do with football. What I wish for all of us Saturday, players especially, is the indescribable elation that comes from pouring out best effort and energy. Anger, verbal abuse, and cheap shots have no part in this.

Finally, to our soccer and cross-country teams, already heard from, you need no prophecy from me to see your way to victory. What marvelous seasons you have both put behind you already.

The prospect of three fine wins on Saturday quite overwhelms me. I do believe I might be so undone by it that a full Free Day might be required for me to recover. The faculty and I hate to waste that good instructional time, but we shall have to see what transpires.

Let's all of us, players and spectators alike, have a glorious weekend at Haverhill.

John:

26 October

MEMO TO: Coaches Kreble, Shire, Tomascek
           Athletic Department

Just a note to wish you well at Haverhill and to thank you for your good, long hours in conducting your teams through exceptionally classy seasons. It's easy to be proud of athletics at Wells this year.

One caution: not-so-veiled rumors are already rife among the players about the "traditional" post-season "bash." We have got to squash this. Let's find a minute to talk to the teams, preferably before the games, to drive home the point that we don't want to lose anybody at this point in the year to discipline or injury or anything worse. I'll have a word with dormitory faculty on the subject too.

Onward!

J.O.G.

Meg:

School House

Decision to make. Oncologist says it would be OK to delay last course of chemo for a few days in light of my being so ravaged last time. Appealing, but I wonder about the value of gaining a mouse-increment of strength before the next siege. Better maybe to get the hell of it over with. Truth is, I don't want it at all, ever again. What's wrong with me, anyway? I am not apparently of robust stock, but it was always hearts in my family. How did I get to be the cancer type? Why can't I at least have been a Kelsey type? I might have been gliding seraphically over bright gardens in Vancouver, mentally picturing health. How is it that sitting in the gray gloom of this kitchen over a rather bitter cup of tea (out of milk, again), feeling stuffed with stale straw from chin to toe, I can still be smugly dismissive of imagined Kelsey initiates with their mantras of lovely thought? I don't feel superior to them so much as annoyed at their willingness, for their aging bodies' sake, to be sweet and simple. That's exactly what's wrong with me—a refusal, a constitutional inability to be sweet and simple. I may have just answered my own question about why I am the cancer type.

Here's another puzzle I'd like to figure out, and I have a powerful premonition I'm going to figure it out whether I like it or not. How come, since I can't even remember when—last March? Possibly even last fall—I felt normal or "well," I still know (even though I can't feel) what normal and well are? I feel bad, chalkily, ashily bad; it's like a droning in the tissues, almost a current telling me *wrong, wrong, wrong, wrong.* So in Deep Meg headquarters something knows this whole cancer-malaise feeling is wrong, but in order to know it, *it*—the knower—can't itself be wrong or sick. So something deep at the core of me is neither sick nor wrong. Here's the puzzle: what is the relationship of my not-sick knower to the sickness. Why is the sickness prevailing over the knower in my sour, shrinking body? Will the knower always know, always be well? And if so, won't I hurt and suffer titanically when the body gives up and finally fails altogether? Because the knower will register that, too. I have a feeling what the Kelsey cult wants to do is pacify and charm the knower into taking healthy charge of the body again. The method is to be sweet and simple and thus give the knower a kind of prayerful nudge to step up to the task. I'm pretty sure this is Mary Baker Eddy's terrain as well, although her approach was more daring, literally out of this world. She decided that the knower was the only self and thus always and forever well. Whereas Socrates said, I always felt sensibly, that we have a divine and thus immortal spark in our mortal souls, MBE says that's the whole soul, whole self. The rest—and I have always loved this—*isn't even there.* My cancer, my jumpy, tingly skin, my rasping pipes are all an illusion. Meditation, faith, and prayer will help me to see this. But when they don't—and they don't—the illusion is awfully hard to put aside, especially when you are sicking up pure bile and passing black blood into the plumbing.

Again, it's the whole relationship between the whole and well knower and the sick known I want to understand. Does my knower stand in relation to my cancerous system as God stood in relation to Job? He was there, all right, but he wasn't, until the suspect epilogue, eager to interfere with what was going on. I shouldn't speak for animals, but I am certain that when poor old Chester met his maker at the vet's, he was just plain sick. He experienced it all, every grating pain, but he didn't also know he was sick and what an awful insult that was to the true Golden Labrador condition. How do you know, the Sophist pipes up? Chester too may have gone into that good night in profound doggy bitterness and despair. But he didn't. He just didn't, and I know it. I was there. He was on my lap. Chester exhaled the breath of life right over the back of my hand. He was sick, but he was untroubled by any knower. I could see it in the beautiful golden pools of his eyes. Even those last days when he could not raise his back legs off his smelly mat, he wriggled himself in reflexive joy when he heard me rattling the biscuits bag. And in the morning when I'd come downstairs he was as generously happy to see me as when we first brought him home. But he couldn't get up. His eyes beamed and then they ached at me, not because he was failing and he knew it, but because he couldn't get up.

Old Meg does not mind eating meals in which wood chips and ashes pass over sand paper down into cramped and roiling depths. She doesn't mind hummingbird sleep. She doesn't mind the actually fascinating image of a startled, balding owl in the morning mirror. She minds the *fact* that she is failing, diverted from keen sensation, wonder, and love by something purposeful and rotten that's taken hold of her. She is even failing ahead of schedule for females of her culture. She minds because she knows. She knows better.

A bad, no maybe a good, cry. I don't know. Why bother thinking—you only fall apart. I suppose it's the specter of the next chemo and having to make a decision. Oh, come home, J. Come home armored from niggling, needy, greedy Wells. Come home to needy, greedy Meg. She'll rig up her most tantalizing kerchief. There will be candles flickering over the canned tuna and celery. Anyway, there will be a drink and a fire and at least one good thing. Come home. Come home, come home, come home.

John:

30 October

I would like to conclude this morning's assembly by saying I am glad we won our contests with Haverhill. I cannot be as ecstatic as you are because, if you recall, I knew we were going to win. Do not misunderstand me. I am not gloating. I take no personal pride in being prophetic. For prophecy, you know, is a gift. I am merely its location, its mouthpiece.

So in closing, let me repeat that I am very pleased with the fall teams, the way one is pleased that water falls or that a sail fills with wind. I would normally dismiss you for First Class, but I seem to recall a promise...

Now, you may either remain here in assembly hall where some of the faculty and I have prepared a very informative presentation on seventeenth century breakthroughs in natural science, or you may go off and do whatever you please. I believe hot chocolate and donuts are available in the refectory for anyone interested.

Good morning.

Meg:

School House

Bad day all day, because of church.

Drove in to St. Stephen's in Cos Cob for, we believed, the choir, but we only got the children's choir. Dispirited and oddly harsh little voices, the wayward, contra-musical sound that can only be produced by children singing against their will.

But that was not the problem. The problem was probably me and the poisonous attitude I no doubt carry with me everywhere. I felt myself sitting in that pew just like an ill and cranky old woman. Who *was* that agitated little sour puss in the odd kerchief? My hopes for the service were probably unrealistic. I wanted worshipful quiet. In that worshipful quiet I wanted to pray. I wanted to pray for grace and strength as I went into the next chemo. But it was impossible. I'm not sure why it surprises me that you get no rest in an Episcopal service. Somewhere early on the Anglican fathers thought it was a good idea to keep folks standing up and sitting down. Perhaps they believed this would keep everyone alert. Between the standing up and sitting down and kneeling there is very little time to juggle the service leaflet, The Book of Common Prayer, and the hymnal. Am I the only Episcopalian who feels the need of a desk and a secretary to negotiate the liturgy?

Everything made me mad. Even J. gave me a funny look when I declaimed, probably too loudly, "all things visible and invisible" over the new mistranslation "all things seen and unseen" in the Nicene Creed. It's not a small point. My Lord of the universe created things mortals can never see, strictly invisible things. The *unseen* includes things people just don't happen to notice. What problem to mortal understanding did the words 'visible' and 'invisible' pose? I suppose continually altering sacred, familiar texts is part of the same approach to worship that wants you standing up and sitting down all the time. I know what I need. I need to find a quiet, ill-attended Catholic church, preferably in the middle of the week when there is no hint of a service. I just want to sit in the close and holy dark, maybe light a candle for my beloved, and pray until my heart breaks. May the Catholics forgive me. God knows.

The sermon was disgraceful. It was about what it means to 'fear' God, when God is love. Not an unpromising puzzle, but in the logic and language of the young associate rector, who, J. tells me, runs the parish youth program, although the youth don't like him, it all turned to mush. He did give one good example, though. He talked about how he was really afraid to come unprepared or to submit superficial work to an esteemed professor of his at college. This kind of fear, it was suggested, was compatible with a loving, if demanding, deity. But then the associate rector badly lost his way. He had read some little self-help book—or perhaps several of them—and he had pounced on the bromide that it is possible and usually best to love opposite or mutually antagonistic things. This, he said more than once, smiling like a jack-o-lantern for emphasis, was 'both/and loving,' which was to be commended over 'either/or loving,' which he found culturally narrow and outdated. Both/and: Belfast Protestants and IRA, Bosnians and Serbs, Palestinian Arabs and Zionists. It didn't help that I was also feeling very queer—a line of sharp discomfort like heartburn moving in waves between breastbone and belly. Suddenly I was soaked in perspiration and was about to ask J. to leave, when it abated a little. Could have been divine retribution for uncharitable thoughts.

The offering was welcome because you got to sit still, and Communion was fine, except for the fussy qualifications in the Eucharistic prayer,

> *Most humbly beseeching thee to grant that, by the merits and death of Thy son Jesus Christ, and through faith in his blood, we may obtain Remission of our sins and all other benefits of his passion.*

Which must have been composed by lawyers. I took the sacrament and prayed for grace, for Brian, and for J.

The drive back to Wells was lovely—was, well, autumnal. Bright, clear sky. Leaves from banana yellow to scarlet, but also plenty of green in our valley. Back home, still a little queasy in my midsection. Starvation? Fear of coming chemo? Probably. Also cancer. Too preoccupied and uncomfortable to enjoy the Brahms. Sherry didn't feel good going down.

Miserable, self-obsessed, worthless woman. So sorry. Help me. God help me. The way out is through, or so I've always told others. Learn from this. No matter what, learn something.

To Boston at six a.m. Poor J.

John:

5 November

Mr. Robert Lavell
CBS Television Network
51 West 52nd Street
New York, New York

Dear Mr. Lavell,

Thank you for your inquiry about Wells as a potential site for your *Here and Now* special: "The Last Boys' School."

I am afraid I must decline on the school's behalf. A school year, once in motion, establishes its own rhythm and momentum, and the to-do involved in being filmed might just spoil ours. Also, for whatever it says about us, we are rather avowed foes of television viewing during term. We do not recommend it in general, nor do we allow it here, either as a diversion or as a rival source of information to books and talk. We have no TV sets in our dormitories or lounges. Of course our policy reflects only our view of the relationship between television and school; the larger place of television in society is rather beyond us. In light of this, I don't think it would be very consistent to be an enthusiastic subject for television.

For what my personal observation is worth, my impressions, spotty as they are, of the *Here and Now* approach is that the point is to "see through," debunk, or, at most, to portray whatever is under scrutiny with such apparent detachment that the result is heavy irony. I may be mistaken in this, and as I say, I seldom watch television. But has *Here and Now* ever celebrated its subject? If I were a skilled film maker and knew what I know about school life, I think I could make a documentary that could show anything I chose. But what would be the point in that?

Greeves Passing

So if not at Wells, I wish you luck with your project. And I hope you are able to celebrate what is fine in the school you settle upon.

All good wishes,

John Greeve
Headmaster

Meg:

School House

So light headed and wobbly on my feet. Cancer and its poisons aside, how could a body stoke itself to rise, walk about, see and think clearly with so little real food—without the whole healthy complex that *wants* food, wants anything. Life=desire, in case anybody forgets.

Head full of soot and fog, I made my jittery way down to the kitchen in late a.m. to address the folder of *Wells Quarterly* proofs. For an eternity it seemed I sat there looking at the folder and my two red pens. Then lugubriously I began to shuffle through the articles, not one of them remotely interesting to me. There is a deadline, no less—day after tomorrow. Firing on any cylinders at all I could do this work in ninety concentrated minutes. This a.m. no cylinders churn; they sit corroding in their sleeves. I pick up my pen—sheer deadening will—scratch, scratch, scratch.

I don't think I've made much of a mark as a worker. Funny, I always felt like a dynamo of productivity as a student, and I suppose if J. had not married me and carried me off to Milton Academy, I would have finished the graduate program in Eng. Lit. and probably taught it somewhere. No regrets about that, I think. The more I have seen of life, granted from pretty remote hideouts, the less I think of academics and academic life. For every ten thousand tenure-track college professors, there may be two or three true scholars. They're probably both Jesuits. The rest turn out more or less serviceable text books and secondary material and contribute to journals that exist only so that people who are professionally obligated to publish their 'research' have a place to put it. Probably a hundred of the ten thousand are also superb teachers, an attainment that usually serves to put less gifted colleagues on edge. Inside their 'fields" university-level academics can only, and only to a limited extent, talk to themselves. Outside their fields they can be almost imbecilic, baffled by and suspicious of commerce, usually unable to make mechanical things work, arrogantly sure of themselves on political matters. Most of them hold views on the leftward margin of American liberalism, and they are so cocooned in like-mindedness that they mistake their unexamined assumptions for objective truth. With a tiny bit of reflection they might see that they are liberal-left because that political and economic point of view is the only one that likes universities as they have evolved. Academics don't like authority, even when it is necessary and right. They don't like their chairmen, their deans and provosts, the president or the trustees. They tend to see their community, state, and nation as larger, stupider universities, and correspondingly, academics don't like civil authorities, legislatures, high courts, and presidents. Academics are therefore not very good citizens, but they tend to feel they are the best citizens, like Socrates. In their unreliable citizenship academics are a lot like artists, but without the saving grace of art. And I have no doubt that if John Greeve hadn't whooshed me off to Milton as I was inching toward orals and my thesis at Cornell, I would have joined the legions of university academics, staking out my own fussy claim to something like Women Poets in the First Quarter of the Twentieth Century (or, Edna St. Vincent Millay and anybody else I could find to like). Didn't want it, don't miss it. Not that I was asked.

But such a shamefully tiny contribution! I have barely worked. Maybe the nicest part was tutoring the younger, weaker writers at Milton. I remember charging five dollars an hour, more, I consoled myself, than a babysitter gets, except babysitters get more hours. I think I was a good tutor. Or maybe it was that Milton students were so generally sound that the weaker ones were just fine. In English I never saw much difference between the weakest and the passable next tier, either at Milton or at Wells. Almost all of them, bless them, read what they were asked—interesting books generally: *Great Expectations, Jane Eyre, Catcher in the Rye*. Moreover, I have to say, most of the assigned paper topics were also interesting: How did Jane Eyre's Lowood education prepare her for the world beyond? Were Pip's expectations finally great? Was Holden Caulfield disturbed, or especially sane? So far as I could see even the dimmest fifteen- and sixteen-year-old boys of Milton's boys' division were open to thinking about those questions, in fact thought about them rather well. What my tutees lacked was strategy and polish, and I believe I helped them on that score. The trick I always felt was to keep it bone simple. "This paper," I would say, "involves making a list and then writing it up." Simple as that. Then we made up the 'list'—passages that showed the formative incidents in Jane Eyre's schooling, then the ones that showed how she got through her adult trials—and presto! The paper was in the bag. Just write up that list, boy-o. The polish came a little harder, since most boys in my experience don't care about polish. Once they think they've seen the point, they lose interest. Standard Written English was regarded at best as annoyingly required, at worst merely decorative. But here too chirpy Mrs. Greeve was good and simple: any damn fool can write a clear, correct sentence, Chip. That's all an essay is, a string of sentences. But in practice it was not so simple, especially when a boy had no conception of, or language for, sentence components and parts of speech. Even in those days progressive junior high schools were skipping systematic instruction of grammar fundamentals—in favor of what? Building little villages, replicas of Viking ships. "This sentence has no subject" or "Subject and verb don't agree here" create only bewildered sadness in a child who has never experienced the empowering distinction of subject and predicate, noun and verb. But we polished away, those nice lumpy Milton boys and I. Who knows. I think the good part was that I liked them, and they knew it. Faculty were pleased. J. and I used the money for symphony tickets. I guess that was a job, although it didn't feel like one.

Being assistant, then associate, librarian to the Adrian Bourne library of Wells School felt like a job, although I'm sure everyone knew I was mainly John's tag-along. It felt like a job because I was expected to show up at specified times and got paid mid-month like other Wells staff. Just drifting downstream. Ordering, within the budget, new requisitions, not from passionate hunches and convictions, but after guarded consideration of what the library journals recommended and what the few interested faculty cared to suggest. Indexing and cataloguing the books and periodicals when they arrived. I thought it would be very nice to work with boys on research projects, but the occasion was rare. Wells faculty don't assign much research. When a boy needed help on Islamic fundamentalism or the crack-up of the Soviet Union, Wells' few thousand volumes almost never filled the bill, and inter-library loans from the University at Storrs were always a little cumbersome. Now with computers, I fear that these will become forgotten concerns, that one day all the texts and data in the world will be but taps and clicks. God, please don't let that day come. Make us keep reading, God. Make us keep reading.

But it takes a discerning mind to make any sense of it all. How does a Wells boy know when to stop the flow? Who will tell him this bit is important and true; all the flashy bits false? This bit true but small; this bit huge. This bit is a conclusion, derived from some other undisclosed source. When computer screens have the authority of texts and when the texts are too numerous to contend with, what will a Wells boy do? He will skim the flashier bits, cut and paste with some kind of electronic Elmer's glue. He will try to get the whole business behind him as quickly as possible.

I would be of little help in that business, not that I ever really faced the problem when I was in the Bourne library. I have never had an interest in All The Information There Is, only in the selected fragments that have by chance or destiny printed themselves on my heart. I felt almost deceptive sitting in my librarian's post. I am bookish, and my rooms have always been heaped with books, so a library would seem the most natural setting imaginable for me. But the library was only camouflage, Wells' little gesture toward All The Information There Is. My books at home are secret Meg documents, dark and exciting alchemical texts, books like fires which, when I put them aside, still kindle and bubble in case

I witchily wish (*witchily wish*, yes!) to 'do' something with them. My books are like the dangerous kinds of drugs, promising sex, transcendence, ecstatic possibility. I have lived dangerously in my books. The library felt like a benign prison, heavy with safety. And truth be told, I was lonely in there. It was not just that by any measure the stately new fake Georgian building was under-used by the boys. Libraries expect patrons to sit quietly and pay no attention to anyone else. One goes to a library to become unrelated. When Brian was an underformer he came in once or twice, and my heart soared, and then he stopped coming.

I can still feel the acute awfulness of standing at the check-out desk, peering through the gray light of winter afternoon across the length of the library. If there were one or two heads visible at remote tables, it made the room all the lonelier. I was doing, I realized, absolutely nothing. I was hanging around, waiting, and if I wasn't careful, I was going to realize this in all its force, and then the hiss I was holding at bay just beyond my ears was going to mount to a roar, and I was going to collapse inward into a final hell. Standing useless and without desire at the check-out desk, I was dying in full, unbearable consciousness.

I quit that afternoon. For appearance's sake and not to reflect too badly on J., I took on 'other duties': copy editing and proofing the *Wells Quarterly*, my alleged eagle eye for the textual error leading to other editing and proofing jobs as they came up. Bearable. The important thing was that I was *out*, escaped, able to breathe a little.

J., who has a knack for the sudden loving gesture, told me one evening out of the blue that the faculty thought I was a 'remarkable woman.' I told him that Lizzie Borden and Christine Keeler were remarkable women, but I knew what he meant. He wanted me to know that some of his colleagues, who were always wonderfully kind and I think a little afraid of me, thought I was awfully smart. No one would utter the dark formula, but I knew what it was. Intentionally and visibly withdrawing from school life, when the very ethos of the place was to participate, contribute, sacrifice beyond reason, opened up the dawning possibility that there was a great, possibly superior Other World, and Margaret Greeve seemed to dwell in it. Retreating from Wells made me exotic and strangely important to the community. This is not what J. meant by passing on the 'remarkable' compliment. He was speaking, I recall, of the responses to a snippy but pretty effective Op. Ed. piece I had just published in the daily NYT: "Using, not Playing, Your Head," about the gains in mental power when a child detaches his nervous system from anything that electronically moves it, so that *it* can begin to act on the world. Many offers to reprint. I got, in sum, a little less than a thousand dollars. This piece, combined with my three published lyrics (Edna SVM imprisoned in a Connecticut village) in the "This Singing World" column of The Hartford Courant, are my entire literary oeuvre.

That and you, little book.

Still, I would like to have earned my keep. I hope loving J. has helped him to earn our keep. Good, though, to have been low impact, no?

Some rest now. Bathe, collect myself. J. home at seven.

John:

10 November

Mr. William G. Truax
President, Fiduciary Trust Company
New Haven, Connecticut

Dear Bill,

As promised after the board meeting, I am enclosing for you, and have already sent off to Seymour, our complete records, including a chronology by me of the Charles Stone disciplinary proceedings. I am very sorry it has come to litigation. I can't imagine it will cost us anything, since, however marvelous their attorneys, there isn't much of a case for the boy. As I understand it, the Wilcoxes are attached to the suit just for the ride. Mrs. Stone is footing the bill. Seymour told me over the phone that damages have already been awarded in Connecticut to parties who have been shown to be "deprived of educational opportunity" after being "publicly" defamed by school officials. If this means we can no longer address the school about important events in school life, then the whole system has gone to smash. (Incidentally, I believe I have already sent you my remarks to the school on this matter.) I hope Tim Shire and I are not tied up for days in court. I personally cannot afford that at the moment, and Mrs. Stone does not deserve the satisfaction. You know it's historically true that every Western society from 4th century B.C. Athens to the present has been obsessed with litigation at the same time it has been in accelerated decline. The letter killeth, but the spirit giveth life. Bloody-minded woman.

I really appreciate your concern about Meg. You are by no means negligent in not inquiring sooner. I have actually taken some pains to keep the nature and extent of her illness something of a secret. This may not be fair to good friends, but it has served the narrower purpose of keeping both of our lives a degree calmer. We have not yet had to undergo the trial of seeing our sadness and fear reflected and magnified in the faces of everybody we know. There will be time for that, I am sure, but I am not quite up to it yet. For the present Meg will remain with me here at home under nurses' care. She is stable for the moment, although very weak and not very comfortable. It is the nature of this cancer that she has practically no resistance or immunity to anything. Hepatitis, pneumonia, or even a virus is a greater immediate danger than the cancer.

Again, I am touched by your concern and by your generous offer to relieve me of school duties for an unspecified interim. For the time being, I would like to pass on that option. The rhythm of work at school is, besides taxing, an ordering factor in my life. I am not too proud to admit that I frankly need the work, for the time being.

All good wishes,

John

Meg:

School House

J. here every minute he can. Bless him. The greatest kindness is not nursing, it is mute loving witness. Not what he does, says — that he's here.

It's over, little book. No more chemo. Not ever will they say, "She *fought* cancer." This isn't fighting. I am the dumb feeble witness to a toxic purge. I succumbed without firing a round.

Where is cure in this? What is left of me well and whole enough to revive?

I take in a little water, rice in broth, nibbles of fruit. I pass unmentionable gruel through scalded passages.

Strength, please. Body no help. The poisons are over. Over, over, over, over. I will think about Brian, fix image after image of him. I will day by day, by grace, prepare for Brian.

Brian:

Tangier

The gods of travel are turning against me. I woke up way down because I'm still feeling lousy, carted my pack and duffel down the lobby and checked out. Big effort. I thought if I could just get on the boat, find a chair, and sit still, I'd be rested enough to make my way when I got to Tangier. No such luck. There was a long line to get through customs. Most of the people, including all of the families, went right through. The customs officer gave me a long, fishy look and asked me how long I planned to stay in Morocco. I said several weeks. He wanted to know how long exactly. I told him I really hadn't decided. Sure enough, he took me off to a kind of barracks and started asking me more questions. When I told him, politely I thought, that the information he was asking me for was all in my passport, which he had taken, he got testy and said that if I wanted to travel in Africa, I would have to cooperate. By now I was losing it, sweating like mad. He called another officer over who took everything out of my duffel and pack and started going through it, including the ledger. He asked me what it was. I told him it was a diary. He asked me what I was going to use it for, and I told him one day I would show it to my children.

I was worried now that I was going to miss my boat, and the customs officer said there was plenty of time. He was right about that. Forty-five minutes later they let me repack my stuff, stamped my passport, and said I could go through. They told me that I should tell the Moroccan customs officials in Tangier the precise length of my visit, or else I would be detained again. Weak as I was, I wanted to get those guys back. I looked for a badge or an identifying number on their uniform, but I couldn't see anything. They wear cloaks, so it's hard to see their chests. I wanted to ask them their names, but the last thing I needed was more flak and delay. But I fixed them in my memory—weasels.

Weasels in little caps and cloaks. Certain kinds of people should never be given uniforms.

I was anything but late when I finally got aboard. The ferry takes on cars, and there was an endless line of German vacation vans to load, about one every ten minutes. All the deck chairs were taken by the time I showed up, but I wedged my duffel and pack against the rail, and sat there, back to the sea. I think I dozed off for a while, and when I woke up the boat was hooting and starting to lurch away from the wharf. For a minute I thought the diesel fumes were going to make me lose it, but it got better when we started moving forward.

I got up to see if there was anything worth seeing, and a hand clapped me on the shoulder. It was Avery Fish, already talking a mile a minute. He seemed to know all about the ferry and Tangier. It occurred to me all of a sudden that maybe Avery Fish could do me some good. I told him I had a bad cold and was looking for a place where I could get some peace and quiet. He said I would be better off in Switzerland. I said I couldn't afford it. Then he got serious and told me there would be no problem finding someplace quiet and cheap in Tangier, but if I really wanted to rest, and if I felt like pushing on another three or four hours, Essaouira was the answer. He said it was his favorite Mediterranean city, that almost nobody knew about it, and that you could stay there in comfort for less than five dollars a day. I made him get specific, and he sounded as though he actually knew what he was talking about—and of course he had "good friends" there. I wasn't so sure about the extra three of four hours, though.

But for a start, Tangier.

Meg:

School House

Sports weekend again. J. sent nurse Ritchie to sit with me. I let her go when she got a call saying a Wells soccer player got a concussion. Boy apparently fine now.

Sad somehow that nurse Ritchie knows. Now all Wells knows. Boundaries down, there will be well-meaning trespasses. Don't want that, can't do that. Vital, mobile people make me feel weaker, more anxious. But where can I go?

> Home is a place where,
> When you have to go there,
> They have to take you in

There isn't any place else.

Brian. Live this day for Brian.

John:

24 November

Mr. Jake Levin
R.D. 3
Petersfield, New Hampshire

Dear Jake,

I'm late getting back to you, not because of a crush of work—there's a little of that—but because of the damned poetry. Truth of the matter is I can't finish the cancer piece. It's not because of the symbolic heaviness of doing it—to finish it would be to kill it, thus killing Meg, etc. It's not that. It's that I don't have anything more to say about it. Some of the images of being ill and hopeless may be arresting in a morbid sort of way, but they are not on their way to meaning anything. It seems to me that the only poems that work are the ones in which the meaning comes straight out at you. They are "overdetermined," like Freud's dreams. The good bits, the lucky images, etc., all participate in the larger meaning. In that way, too, I suppose, good poems, like dreams, are generated unconsciously, in the sense that they aren't worked out in advance or planned as wholes. This is not to say good poets aren't conscious of what they are doing. I think they are, and that the poem, the meaning, does come out of their deepest knowing, but in the actual act of their best writing, poets are on auto-pilot, the poetics tending to attach themselves to the rightness of the larger enterprise.

Anyhow my cancer poem doesn't seem to be the right kind of enterprise. And meaninglessness or meaning-groping isn't itself a poetic enterprise—although I'll bet you've taught many a bearded Dartmouth seminarist that it is. A pack of images organized around a voice does not a poem make, although this formula seems to cover every contemporary poem in every journal, except the Catholic ones, that I have read in the past ten years. Agree? We don't get themes and meanings any more in poems; we get voices. And since most voices, even tarted up with odd punctuation, surreal images, and curious arrangements of type, aren't very interesting, there has been a premium on spooky voices. I suppose this is why practically every poem in the New Yorker and the fabled quarterlies is in the present tense—in the New Yorker even the stories are in the present tense—and very likely in the *second* person, a hopelessly illogical and irritating device—

> You wake to fog but there is
> No fog you move to a mirror and
> It is a window and through its fog
> You see clearly
> A light in a window
> Framing a man
> Standing at his mirror
> Lost in fog

Admit it. Admit it is no better or worse than practically everything you have read in the literaries this year. It is not only bad, it is derivative. Robert Service was less derivative. There's a moral dimension to it, too. All this standing about, being a "voice," reporting surreal nonsense or, worse, reporting the commonplace as if through the eyes of a dinosaur—

> Her fingers alight on the pale ovoid,
> Extract it from its half-hole.
> It is cool on the fingers' pads,
> On her palm. Against the black iron rim
> She half-drops, half-holds it
> Running, escaping now from its center,
> Widening, now viscous pool
> About an orange-gold sun,
> Becoming, yet no longer, egg.

Fascinating stuff. Morally, if all this voicing and dumb gaping are taken seriously, it amounts to a kind of pantheistic embrace of everything. I read a prize-winning poem this month about the clubbing to death of a dog. There was no esthetic or ethical framework for this, it was no canine "Out, Out"—just a starkly rendered, highly specific animal mauling. Contemporary art. Onto which heap I don't care to throw my impressionistic pastiche of images of having cancer. There is of course a theme, a point to cancer, not only to cancer itself but to every particular cancer. But I don't happen to know what it is, haven't the courage or intelligence to know, or whatever it takes. No poem in that, which isn't to say I couldn't win a prize.

I would like to know what poems you need. What in your heart of hearts do you go to for nourishment? I want the truth. The poem I have read with the deepest satisfaction this year is Arnold's "Thyrsis." It is about resurrection and striving and hope. He believes in them. He half has it and teases you in after him. You must agree that if those lines are dead, we are all dead—yet nobody is writing them. Too hard, I suppose, too big a risk. And no prizes.

Forgive the grousing. I feel I am doing more of it these days. The headmaster is a crank and a reactionary. I am actually, strange to say, a little stir crazy. The boys have been gone for four days and won't return till Sunday p.m. I've been in the study—crackling fire, whiskey, dozing, desk work of a not too taxing kind—usually just my kind of thing, but I'm finding it eerily unsatisfying. Outside the study is another world, quite divorced from mine, a uniformed little system orbiting around Meg. It covers front hall, kitchen, laundry, stairs, landing, upstairs sitting room, and master bedroom (now Meg's). Anywhere outside that beaten path is all mine. It's strange that Meg's nurses and Meg seem to belong legitimately in the house, but I, for some reason, feel like a trespasser, sometimes even a shade, as I pad around in slippers, embarrassed to meet a nurse. Going out is worse, though. In a fit of laziness I went out to lunch at a popular restaurant hereabouts which features crepes of all sorts (crepes rhymes with grapes in our region). Terrible experience. I didn't know where to look. Never go to a restaurant alone without something fascinating to read.

Meg and I will pass a quiet Thanksgiving together, both trying not to swell up with confusing feelings about Brian and extended family, with whom we normally spend our holidays. The fact of Meg's cancer is now so pervasive that it has lost any power to frighten us. We can talk about it almost the way we talk about inflation. In all, we have about an hour of concentrated conversation every day, perhaps a half hour at the longest single stretch. We talk about topical things, my news from school and from the papers, hers from the nurses or television. So keen is Meg's intellectual acumen that she can derive amusement and generate good talk from watching television. I hate it in the abstract but it has been a godsend for her. It is marvelous how her naturally literary approach to life transforms what she watches. Since nobody on those stifling day-time serials or on the talk shows seems to be credibly connected to a world of work or to flesh and blood companions off camera, Meg is able to speculate hilariously about what the physicians in the soaps would be like in a consultation with, say, Arnold Lieber, the school's maintenance director, or how they might work alongside one of our household nurses. It is her feeling, based on fairly close viewing, that Johnny Carson is not nice. She notes how, when a guest is boring the audience and him, he mugs in that well-known way of his, but there is also a real, icy cruelty in his eyes. She finds him 'lupine.' I admit to coming around to her point of view after watching him a while in her company. He could probably not maintain his stiffly jocular approach to life off camera; the strain would kill him. He is undoubtedly cruel and lupine, if only to relax.

I was about to say that television was not getting to the essential Meg or to me, but in reviewing that last paragraph, it is very clear that both of us have been deeply affected.

We have heard nothing from Brian, and if I don't hear something this week, I am going to step up my worrying. He has never failed to greet us in some fashion on a major holiday. It is hard for Meg to imagine dying without ever seeing him again, although I personally dread more conveying to Meg that something awful, including the worst, has happened to him.

But enough of that. How's tricks in the woods? Did you shoot your own turkey, or is that no longer ecological? I meant it about wanting to know your reading. I am not evaluating your soul or measuring your taste. I am out for nourishment myself. I dearly hope *The Eve of St. Agnes* passes its annual test later this evening.

A nurse calls—most unusual. I must go.

Best to you,

John

John:

28 November

Mr. Francis McLaughlin
Poetry Editor
Commonweal
232 Madison Avenue
New York, New York

Dear. Mr. Laughlin,

I am submitting the enclosed poem for *Commonweal*.

I'm not sure if you require personal background from those who submit unsolicited material, but for what it's worth, I am a schoolmaster who has published some poetry and criticism in "little magazines" and professional journals.

Because the enclosed poem has a living referent, I wonder, in the event you decide to print it, if I may use a pseudonym. If so, "J.G. Oberon."

My Good wishes,

John Oberon Greeve

Richard Hawley

THE DEAD BURY THEIR DEAD

Here lies a woman dying.
One thing, then another, is taken away,
And she becomes the knowledge of her disease,
An apple feeling where its worm has been.

The presence of this process
We solemnly attend,
Repeating till our worry wilts
A story about ending.

A story about ending,
Death: a dream we dream to deny
The itch, the bursting, the bloom,
The apple, the eating, the worm.

Brian:

Tangier

The ride over to Tangier was actually nice. There is plenty of air in your face, and the water is beautiful, a dark blue-green, and the sky overhead was a perfect blue. I felt normal for a change.

Avery had a lot to say, but it was good to have company. I can't tell if he's the most experienced boy-traveler in the world or a phenomenal bullshitter. He told me Tangier is a city of "many pleasures." He said it about six times. I think maybe he's seen a few movies. He did give me one good idea, though. I told him about getting hassled by customs police in Algeciras, and he suggested getting out my blazer and tie and wearing them. Sure enough, when time came to pass through Tangier customs, we were waved straight through. Purpose of my visit: tourism. Expected stay: twenty-six days. Merci beaucoup.

Tangier is something else. The movies would actually be a good introduction. When you first see it spread out on the hillside, it looks just like *Casablanca*. Everything is the whitest white. We chugged in around midday, and from across the water the buildings seemed literally to gleam.

The gleaming is deceptive, though. The place is swarming with hawkers and peddlers, most of them kids. You can hear them even before they tie up the boat. Getting out of the customs pavilion was a shock. First the bright sun and the white buildings sock you in the eyes. Then the smell hits you—very strong and actually pretty bad, a mixture of sweet and rotten, like spoiled meat, but also smoky and spicy. It's not just an interesting smell, but like something gone foul. But the main business is getting past the hawkers. "Hey, Johnny! Hey, Johnny American!" They shout in English and French, a little inefficient, I think, since nearly everybody on the boat was German. The kids are wiry, energetic little guys wearing old American-looking running shoes, shorts, and tee shirts with things like The Who and U2 and Red Sox Nation written on them. They were hawking tours, hotels, polished boxes, leather wallets, kif (dope), "nice girls," and (I think some of them) themselves.

Everything's uphill from the docks. I was glad to see there is a wide beach along the water line as far as I could see. Almost nobody swimming or sunning, but there were clusters of little Arab boys running in and out of the surf, so it's obviously swimmable. I asked Avery if he swam, and he told me never—he "detests" all forms of exercise. Avery is a piece of work. Maybe a hundred yards from the ocean, a railway line and a road run parallel to the shore, and beyond that the land slopes upward to the walls of the city.

I didn't feel too well slogging up the incline. It was hot, and it felt like we were going uphill for blocks, but Avery said he knew just the hotel, and he did: an anonymous little place called The Aladdin, close to the casbah. He proposed a minor scam by which one of us would check in and get the key, then the other guy would slip in later, without registering and we would split the cost. The whole idea made me tired, and I also really wanted a room to myself, but I agreed at least to try it—as long as I was the person checking in. I felt about ready to lose it.

First we had to settle Avery in a café down the street—pretty interesting looking place, actually—while I hauled his enormous trunk, plus my duffel and back pack to The Aladdin, since it had to look like my stuff. Coming in off the street, the place was incredibly dark, with almost no room around the reception desk. The Arab clerk spoke to me in French, and I answered in English, and somehow we got through it. Like the tiny lobby, the corridor was cramped and almost pitch dark, so I banged the bags around quite a bit getting to the room. It was long and skinny, but I noticed there was enough room on the floor for me to pull the mattress off the box spring so two of us could sleep. A basin. Lavatory down the hall. I don't know if the place is really clean, but it's not disgusting. Sixty five dirham, which is about eight dollars; split two ways, four bucks a night. Nice going, Avery.

When I went back to the café to get him, I was feeling pretty terrible; maybe I had a real fever. Avery had joined a table of young Arab men in suits, and they seemed to be having a lively time. They invited me to join them, but I begged off. Avery told them I was under the weather. He obviously wanted to stay, and I couldn't give him the key, so I told him I was going back to the hotel to sleep. I'd leave the door unlocked.

Really not feeling great. I sleep, wake up in a sweat, wash, read a little, then sleep some more. Hours pass, and no Avery. Finally, when it was nearly dark, I roused myself and made my way down the street. I looked into the café where I had left him, but he was gone. I had some clear broth, ordered some kind of lamb mixed with rice and pushed it around my plate. I bought a Paris paper and drank some red wine which I cut with bottled water. No appetite, no energy. I just watched other people. No Ingrid Bergman.

Meg:

School House

Sunday. J. home all day. Much better. No church.

First good thing: long reverie, for some reason, about our travels. The curious trip to England when Brian was fifteen to visit literary shrines. Such a pleasure, if a ghostly pleasure, to stand beside the inscribed stones of the poets in Westminster Abbey. Amid all the fumey clutter and clatter of modern London, the monuments, like the poetry, seemed so majestically accomplished, there forever. Bloomsbury streets, then down south, standing before Jane Austen's desk, up to Yorkshire to the Brontes' house, the moors, Wordsworth's lakes, Hardy's Stonehenge at summer solstice, Chaucer's Bath, Glastonbury, where "did these feet in ancient times..." Each called up something like "yes!" from deep headquarters. It made me feel very small but very happy to make these modest, touristy homages, but my heart broke a little for Brian who for the most part seemed politely lost. He had read only a little of the work in school. Through his eyes it must have felt like too little to do. Even the hiking in the Lake Country, with his mother and dad, was I am sure a confining—he would have said dorky—thing for a fifteen-year-old boy to endure. He couldn't seem to find food he liked and found pub lunches mystifying, bangers and mash an affront, cream teas no kind of treat at all. I could feel his wanting to break out and do something—climb something, take a train somewhere on his own. Of course he would. I think he liked the shows in London, and he had a diverting afternoon trying to make a punt go forward on the Cam. That was the day he asked what I thought was such a hopeful question: "How does an American get into a place like Cambridge?" So the fens and water meadows, ancient courtyards and dreaming spires were probably not entirely lost on him. Painful to recall those evening meals, though, when there had been woefully too few "highlights" to exalt in, fiascos to laugh about. It hurt me, and I know J., to be traveling as a family but at the same time failing to make the experience work. Brian I know kept a journal of the trip. I long to know what he wrote.

The best trip, the magical trip, was the following summer doing Switzerland and Italy. This time just J. and I. I was utterly unprepared for such color and light, for the very feel of the air. It too was ancient, its genius already accomplished, but whereas the pleasures of England felt to me like recollections, passing through Switzerland to the Italian Alps was entirely Other. I must have heard, read, used the word "longing" a thousand times before that summer, but from our balconies overlooking Lake Lucerne and Lake Como, I longed. Pale pink, pumpkin-tinted villas reflected the ripples of those honey stone lakes. There was something so numinous, so urgent there, I *longed*, I worshipped. I wanted to give up everything, hearth, home, Wells, respectability to wake up every morning on Lake Como. I would have served at table, taken in laundry. I don't know if J. felt it too. I hope he did. No—I hope he didn't. Wells has been hell enough without a beckoning alternative. We did talk a little about Lake Como being our Afterward. Then somehow Little House and the boat got to be the Afterward. Never went again and won't, I'm afraid. Amazing to me how brightly I can still see it.

Second good thing: J. got hold of the P.B.S. videos of *Anna Karenina*, and after a little soup, toast, and chicken bits, we got lost in nearly three hours of it. It is phenomenal how not having a working body heightens the ability to participate in visual story. Disbelief was totally suspended. I savored every silver hair brush, every porcelain basin. I loved, in appropriately different senses, all the men. For I of course was the very beautiful, most affecting Anna. Being so insubstantial, I was swept like a butterfly, like a gnat into the wake of her beautiful mess.

I'm very sleepy, little book, and I have a taste in my mouth like mustard powder, but I am still thrilled by AK. There is no frigate like a video. Maybe I'm not dead yet. Night.

John:

2 December

REMARKS TO THE SCHOOL

Welcome back.

You look to me well-fed and rested—at least you boys do. The faculty, if you will observe closely, look pale and wan. I am sure this is due to their feverish grading of your exams. Believe me, taking them for four or five hours bears no comparison to the tedium and stress of grading them for forty. It's a wonder we do it. Incidentally, for those of you changing classes or sections this term, do collect your exams and other first term work today, if possible. Today, remember, is the first day of winter term, not last day of fall term.

It's important to make each day count, considering that there are only 19 shopping days and 17 school days till Christmas. This odd, inconvenient wedge of time between Thanksgiving and Christmas is always, for some reason, the best time of year. I don't quite know why that is so.

The most obvious answer is that it resonates with old, cozy childhood associations with the holidays, visions of free time, sledding and skiing and loot. But it is more than that, because actual school life is fun, too. It might have something to do with the launching of winter sports: the *first* basketball game, wrestling and swim meets. And the upper former play is always especially powerful for falling when it does. At least one good, authoritative snowfall usually helps, too. There is of course our last night's Candle Sing, but that's just the capstone, the *recognition* of what feels so good. I'd like to think the spirit comes a little from the Christmas drives, from the glorious theme of giving things away that is so hard to summon up during the other months. Whatever it is, it is wonderful, and I hope that each of you can find a way to play a part in it.

On a more somber note: Seniors! Contrary to all pernicious rumor and false tradition, the academic year is not over. College admissions officers do not read all but the last two columns of your transcripts. Do not slump. I repeat, do not. No matter how far you think you have come, no matter how great the sophistication, it is as easy as sloth to turn stupid again overnight, just as in some sort of academic fairy tale. I have personally seen it happen hundreds of times. So be warned seniors—models, leaders, examples to others, etc.

And to the rest of you, a very good morning.

John:

2 December

MEMO to Arnold Lieber
      Maintenance

Arnold,

I am afraid it is time for the Christmas tree again. This year, for a novelty, let's not make war about this. We need a full size, at least 15' spruce for the commons. The boys will trim if you and Andy will haul out the ornaments. Please do not ask me about aluminum trees, and please do not remind me of how many aluminum tress we could have purchased for the price of the last dozen real ones. We could save even more if we put up no tree. In my opinion, aluminum trees are not trees. They don't smell right.

Merry Christmas,

J.O.G

John:

2 December

Ms. Camilla Lang
Editor, Home Forum Page
The Christian Science Monitor
1 Norway Street
Boston, Massachusetts

Dear Mrs. Lang,

I enclose for your consideration, I hope not too late, a short Christmas poem.

I am not sure if you require background material from those who submit unsolicited material, but, for whatever interest it provides, I am a schoolmaster who has written and published occasional poems, essays, and reviews for magazines.

My good wishes,

John Oberon Greeve

    THIS CHRISTMAS

    For it to be true
    And for us to know it,
    Wouldn't it occur in the cold,
    In a near absence of light,
    Eclipsed, perhaps, by a festival
    Of carols and all our gaudy hopes—
    Like this?

Meg:

School House

Not feeling right at all, little book. It's up and down my chest and belly. The worst is I can't tell what's discomfort and what is anxious mood. Perhaps they are one. All night and all morning like a current or buzz: wrong, wrong, wrong.

J. and I will drive to Hartford for scans and tests to see what the chemo has accomplished. Brain is so feeble and my horizon so near I can't imagine caring what they find. I don't even want to ride in the car an hour each way, although I know J. spent time he could ill afford arranging the appointments in Hartford instead of Mass. General. Will my spirit soar if they look at the pictures and say, "Amazing. Not a trace of a *–noma* anywhere!" What would be the meaning of that finding while I am held fast in this sickening hum? Where exactly is my spirit anyway? Seems to be lying awfully low. Can't imagine it soaring, or even peeing.

Just read over my last entry, and I am ashamed of myself. The puffed up diatribe against academics—who was that speaking and what on earth does she know about university life? If it took ten thousand aspiring scholars to produce two immortally good ones, and if that were going on continually, we would have all the scholarship we could ask for. And if the work of some is mulch for others, God bless the whole garden. And as for "a hundred superb teachers"—what a blessing.

So clear that my sour braying is only about me, not about academic life. I was no doubt fleshing out the kind of colleague/ scholar/teacher I would have been had I remained on the treadmill. No one is quicker to inflate than old Meg Greeve. Weak, sick, useless, and immobile, she rattles her one last rusty saber, her overvalued, by-default habit of cerebration at a whole thriving world of men and women who have done her no harm. No more of that, please.

In a suitably penitent spirit, I finished the *Quarterly* copy and called to have it picked up.

I must set myself to sleeping, or at least resting. Also quarts and quarts of water. Surely good clean water will flush the rot away, a Kelseyan image I rather like.

J. home at six, then gone till 8:30 or 9. Hope I can rally for the rest of *Anna Karenina*. Actually, the fall of darkness, the night table lights on, and J. moving around the room are all I want.

Meg:

School House

The new killer word is "mass." There are still masses in me, whether mere husks or still cooking, where esophagus meets gut, where guts meet intestines, hunkered up against my uterine wall, very faintly staining the Cape Horn on one lung. My brain is still clear, and while nobody mentions it, one of my pamphlets suggests this might be the way to go. Quickest and least painful. But would I have to go mad? Would I randomly speak out to world figures now dead? Would J. murmur an endearment to me and would I bark like a dog? Don't want that. Glad my brain is not massive.

The idea, as we discussed before chemo, is to zap the masses with x-ray. These at least will be quick and painless and can be administered in a clinic near Wells. Compared to the chemo, x-ray side effects should be a piece of cake, although Dr. Felice suggested I might feel "a little punk." I asked whether that meant *altogether* a little punk or whether I would be adding another small increment to the all-being total punkness I already feel. Dr. F. appeared bewildered by my question. He said, among other things, that I might feel weak, dehydrated, and that food might not taste right. He was more than bewildered.

J. asked the good questions. Before rising to leave, I had to ask, with what I hoped was bluff good nature, "So how am I doing?" He was utterly expressionless. Then he said that the best sign is that there is no new growth or involvement. He said he was concerned that there was so little reduction in the tumors. This, he told me again, is what the radiation is for.

Riding home to Wells, it settled on me with great clarity that Dr. F. had not offered any hope. That, I realized, is what must be behind physicians' reputations for coldness and insensitivity in dire circumstances. There is probably no special lack of warmth or empathy; when they know perfectly well the picture is hopeless, warmth is an imposture and empathy unbearable. If they loved you, they would embrace you and conceal the terrible truth. If they are physicians, they state and restate the data and related protocols.

Proceeded quietly to Wells, reconciled to hopelessness, feeling actually a little better.

Quick cup of tea at School House—herbal for me, real for J.—before he headed back to the office. Alone, I feel like reading something vague and majestic, maybe Marcus Aurelius or Boethius. Then the prospect makes me laugh out loud. Instead, I reach for Alice Munro's collected stories, hoping I may have forgotten them enough to love them again. But so sleepy.

Meg:

Little House

Feeble again today, so I may have to peter out soon.

This a.m. I overcame an unexplainable aversion and started into the Kelsey books again. At the heart of it I think was a desire to know if they ever reclaimed anyone with prospects as dim as mine. Looking hard for the worst cases, I found some pretty dramatic messes, including a few who had turned to the Kelseys after surgeries, but each of them had seen the Kelsey light much earlier in their treatment. There was nobody I could find in the done-all-they-could-medically dept. Also, nobody who came to them after chemo. Maybe the chemo zaps, along with everything else, your curative essences. Nice thought. Nevertheless, I found myself warming again to the idea of addressing illness soulfully and gently. It is now not sounding to me silly at all to wonder about being perhaps nicer to my tumors. Such thoughts before chemo would have been sheer wishful thinking and cowardice, but now I think I've fairly earned my right to think such thoughts. I can conceive of my body undoing a tumor. I can conceive of soothing myself to a point where benign, restorative forces within me were liberated for the good. Unfurling. Healing should feel like unfurling.

Everything good in my life, everything deep and transforming and astonishing has felt like an unfurling. There is never any hurrying a true unfurling, only witness and wonder. Crystal Foote, for instance. Crystal Foote! Amazing to think that was—sixteen years ago, when I was forty. Sixteen years since an unfurling. Now, if you'll excuse me, I'll have to go get my forties little books to see just what unfurled.

Little book! I was on fire. And how happy I was, even then, having fun with the name Crystal Foote, which was and is absolutely the best name for an ethereal yoga teacher. I see that I fantasized about her deep into the night. Dark, lithe beauty in her black leotard, sitting straight backed and pretzel legged in the lotus position. In my fantasy then, at least in the dead of night, white diamond light flashed from a crystal foot.

I seem to have got onto yoga matter-of-factly enough. Val had been yammering on about it during our August cruise on the Valmar. She was rhapsodizing miracles on yoga's behalf, and I felt obligated to talk her down to earth. How come, I asked her, if it's hard and even hurts, it's so restful? And if it's so restful, why is it so energizing? And if it's only restful, what's wrong with a good, no-guilt nap? Val was sweet to ignore these nigglings. She really wanted to share yoga with me, and the good will struck deep, because after all my sophistry and teasing, I went home and went on the prowl for a yoga class.

The Wellness Center in Kent, when I visited, was about as suggestive of the Mysterious East and deep inner knowing as the Stop 'n Shop. But there were, as advertised, four yoga classes per week, and the instructor was Crystal Foote. Crystal was beautiful to the point of being disturbing—and it wasn't only me. She was rather tall, 5'7" or 5'8", and she had wonderful shiny honey-brown hair worn long and straight, to about her bottom, except for class where she did it up in a stylish twist, somehow arranged in about two seconds around something like a chopstick. In little book #81 I see I referred to Crystal as a "colt," and I can remember deciding reflexively that she was too thin, then realizing that she wasn't. She was instead light, wonderfully light. She moved lightly, she was light on her long brown feet. Willed and forced thinness always betrays itself in harsh, worrying concavities, an effect of ravaged scrawniness. Not so with Crystal Foote. Arms and legs were both somehow slender and full. Her belly was flat, and her waist seemed tiny—although she had two babies under four. No cosmetics could create that rosy flesh along her jaw line. Crystal Foote was, and no doubt still is, beautiful in a way that has always made me want to give up trying. Straightforward and sweet as she was, it was an effort at first not to resent her.

And then there was the yoga. My skepticism lasted about a minute. Even when I couldn't bend where Crystal bent in the early sessions, I was rapt. I loved my little rubber mat. I came to love everything. There were usually about eleven or twelve of us, a gaggle of women in their thirties and forties—and one man, Lonnie. Lonnie was doughy and bulky, and in the months that I observed him in yoga, he never seemed to be able to do anything at all, the configurations of his hulking arms and legs in no relation whatsoever to the positions Crystal demonstrated. He was always idiotically cheerful. In the closing silence and meditation, he usually fell asleep, his deep, troubled inhalations and exhalations a bearable distraction. Who would have guessed that Lonnie would surface again in consciousness?

It did not take long for me to become devoted to the yoga and to Crystal. It was more than a little hypnotic, and it also felt, as Val said it would, wonderfully invigorating. Such a wonderful, wonderful feeling of time—that is, no time—passing. The sessions were ninety minutes, including the closing meditation. It could have been a minute, or hours. Every cliché about yoga is true. One *is* "in" the moment, every moment. One *is* "in her body." I was in my body. I was also, it turned out, mighty supple. Yoga! I can't begin to imagine, sitting up in this bed strewn with old little books, how I managed to get so far out of my body. Could a dedicated yogi ever get cancer? Is there a yet retrievable yogic principle for me? Hard to imagine.

But there was, when I was forty, that definite unfurling, and it wasn't yoga itself; it was more what the yoga let loose. It wasn't also, entirely, Crystal, but she was an angel to unfurl to. I don't think I quite knew, and certainly never named, what was happening. It was good enough just to feel it. But I was falling in love with Crystal Foote. If I had been a little more finely tuned, I would have realized that I was picking up the currents and undercurrents of the whole class, excepting, possibly, Lonnie. Everyone was in love with Crystal, in love with loving Crystal, in love with the slow, yogic extension of that love. How could you not be? The beautiful bones of that face, dark hair, bright dark eyes, the balletic perfection of her movements. Her movement was a kind of language. Of course I moved to it, compliant, worshipful. Of course it was sexual. I don't think I really fantasized about "running off to the Caribbean with Crystal"—although that light hearted aside (little book #82) would turn out to be a little prophetic. The combination of my eyes swimming attentively all over Crystal's perfect leotarded body and my own serenely invigorating exertions released terrific libido. "A new, or recovered (?) Sapphic impulse in Mrs. Greeve?" I noted in Feb., little book #82. Didn't really trouble me, actually never has. It was altogether invigorating. Brian was oblivious, but J. knew something was up. I was becoming positively adventuresome and frisky in bed. J. pleased as could be. Nice all around, I think, but, as I said, I should have been more respectful of the currents.

Of course all that new libido, the whole unfurling, would have to go somewhere. Several of us yogists had become rather tight, were meeting before and after classes for tea and talk. We felt smug and good and cultic about what we felt but could barely bring ourselves to name. To me, and I'm sure them, more time with yoga friends felt like more Crystal time. Talk came up of other "body work," deep breathing, massage, group aerobics. I was, we were, for all of it. Three or four of us, sometimes with Crystal, sometimes on our own at Devon Bemish's house, would get together and breathe deeply in sync for half an hour or more, until one of us was thoroughly altered. I remember being afraid and then fascinated when my fingers grew stiff and curled up in tetany and Crystal saying no, no, it was fine, it was supposed to happen; breathe through it, breathe, breathe. Devon would reach a point where she would sob convulsively, and we would hold her to us and rock her. We were, we believed, "getting clear" of traumas and blocks held in the soma, prior to consciousness. That's what I picture now, us standing in pairs, breathing rhythmically, looking into each other's eyes, perhaps clasping hands, occasionally embracing, perfectly glad to open up to what kept unfurling.

J. home—it's dinner time and I've been sitting up since noon. Best day since cancer. Back to unfurling tomorrow? Legs all pins and needles. Come up, come up, J. my love.

Meg:

School House

Clinic this a.m. for my silent zaps. Radiologist and technician girl are good, I think. We waste no time. My wretched masses are in such a variety of parts of me. I have to get into the damnedest positions for them to line up the targets in their sites. Astonishing that they can focus their killer rays with such pinpoint accuracy. At least I hope they can. Click, hum, "all right, Mrs. Greeve, now if we can..." All under the brightest, yellowest fluorescence.

Home by ten and J. off to school. He can't get past the endless mess of the LSD boys. J. sees it as a Sisyphean boulder. He has to help the culprits and the school see the point of the discipline — sacking the users and supplier — and of course he has to break the parents' hearts. At least one of them is being venomous about it and is suing, so J. has to negotiate with the board and school lawyers about all of it endlessly. J. doesn't even have to say that in the aftermath of every bigger-than-usual stink, the school's collective mood dips to the floor, with the usual projected charges of inequity, inept handling, soft-headedness/lack of compassion. Enough of these and the invisible black banner of Bad School is hoisted ominously above the campus. All J.'s fault, all his to bear. Too often I have hated what this school and this work have done to him. Day after day, night after night, he goes back to it.

This morning I was thinking about the boys, one of whom, Marc Slavin, a little ferret of a boy, I got to know a little. What would he have been thinking and feeling in anticipation of getting hold of his little lick of LSD? Was it the outlaw risk of acquiring it? The rumored thrills and scrambles of the trip? Obviously, all delinquency and puddingheadedness aside, he wants more of something. More what? What are the real rumors, boy to boy, that make the risk so irresistible? Is it a longed for, instant unfurling, a short cut to that? If that's it or even part of it, however unsafe and unwise, I understand it.

Yesterday's unfurling. So strange to go back there again, to Crystal, Devon, and the girls. The yoga, the breathing sessions, feel, touch. It wasn't quite a year, but it seems a whole epoch of life. Center of gravity shifted from Wells to Kent, though there was no real betrayal of J. I don't remember even feeling a concern about that. Devon was just divorced, and some of the other women were not too firmly rooted in their outwardly conventional families, but J. and I were elemental, deeply safe, a good place to unfurl from.

And unfurl I did. Devon, who seemed to have money, managed to get me to a spa she went to where we were massaged with silken hands at a heavenly tantric pace that carried me past any sense of time. There too I was tanned by bright lamps while lying naked in a closed metal cylinder. I was shampooed, facially wrapped and, once, made over. J. was incredulous, also stirred (!). In the course of massage, which was almost sex, tapes were played of rising and falling gusts of wind, breaking waves. Scents—incense, aromatic oils. Yes, yes, yes to all of it.

With Devon, now my best, best friend, it was more than almost sex. Devon herself was studying massage. She practiced shiatsu and another wondrous kind in which the masseuse's hands don't even touch the subject's body; the hands move intuitively along the spine and other planes of flesh, transmitting and eliciting putative "energies."

One late a.m., after yoga and yoga tea, Devon asked me over for lunch. She wanted to give me a massage, which I thought was a wonderful idea. She would in the weeks ahead indeed give blissful, ultimate massages, but that first one was disrupted and overwhelmed by other impulses. Probably because we had wine for lunch. Not just one chilly glass, its water-beaded bowl dangerously full over its skinny stem, but two.

Greeves Passing

Devon spread a comforter on the floor of her spare bedroom and covered the comforter with a sheet. I undressed and lay out on the sheet. She went off and when she returned with arms full of candles and oils and god knows what, she looked down at me and said, "Oh, look at you." As a person to be massaged, I assumed an attitude of utter compliance. Devon drew the shades, placed candles in little bowls all around the perimeter of the sheet. A tape was inserted, some white noise and then a barely audible flute. Devon knelt beside me. I heard her moistening her hands with oil and then the good surprise of her hands on the small of my back.

Happily, unfurlingly lost. When it came time to turn over, I was very torpid and slow from the wine and the touching and the darkness. I noticed that Devon too had taken off her clothes, the candle light creaming her white breasts in contrast to the tan of her midriff. No surprise at all then that after a tensing minute or so I was touching her too, ecstatic, starved for it. Absolutely. Oh *yes*, I thought, and oh yes, I said, and then it was no longer massage but sex, new but also not at all new. Completely affirming, no edges, no urgency, the best kind of opening up and exploring. I was pleasuring Devon extravagantly—belly, fingertips, my toes up and down the length of her calf—but I was not primarily engaged with her. I was swimming, now really unfurling in the buoyant, yielding medium of this lovely sex.

Little book, as God is my witness, there was no guilt, not while we scissored and caressed, stroked and slid, or afterward driving home to Wells, or at dinner, or in bed. Whatever Devon wanted from me, she seemed to have gotten. She was the same sweet, loopy Devon when we embraced at my car as when we poured out those first chilly glasses of Chardonnay. "Lesbian, lesbian, lesbian, lesbian," I see I wrote in March, little book #82, then: "I don't really think so." Bisexual then? I suppose so, on the evidence, but the obvious and affirming fact of the matter was that I felt utterly the same, fundamentally unaltered, just more realized in the body department, and, in Deep Meg, decidedly and thrillingly unfurled.

But not at all life-changed. Devon and I had each other perhaps a half dozen or more times, each of them at least tenuously related to the yoga/body work dream. After the first marvelous secret time, I remember rising after yoga meditation as Crystal made her way to my mat. She clasped both my hands and looked into my eyes without speaking. Then at last she said, "You're doing well, aren't you?" Could she tell? Would Devon have told her? Were they that close? I gave Crystal such a hug.

That spring a few weeks after, it all fell apart. Rather, it flew south. Crystal, who was married, or possibly partnered, to a man who was developing some new fitness apparatus, told us one morning that she was moving to Key West. She spoke to us very deliberately, as if to acknowledge that she was dealing out more than a routine emotional blow. She was, as reasonably realized women usually are, aware that a complex relationship of some weight had come to be. She was its center, and she knew it. As she outlined the availability of other yoga classes in the region, the whole good dream seemed to float off like a bubble. I didn't know if I was sad. I remember hoping I would stay unfurled. Alone I think among the inner circle I was unaware that a group migration was in the works. Devon and three others were following Crystal to Key West, families be damned in two cases. Afterward, it left a bad, though highly localized mark, almost a scandal. Opinions were voiced and even printed in Kent that something unsavory had occurred at the Wellness Center. There were suggestions of feminism darkly and seductively at work, a feeling that women idle enough to assemble at will and otherwise indulge body and whim were not good for the community. Yoga, as the common practice linking the women making their sudden exodus, was vilified to the extent that classes were not resumed at the Wellness Center.

Just like a bubble rising into bright sky and disappearing. Off flew my yoga and Crystal and funny, silky Devon and that gift of lightness itself which visited me without resistance when I was forty.

Greeves Passing

I always believed I would tell J. about it, really about it, about Devon especially. The lovely thing is that I always could. Few of his friends or colleagues understand him well enough to know that he could hear it, hold it, take it deeply in, let it deepen us. No unfurling would diminish me for him. That is your great, great goodness to me, J. You have always wanted me unfurled. Have I ever for a second been that generous? I am afraid not.

No earthly point in telling him now.

He will be home soon. I must divert him, as I hear the LSD flap is getting even worse—gloom, mess, and lawyers, no less. Rise to it, Meg. Grow hair! Maybe some videos.

John:

5 December

REMARKS TO THE SCHOOL

I must precede these luncheon announcements with some very sad news. As some of you have already heard, this morning during the third class, there was an accident in the pool in which a fourth former, David Lewandowski, was killed. This is still such a surprise and a shock to us that it is hard to tell you much about it.

Three boys, including one with Senior Lifesaving, decided to take a swim through the midmorning break. David, while swimming in the diving end, may have had a convulsion. Whatever happened, his friends were unable to take hold of him in the water, and by the time Mr. Kreble was called to the scene, David was unconscious. Mr. Kreble and Doug Froehling applied resuscitation until an ambulance arrived, which took David to Three Counties Clinic, where he was pronounced dead on arrival.

I have just talked to both Mr. and Mrs. Lewandowski, who are on their way to school and should arrive early this evening. Those of you who knew David may want to talk with them after dinner. I know that would be a great comfort to them. Right now, as you can probably imagine, they are simply numb with shock and hurt and loss.

Tomorrow's chapel will be a formal one in David's memory. The goal for now is to do all we can to support the Lewandowskis, David's friends, and each other on this very sad day.

John:

5 December

DEPOSITION
To Wells Village Police Department
Wells, Connecticut

This morning, December 5, shortly after the start of third class (approximately 10:05 a.m.) three boys, David Lewandowski, Dough Froehling, and Mark Tepler, were dismissed from their geometry class for causing some sort of disturbance in the classroom. They were not told to report anywhere in particular, and since school break follows third class, they felt they would have time for a swim. Free swimming in the pool is permitted if an athletic department member approves and if one of the swimmers has passed Senior Lifesaving. In this case, Froehling has passed Senior Lifesaving. When the boys arrive at the pool office complex, Mr. Kreble, who usually gives permissions, was out. The boys claim some confusion about permission being necessary. They cited other times they had been swimming without supervision or permission and assumed it was allowed.

At approximately 10:25, as the boys report it, Froehling was swimming laps in one of the racing lanes in the shallow end, Tepler was sitting on the pool edge of the deep end, and Lewandowski was diving off the low board. As Lewandowski surfaced from one of his dives, he began thrashing about in the water. Tepler noticed this first, but paid little attention, as he assumed it was only energetic fooling around. When the thrashing persisted for what Tepler estimated might be a minute or two, he began shouting to Lewandowski asking if he were all right. Lewandowski was by this time "out of control" in Tepler's opinion, and was periodically going under. Tepler, who is not a strong swimmer, swam out to Lewandowski and tried to hook his arm around Lewandowski's waist and haul him to the side of the pool. At this, Tepler said, Lewandowski locked an arm around Tepler's neck and pulled him under. Tepler managed to get free and shouted to Froehling, a strong swimmer, for help. Froehling did not hear the shouts at first, but after a short delay made his way to the deep end and tried to fasten an arm under Lewandowski's chin so as to drag him backwards to safety. Froehling said that Lewandowski pitched over and as with Tepler, the movement forced Froehling under. As Froehling attempted to work himself back up to the surface, he caught an elbow to the side of one eye and was momentarily dazed. Deciding he could not bring Lewandowski immediately to the side of the pool, he told Kreble to find Jack Tepler and a rope or a ladder or a pole.

Tepler thinks it may have been a little after 10:30 when he ran from the pool to find Kreble or another adult. Froehling meanwhile made repeating dives below Lewandowski and attempted to boost him up to the surface so he could breathe. Feeling this was futile, he swam to the side, got out and picked up a wooden bench from against a wall and placed it in the pool, using it as a prod to nudge Lewandowski into the shallow racing lanes.

At this point, about 10:35, Kreble arrived at the pool with Tepler. Kreble entered the water and they were able to remove Lewandowski, who was now unconscious, without difficulty. Feeling a pulse, but detecting no respiration, Froehling and Kreble began to apply two-man cardiopulmonary resuscitation. At this point they realized Lewandowski had swallowed his tongue. They had some difficulty opening his jaw to correct this and, after that, further difficulties in extracting the tongue. When this had been done, they resumed resuscitation until an ambulance arrived a few minutes after eleven. Emergency staff took over resuscitation procedures and took Lewandowski in an ambulance to Three Counties Clinic. At eleven thirty Kreble called me from the clinic to say that Lewandowski was pronounced dead on arrival.

The school had been made aware by the boy's parents that he had been taking anti-seizure medication daily as a precaution against the recurrence of a single seizure his parents reported during the previous summer. His teachers, dormitory master, and coaches were all aware of the boy's condition. Both the Lewandowskis' family physician and the Wells school physician had advised against contact sports, but had allowed others under appropriate supervision. There had been no evidence of other seizures since Lewandowski enrolled in the school in August. Tepler, who is one of Lewandowski's roommates, said he was aware of Lewandowski's medication and that Lewandowski had told him he really didn't need to take it. In light of the date of the boy's most recent prescription, the number of pills remaining in the bottle suggests he probably did not take the medication regularly.

I have questioned Lewandowski's other roommate as well as his teachers, and I am convinced that no other drug or substance had been taken by Lewandowski prior to the accident.

John:

6 December

REMARKS TO THE SCHOOL
In Memoriam, David Lewandowski

Mr. and Mrs. Lewandowski, ladies and gentlemen of the faculty, and boys of Wells School:

It is too soon and too sad to try to put yesterday's tragedy into perspective. What we are feeling now is a numbing sense of loss. There is undoubtedly some great scheme into which the death by drowning of an able, energetic sixteen-year-old boy fits, but if so, it is a design perhaps too magnificent and terrifying for us to comprehend.

What we must all keep in mind is that our grief and dread today are not for David but for ourselves. David's fear and discomfort were brief and are now past. Ours, especially today, continues, and it is hard to bear. A death among us, especially of one so young, makes us question and resent bitterly the loss of so much promise. Anyone who knew David Lewandowski knows that his promise was considerable. The deeper dread, though, is the realization of our own vulnerability, the very real and possible loss of our own promise and vitality. We have been reminded that our own days are not infinite, not guaranteed, not even especially safe. David's loss confirms our mortality, and we don't really want the news.

Difficult as it is, we have got to divert our prayers and thoughts from his fatality to his vitality, for it is in this, not in his passing, that David had something to teach us. Consider David for a moment. He was a new fourth former this year, but there was not, I'll wager, a boy in his form who did not know him well by

Greeves Passing

Thanksgiving. Rarely does a boy take to Wells—and Wells to a new boy—so quickly and so surely. As one housemaster in Hallowell put it, "He was so easy to like." Easy because he was so indomitably high-spirited. No one who has spoken of David to me in the past twenty-four hours has done so without remarking on his laughter, how quickly it would come, how infectious it was, how it was always occasioned by something unexpected or loony—and never, apparently, by the shortcomings of others or at their expense.

David was also a risk-taker, a volunteer. On the campus just twenty-four hours this past September, he volunteered to be varsity football manager. He did this because he wanted to help out and because he desperately wanted to be close to football. It is characteristic of David that practically none of you was aware that he was forbidden, on doctor's orders, to play contact sports. His name also appears, I notice, first among the fourth form volunteers for the Christmas food and clothing drive. He was not yet, as it happens, a first-rate student—in fact, he was a little daunted by Wells his first term. But he was not one to let a set-back get him down. Mr. Shire tells me he found tutors on his own and was in the process of finding his feet scholastically. I am certain he would have done so. He was the type.

So, in the poet Auden's words, "what instruments we have agree": David Lewandowski was a good boy. And what we came to know this fall the Lewandowskis have known much longer. David did, and does, glorious credit to his parents. It is for them, as well as for ourselves, that we so wholeheartedly celebrate and honor David here this morning. Mr. and Mrs. Lewandowski, to you go all our love and prayers and support. We cannot lighten your grief, only share it. We must acknowledge together that this grief could not have been had David not been the boy he was. Let us remember and honor that.

Thank you and good morning.

John:

6 December

Mrs. Florence Armbruster
Mathematics

Florence,

I must ask that with respect to future disciplinary measures you observe the following policy without fail: if you dismiss a boy from class for misconduct, make sure he *reports* somewhere, either to me or to Phil Upjohn. We are long used to receiving such miscreants. If you wish to follow up yourself, ask the boy to wait in our offices until you are free. In the event that either of us is otherwise occupied, Marge Pearse will know what to do with the offender.

This is by no means a suggestion that you have been negligent or in any way responsible for the Lewandowski boy's accident. There is no blame to assign there.

I would appreciate your cooperation on the disciplinary matter. The wrong kind of boy finds it a treat to be dismissed from class if there are no other consequences beyond the dismissal.

Thanks.

J.O.G.

John:

9 December

Mr. and Mrs. Frank Greeve
14 Bingham Drive
Tarrytown, New York

Dear Val and Frank,

This is not a Christmas card. I regret to say it is the opposite of a Christmas card. "He who has the steerage of my course" has for some reason determined to wreck what is traditionally the most lovely passage of the school year, the between-holidays month, when the illusion of good will and anticipated comfort hangs cozily over the old quad like weather. Advent.

Not so this year, I'm afraid. Meg was taken back to the clinic today by ambulance after a night of terrible pain and, late this morning a very bad hemorrhage. I can't even think about it. She is so miserable and tired and angry. What an affront this disease is. I am thoroughly convinced that, almost from the time it was diagnosed, this cancer's treatment has served only to aggravate it. Cancer may have been prolonged, but Meg has not been. Until now, except one afternoon on a cruise years ago, I have never seen Meg nauseated the way these drugs have nauseated her. Not until this have I seen Meg close herself off to others—out of sheer exhaustion, embarrassment, and pain. Meg could never stand to be as bad company as she feels this disease and its "treatment" have made her. Meg was not made to lose her hair and her appetite and her color. She wants to die but rails at the cowardliness of doing it herself. She is not likely to live past Christmas, and I hope to God she is spared the hell of another bout like last night.

Richard Hawley

I can't get it into words, but something is so wrong with all of this. It's not the dying or even the cancer—it's the treatment, or the illusion of treatment. Hurtful and terrifying as it is, Meg's dying ought to be in the same run of phenomena as birth, marriage, and parenting. But I don't know. This hasn't been right for Meg. It's not the way she should leave us.

I'm very full of death. A boy drowned in the pool this week—terrible wild card, nobody's fault. He seems to have been a borderline epileptic who had gotten negligent with his daily medicine and convulsed in the water. A very nice boy, game, very kind, a not-too-bright innocent. The blow to the parents was indescribable, their dignity in the face of it even more so. We put together a quick memorial chapel for them here the morning after. The boys rose to the occasion and to what the parents needed like angels. I've never seen anything quite like it, the parents desperately attaching all their parental affection on each boy they got to know. They decided to bury him here and stayed on the campus three days. Going home without him was the hard thing.

We have heard nothing from or about Brian, and Meg is now unable to talk about him. I don't know if she thinks about him. I hope not. I don't know myself anymore what I expect or what I want from him. I spend hours at a time, at my desk or lying in bed, when I positively, murderously hate him. Perhaps this has always been there, perhaps the real cause of all that's gone wrong. I don't want to believe this, and for the most part I really don't, but it's a possibility. And if true, if that kind of hate is really running my engine, then all this other business, the avuncular reasonableness, the old-shoe headmasterly patter I do, this affection I think I feel for practically all of these boys who have been milling around me for the past thirty-two years—it's all a veil over something pretty ugly.

I've gone over Brian's growing up a thousand times in the last few years. It's all there in bold strokes: only son of a headmaster, like son of a clergyman, finds adult expectations impossible, so end-runs, self-destructs, and compulsively fails. Until his teens, though, Brian wasn't anything more alarming than a little passive and occasionally stubborn. I always think of Brian's and Hugh's respective approaches to performance, whether musical, athletic, or scholastic. Brian would be pleased to master a tune on the piano—would get it note-for-note perfect through solitary practice. Then, when asked to perform, even if only for Meg and me, he would decline. I once begged him to play for company until he wept. Hugh, on the other hand, liked to perform. He was never a show-off, but he always seemed delighted that you would actually like to see or hear something he had been working on. I will never forget one summer evening at Little House when Hugh had haltingly pounded his way through "Bumble Boogie" and we all cheered wildly. Late that night it started to rain, and as I was cranking windows shut in Brian's room, he startled me by saying, "Dad, you know I can play it really well." I don't know what I said, probably something like, "I'd love to hear it." But both of us understood that was not going to happen.

I think I understand pretty well the dynamics of Brian's relationship to me and Meg. It's called passive-aggression in the psychoanalytic literature. All adolescents do it to an extent. The idea is for the adolescent to get you by not performing and thus spoiling your expectations. It is very hard to respond to. Real love and support sustain the passivity by reinforcing it; anger fuels it. It's also hard to be angry at the passive kid because he isn't (consciously) angry, and he is suffering consequences, too: failure, loss of esteem, lack of mastery, lack of recognition. It's deadly. Whole lives are organized on the principle. In my view, a lot more kids grew out of it before drugs. Kids always like to frustrate parental ambitions (even Hugh, who is perfect, is not an entrepreneur yet), but they also like to please and acquire skills—social skills, vocational skills, recreational skills, intellectual acumen—and this requires growing up, knitting onto and joining the adult order. Drugs block this healthy progression. They have done it to dozens of boys I have known well, and I believe in my bones they have done it to Brian. Drugs are made for passive-aggression. In the old world, in which we may be the graying final generation, being high (without chemicals) was the reward of achievement: goal reached, girl won, etc. Now being high (with chemicals) replaces achievement, *is* the achievement—no behaviors necessary, no mastery, no exchange of favors with the world.

School has always been an adult-adolescent battleground, but the battle was so much more invigorating and honorable before drugs. We can only, usually, guess if a boy is stoned. Druggy boys can get us every time. They can play their heads like chemical juke boxes, while we are drilling for order, for esthetic response, for logical subtleties. Masses of contemporary young never get very subtle. Their language and discrimination are fuzzed, perhaps a little, perhaps a lot, but forever. Medical schools, businesses (as you know) will accept them; the arts expect them. Which does not prove, at least to me, that drugs are harmless. Consider the medicine we get. Consider the manufacturing, marketing and delivery we get. Consider the arts. Take Val to the movies, Frank. Take her to *Apocalypse Now*. Listen to the diction and syntax of talk show guests—and of the hosts. I can imagine, without irony, a near future in which the culture can *only* be endured with drugs.

But the hell with the near future. My present is hardly manageable. My near past is what I would like to understand better. I saw Brian grow up sweet, bright, maddeningly private and tentative. But promising! I saw him waver and grow tense at fifteen, and after that I never saw him entirely clear headed again. Which, in our particular Oedipal combat, is just about perfect, since being a clear-headed member of humanity was possibly my only firm expectation of Brian.

I know damned well I'm right about drugs. Historians millennia hence will perhaps cite me in their treaties on the Pax Americana in decline. But I still lose. Passive-aggression and its chemical props beat me easily. Brian has rendered me sad, helpless, frustrated, and angry, and he has done worse—or is it better?—to his mother. He has shown us and our WASPish liberality to be ineffective, and the only cost was forfeiting a comprehending, connecting life. Twenty years ago, passive-aggression or not, Brian would have seen this, seen through it and past it.

Don't let these ravings frighten you, either of you. It's good for me to get them out, and it beats lying awake in bed. Thanks so much for all your support. Am living for your arrival at Christmas. It will be gruesome for you, but I love you for it. Best to Hugh.

John

Brian:

Tangier

Avery never really came in last night—actually he did, for about a minute, which I barely took in, to get something from his bag. Then this morning when I was awake enough to start to read, he came in and crashed. I asked him if he had met someone, and he said "unfortunately, yes." I was pretty curious, but he wanted to sleep. He told me again how it was a city of many pleasures.

Avery is turning out to be even stranger than I thought. Sometime this morning when I was dozing off, he disappeared again. Then tonight around dinner time he came back, talking up a storm about how he met a bunch of French film makers, and how they might want to use him as a location liaison for their film. He also brought back with him a hefty bag of kif, and he did two or three bowls before he took off again. I smoked a bowl myself. I wanted to see if it had an effect on my crud. It actually wasn't bad, at least it carried me out of my sick mood. Went back to the same café for supper, but still no appetite. Head still swimming around from the kif, so I passed on the wine.

Very weird thing happened at the café. I was sitting at my table, making almost no sense out of my *Le Monde* from yesterday, and it suddenly occurred to me that I was afraid to go back to the hotel. There was no reason, no sense to it, but I felt an almost electric fear of getting up, entering that dark lobby, and making my way back to the room in the dark. It made no sense at all. I wasn't afraid that someone would attack me or hurt me—the scary thing was just penetrating the darkness, entering the room, like a nightmare. Maybe it was the dope, but I started sweating through my clothes, and I knew that if I didn't get up right then and walk back to the hotel and head straight back to the room, I was never going to be able to do anything again. I was going to be afraid forever.

Greeves Passing

So I did. I went back to the room. No special panic. It was still early. I turned on the little table lamp and started to read, but I couldn't read. I kept seeing myself from outside of myself, a boney blond kid lying in a bed in a dingy room in a dingy hotel, in a city that smelled like it was going off. I found myself wishing that Avery would come back, but I don't really know Avery. And if he did come back, he'd talk me into a trance, and I'd want him to back off so I could get some sleep. I look forward to his showing up the way I looked forward to getting to Lisbon or Algeciras or Tangier. The next thing is going to be better. Life is turning out to be a succession of next things coming to be, and their being about what you'd expect. Maybe part of the problem is this awful room. It's less like a room than like a drawer.

Smoked another bowl of Avery's kif. I'll pay him back.

* * *

Sucked up my will power and checked out of the Aladdin. It was a little tricky because I didn't want to take Avery's bag with me. I ended up asking the clerk if I could check it until I could have a friend come and carry it for me. I also left a message for Avery, explaining.

He never paid me his half of the rate, but he was only there for a few hours. Not a tremendously reliable guy. No more kif. My eyes feel like they're zooming in and out of my head. When I walked down to the beach today to check it out, it was as if my entire mind was going in and out with the waves. A big one would break on the shore and the water would run up almost to my feet, then slide back down over the pebbles, and I would almost fall down—as if I had to go with it.

Only good thing about my little walk, I saw a place I want to stay, a big, probably touristy hotel called the Belvedere. It's the first big hotel up from the beach, and it's got balconies on all the rooms. Whatever it costs, I'm there for at least two days, and I'm going to get my pitiful body out in the sun.

*   *   *

Excellent intuition. The Belvedere is big and posh and normal. It costs 300 dirham (about $40) a night, but I'm going to live with that. The rooms are as white and clean as the Aladdin's were stale and dark. I think I'm perking up a little too. I'm doing my blazer person imitation, drinking lots of mineral water, eating bowls of fruit. I'm going to lick this thing by an act of will.

I also made a big resolve that I'm going to stick to. I'm going to start writing things on a regular basis. I'm going to bag all the doubts and anxiety about whether it's great or not and just get things down. I notice things. I feel things, so why not? If it's no good, I'll realize that and try to improve. I need to get into a mindset where I'm confident I can do something—anything. I'm going to walk a few miles every day, sick or not. I'm going to swim every day. I'm going to get a haircut, and when I get my next money windfall, I'm going to buy a pair of good leather shoes.

Discipline. The new Greeve. Do your magic, Wells.

*   *   *

Better today, I think. Also obsessed. A family of Germans or Danes passed by me this evening on their way into the Belvedere dining room. There was a daughter, somewhere between fifteen and twenty, who may be the most beautiful human being I have ever seen. Nothing flashy. She was thin with brownish-blond hair down to her shoulders, kind of full and bushy. She had a little sharp nose, a sharp chin, and amazing bright eyes. Wonderful skin, tan but also rosy. She was dressed up in a plain white dress and a white cloth band in her hair. She was so delicate and graceful and clean. I'm not up to intruding into family meals, but I did decide on the spot to dine at the Belvedere. The table they gave me wasn't great, but I made two trips past her, one to the lobby to get a new *Le Monde,* and one to the can. I was disappointed by my own face in the mirror, way too pale. I wanted to look more

Greeves Passing

like a healthy animal. I wanted to look more like her. I thought maybe I'd calm down a little eating dinner, but I didn't. I felt an electric awareness of her and her family across the dining room. I don't think I've ever felt anything like it in my life. I pushed my food around on my plate until her family got up to leave. Then I got up, too, and followed them out. And as I did, I heard what I wanted to hear. Her name: Astrid. Never in the history of humans has a beautiful name better fit a beautiful person.

Weird night. A million movie fantasies. Astrid's family would somehow seek me out to tutor her in English. She would spot me in the lobby reading Rilke's poems, and she would introduce herself to me in a fluster, since Rilke was the poet of her heart. Her little brother gets lost, the family panics, and I find him at the beach scuffling with Arab boys. The family is tearfully grateful. Won't I dine with them?

Astrid. Astral girl. The very physical fact of a person like that tends to burst you out of your cocoon. There is no question, really, of what you should do in life. You do what is necessary to be with the Astrids of the world. If it takes social graces, you get them. If it takes college degrees or courage under fire or incredible pain and sacrifice, you go after it, you do it.

* * *

Bad, sad news. I was heading up from the beach this afternoon, sun-groggy and full of Astrid fantasies, and there in front of the hotel was Astrid and her family. The porters were loading their bags into a car. Checking out. I just stood and watched them like an idiot. I stood there until they drove off.

I never even managed to meet her, not that anything would have happened. I went inside and asked the name of the family that had just checked out. The twerp at the desk gave me a fishy look and said the hotel didn't give out names of its guests. He was a kid younger than I am, but he had a uniform and so was very important. He's also an idiot. Any hotel will give you the names of its guests, they just won't give you their address. Which is what I wanted.

Amazing that the loss of somebody—a possibility—I didn't even know could hit me this way. Maybe fate is trying to tell me something. Maybe it's telling me to get on with it.

Meg:

School House

Not at all right today. Standing up from the bed I almost fell over. Mouthful of sour ashes. Try again later.

Later. Think I'll just lie here and let the world, if there is one, fold in on me. Val called late a.m., so comfortable, so sweet. She really does make me feel all's right with the world, always has. Odd how I listened to myself telling her about my procedures, peeing fire, and other symptoms, and I sound sure of myself, summon up extra force in my voice as I go on. The woman talking on the phone to Val was in control, nothing to worry about. As soon as I hung up, my stomach was all fluttery, and I was perspiring through my nightie. It occurs to me what a physically expensive thing it is to be "managing well." And poor J.

Later still. Arnold is lumbering around downstairs doing about the perpetually running toilet in the powder room. How hard can it be to repair or replace? Sure Arnold has attended to it thirty or forty times since we've lived here. Arnold is always extremely gloomy about the prospect of anything wrong improving. The powder room toilet seems to share his karma. In a peculiar way the whole campus does. Why do I find this *reassuring?* And why do Arnold's footsteps below—even the footsteps conveying pessimism and doubt—make me want to laugh out loud? Is it because I know that, however improbable and grotesque, Arnold likes me? It is.

Four p.m. Arnold gone at last. I teeter down for tea in the kitchen. I am tempted to flush the powder room toilet, but pass it by superstitiously.

Pleasant cup, rereading recent entries in little book. Interesting from a little distance. I was unfurling, certainly, but what a strange thing simply to have arisen like that and departed. There was so little resonance or dissonance with everything else in my life at the time, Brian, Wells, propriety, or whatever I thought propriety was when I was 40.

I suppose I should not be surprised, especially now that I have this Alamo perspective, that the deep truths one stumbles on are always uncomfortable, inappropriate, beyond polite social category. Civilization may be, as Freud thought, more or less bearable neurosis, unavoidable, tragic compromise. The soul and survivable good sense forever at war. And how did my beloved Edna St. Vincent Millay know this so eloquently?

> *So subtly is the Fume of life designed*
> *To clarify the pulse and cloud the mind...*
> *...the poor treason*
> *Of my stout blood against my staggering brain,*
> *I shall remember you with love, or season*
> *My scorn with pity—let me make it plain:*
> *I find this frenzy insufficient reason*
> *For conversation when we meet again.*

Why are we born if our situation in life has already been sorted out and perfectly framed by others? I suppose I did season my scorn with pity in Devon's case. Her letters from Florida were appalling, unreadable, as are so often the written utterances of those we come to know in other ways. She would actually inscribe "apropos of nothing at all" and "anyhoo" and amplify her points with those smiley and frown-faces. And our frenzy was clearly insufficient for conversation if we ever met again. We never did.

Upstairs for sleep before J. On the way, tried the powder room toilet. Still running.

John:

12 December

Mr. and Mrs. Kenneth Ryder
175 Old Church Road
Dedham, Massachusetts

Dear Mr. and Mrs. Ryder,

By now Carl has told you about his latest trouble here in the biology lab. Frankly, we find ourselves baffled by it. We don't know whether it is an instance of childish cruelty, or submerged anger, or of something else. Carl himself doesn't seem to be sure. The startling fact of the matter is that during Morning Break yesterday, Carl made his way into the lab and proceeded to cut off the tails of our six gerbils. Fortunately, I think, he was spotted by Mr. Fiore leaving the lab during mid-break, so we have been spared the unease of wondering who among us mutilated the animals.

The incident raises a number of concerns.

(1) Is Carl a danger to other boys and to property here? We are fully aware that many boys pass through a phase of murderous cruelty to animals. Some boys half-sublimate this into "experiments." Some turn it inward into temporary phobias of mice, spiders, etc. Many let it run its course through hunting, exterminating pond frogs or some other easy prey until the impulse is either dissipated or brought under control. John Steinbeck's *The Red Pony* is very instructive in this regard. Something of this destructive impulse is obviously still at work in Carl. What concerns us most is that he is too old for it. I hope the mortification of being caught doing such a thing becomes a first step in being able to assess his urge self-consciously and thus bringing it under control.

(2) What will it do to Carl's rather fragile sense of esteem to be known, as I'm afraid is already becoming the case, as the boy who cuts tails off gerbils? Such acts, again because they are so unconsciously appealing to emerging adolescents, are not readily forgotten. Cruel or funny labels are often applied, and sometimes they stick long after the event that inspired them is forgotten. Mind you, we do not encourage this, but there is little we can do to prevent it.

(3) Has Carl posed a disciplinary or a psychological problem? Both, I think, but we are trying to treat it more as the latter. I am convinced by his remorse (copious tears) that he is not proud of what he did; getting nabbed just may put the lid on that impulse for good.

But we intend to help him seal that lid. Our terms for keeping him on here must be as follows. He should have a psychological evaluation by somebody acceptable to you some time over the Christmas recess. I would like to see a written summary of that evaluation when he returns in January. Beyond that, we would impose no further discipline or require any kind of therapy, unless that is recommended by his evaluator. However, should Carl be involved in another incident of cruel behavior to animals or others here, we are going to insist that he go through at least one term of schooling away from Wells, during which a regular course of counseling would be required for his readmission. I really do not think that will happen or such measures will be necessary, but their clear statement may help to keep that 'lid' on until maturity settles the matter.

(4) What to do about the gerbils? This is almost too trivial to mention, but the problem is perplexing. The gerbils, now tail-less, appear to be fine and healthy. They serve, however, as a visual reminder of what Carl did to them, and this isn't good. On the other hand, they have become special pets of some of the third formers who would be hurt and incensed if the gerbils were removed — and would hold Carl accountable for any such action. Be that as

Greeves Passing

it may, my own feeling is to buy six new gerbils at Carl's expense, and to find the others homes in Wells village. This should go best for Carl in the long run. I am afraid there is no way to ease Carl's embarrassment in the coming two weeks, but after Christmas, given boy time-sense, the event will seem remote history.

Please write or call if I can be of any further assistance or if I can clarify further the conditions I have set down. I think you will agree they are not harsh; they are, however, firm.

All good wishes for the holidays,

John O. Greeve

John:

13 December

REMARKS TO THE SCHOOL

I could not send you on your way this morning without remarking on the exceptional experience I had last night as a member of the opening night audience of *Murder in the Cathedral*. It was not only the finest production of that work I have ever seen—and I have seen three: one at Harvard University, one in England in Canterbury Cathedral, and one in New York. It is also the finest schoolboy production of *anything* I have seen. Mr. Burgermeister and players have more than done it again.

I don't know why I so easily forget, but I do, that a well-made play is like a potentially living thing, and when life is breathed into it by convincing acting and intelligent interpretation, the experience is always richer and more powerful than one can ever imagine outside the theater. I have also not yet kicked the bad habit of thinking, before the action begins, that I am about to watch a *school* play, rather than just a play. I think last night's performance may have cured me permanently of that. As Plato liked to point out, a perfectly tuned string is tuned regardless of who happens to tune it; similarly, a play brought to life by talented and bright adolescents is as *done* as a play can be. The Royal Shakespeare Company itself could not have come closer to Eliot's heart, and through that, to the truth, than our Dramatis Personae did last night.

It has not really been a happy time with us lately, has it? And I must say that I myself, for a variety of personal reasons, have probably been gloomier than anybody else, but that experience last night of getting vividly in touch with ideas and with meaning—well, that was a tonic.

Greeves Passing

I will be there again tonight, I've decided, and hope that all of you who have not seen it will join me.

Good morning.

John:

13 December

Mr. William Truax
P.O. Box 121
New Haven, Connecticut

Dear Bill,

Thanks for your letter and for the copy of the Durham School plan.

I wish, though, that you had at least commented on the substance of the plan, which I presume you have read and of which, I further presume, you approve. I am afraid receiving it makes me feel a little like a dull student who has been given a brighter lad's composition to look over for instruction and inspiration.

The Durham plan is certainly streamlined, and the "hard data" awesome, but it projects some awfully worrying things. If this plan comes true, Durham is going to cease being a real school and instead will become a way station for clusters of all kinds of boys and girls who will go there to "tool up" in Durham's lavishly equipped "resource centers" and "research mods" for six weeks and then return, tooled, to their own less streamlined schools.

Although the plan doesn't say so in so many words, Durham, if they actually do this, will no longer properly be a school, but a national "resource" for a few of the nation's lucky, far-flung children. Let me tell you what I think of that. (1) It's rather condescending to other schools which are also, most of the time, engaged in skill-building and research activities themselves. (2) Big and rich as it is, Durham isn't big enough to process more than a negligible fraction of the public/private school population they are aiming at. (3) The proposed "mods" are too expensive to attract many students beyond the ones who are already clients of private schools, posh public schools, or already enrolled in diversity get-ahead programs. (4) Durham will no longer be interesting once it recomposes itself. It will not be a community of scholars, nor a community of teachers. At the heart of it, I think, is that Andy Ames has been embarrassed about heading a powerhouse prep school like Durham ever since he took over. He is a man who did not make his reputation in schools but in something much more grand called Education. He said so many brave new, anti-elitist things from his throne at Columbia in the sixties that he has now got to reconcile his contradictions. I'm all for that, but I don't see why a great (if too big) American school should have to go down the drain for it.

But I am undoubtedly mouthing off for nothing. Perhaps you just sent me Durham's plan just to show me what a proper job looks like. It's a hell of a plan, I agree. Ames is a giant among planners. If I had the money, I'd lay him on to ghost a plan for Wells, but I'm afraid a kind of hotel-hospital for burnt-out teachers might result. Better yet, we could become a traditional-school lab, in which everything would be more or less as it is, except various administrators-in-training would come through and practice making innovations. I would prefer this because there would actually be a role for me. They could bring me in between innovators to restore torpor and aimlessness.

Bill, I am not being defensive. I don't want you to think that for a minute. I'll plan, I'll plan.

If I can be serious for a moment, I am awfully concerned about the Stone-Wilcox suit. I am even more concerned about Seymour's handling of the matter. According to him I may have made Wells vulnerable to an unfavorable ruling in a number of ways, but first and foremost by announcing what had happened and who was involved before the faculty and student disciplinary recommendations were made. I cannot believe there is much to this. For one thing, the boys had already admitted everything I told the school, and they had also told their friends. Moreover I did not pass a character judgment on any of the boys involved, nor did I indicate what their "sentence" should be. In no way did I depart from the stated and traditional due process of the school or from the disciplinary contract all parents sign, including Mrs. Stone and the Wilcoxes. That contract states, in effect, that expulsions are made at the discretion of the headmaster, who may seek student and faculty counsel as he sees fit. Bill, if Seymour can't win this case hands down, there will be no effective disciplinary process in the future. This is perhaps the neatest and most routine expulsion I can remember.

I wish to make no cash settlements or other substantive compromises out of court. Seymour has led me to believe that Mrs. Stone's principal aim is to correct what she feels has been personal mistreatment of Charles and of her: my addressing the whole school about Charles' drug deal and perceived slights in my subsequent letter to her. I regret now that I wrote her the same letter I wrote to the Wilcoxes, but it pertained adequately, and I was pressed. Seymour says that if I alter the status of the dismissal to a voluntary withdrawal and draft an encouraging letter of recommendation to the colleges of Charles' choice, she might, for lawyers' fees to date, drop the suit. I sense that Seymour likes this, as it will keep Wells and its associations with drugs out of the New York and Boston papers. No mean consideration, I agree. But wrong. We did right by Charles and by Wells in this case, and it's important that we don't forfeit that gain. Why should Mrs. Stone—for those motives—get satisfaction? Please support me on this, Bill. I don't want to see Wells smeared, and I don't want to see Mrs. S. have the satisfaction of hauling me into court to defend myself, but the principle is worth it. In fact, I dread the prospect of court. It couldn't be a worse time for me, although I understand we are getting delays until January. After we win the case, or she drops it, I will be glad to write to Mrs. Stone apologizing for the inadequacies of my letter. I'll also recommend Charles to somebody some day, if he ever pulls himself together.

Why does so much about school life feel like a fight? And why doesn't it feel like school unless it's a fight?

Thanks for your kind words about Meg. There is too much for me to say about that right now to say anything. She is very bad, Bill, and unlikely to make it through the holidays. My brother and his wife are coming up here for Christmas, and we are going to hold each other together. You and Marguerite have been a terrific help. I think you know how Meg feels about you both.

Have a joyful holiday,

John

John:

14 December

Mrs. Herman Triester
2006 Apple Mountain road
Williamstown, Massachusetts

Thank you for your frank and thoughtful comments on my "Headmaster's Notes" in the *Quarterly*.

I think I may be less guilty of espousing the bad ideas you attribute to the article than I am of being insufficiently clear about what I did say. By no means did I want to suggest that "grade-grubbing" was a welcome development—for itself—at Wells. I did mean to say that on balance the boys seem willing to work hard again, and there might be some good in this.

I am no foe of "learning for its own sake," although I happen to think the term is tossed about a good deal as an intrinsic educational good, but rarely examined for meaning. Considered seriously, the notion poses problems. Learning seems to me to be perfectly instrumental, to be invariably for the sake of something else: reward, promotion, amusement, mastery. Different souls learn different things for different ends, and some ends are undoubtedly nobler than others, but learning itself is never the end. An eight-year-old learns multiplication tables so as to feel competent at an age-appropriate level, not really out of a desire to get out and perform the practical tasks multiplication might allow him to do (which is still instrumental), and certainly not out of love of arithmetic elegance. We learn these basic things because we are supposed to, and because we'd be ashamed not to. And so it goes with other enabling skills. Without them, learning, however it was acquired, would only be what accidentally accrued as one pursued impulsive desires. Of course there is an educational theory in that, revived from Rousseau and plunked down in the nineteen sixties, when there was a new population willing to believe that if you don't block the youthful learning engine with stultifying conventions, it will run, run, run to the benefit of the learner and his society. This has always sounded marvelous, but it's false, and the desired result never happens.

There is an occasional practical genius like Edison who was genuinely uneducated but who nevertheless synthesized experiences in such a way as to contribute to the culture, but he is one in a million, perhaps one in ten million. My own feeling, based on a fairly interested reading of Edison's life, is that ordinary schooling would have imposed little on his technical aptitude and might by way of compensation have added some order, perspective, and appreciation to his badly muddled adult life. Rousseau, by his own *Confessions*, was worse: the genius of progressive child rearing gave his own away; he had no time for them. You also mention da Vinci, who, while incontestably a genius, was hardly unschooled. He had a marvelous humanistic education from Florence, just as Socrates had from Athens.

One can't know these things for certain, but let me offer you two basic propositions. (1) Boys who work hard or are made to work hard acquiring verbal and logical facility at school will be more productive in any endeavor than boys who do not. (2) Boys left to their own devices, especially adolescent boys and adolescent devices, seek only gratification of their impulses in the most sensational, yet most effortless, ways possible. Consider any example, historical or contemporary, of adolescents left to their own devices. Adolescents, at least half of them, grow out of adolescence, but if they are unschooled, they are crippled in taking up their life's purpose.

Of course I am laboring, and probably blurring, my point. In large measure I agree with you. Nobody is more heartened to observe a student "see the point" than a schoolmaster. My experience, however, has taught me that the odds of seeing it are greatly increased when the vision is trained. I don't worry about the self-esteem or the sensitivity or the "creative potential" of any boys working doggedly at school. Hard work brings achievement, which is the only sure source of self-esteem—I say this in spite of the odd theories afoot that talk about self-esteem as if it were a wonderful visceral potion, somehow stopped up by pressures to perform and produce. As for sensitivity and creativity, my experience again is at odds with popularly expressed sentiments. My own view is that sensitivity and creativity from the young are rarely welcomed by anybody. If you are talking about creativity in the sense of acting like an Alienated Artist—Byron, Shelley, Joyce—then the best bet would be to enroll the prospective artist in a perfect prison of a school, a place with no outlet whatsoever for their finer sensibilities. Seemed to work for Byron, Shelley, and Joyce, and for many lesser lights. I would also be intrigued to see a school designed for Byron, Shelley, etc. I think it's possible. I can see, in fact have seen, the curriculum that would make every provision for creativity, set aside appropriate modules of time for spontaneity. Ah, give me Tom Brown's Rugby, and I'll give you not only Robert Hughes (who wrote the book), but Matthew Arnold (the headmaster's son).

Please forgive this garrulous reply. You have struck my one chord (maybe only a note).

Again I appreciate your letter, criticism and all. Would you mind if we printed it in the spring *Quarterly*?

Best wishes for a joyful holiday,

John O. Greeve

Meg:

> West Hartford
> General Hospital

Cruel surprise. J. drove me to the clinic this a.m. for what was to have been the last radiation. Pictures showed something big and terrible at the base of my stomach, where my trouble was before.

So, here I am again in Hartford, imprisoned in white, wired up to fluids. Apparently they need to get at this thing, cut it up, and "clear it." I have held firm from the outset that there will be no holding-action surgeries, but they make a case that they can sneak into me with little wiry tubes with even smaller snippers inside the tubes and get at the thing. I'm worn out, little book. Let them at me. Let them take me snip by snip. Just let there be morphia.

Poor J. is frantic. He wants to stay, and he has to go, Wells is needy as a big crabby baby. I hate this more for him than for me.

They will do the snipping in the a.m. I told J. just to call. This will undoubtedly not be the worst. Hell and blast. Where's Rilke? I'm going straight to Rilke, so back off, nurses. No samples or souvenirs for at least two hours. Medicine indeed.

* * *

You don't want to know. Snipped into something toxic apparently, and now I am septic all over, septic in my mouth, septic in my teeth. Foul, weak, dim past caring.

I am a septic product of this septic place. I want the quiet of my own bed. Oh God, let me go home. This was wrong, I was all wrong about this. These people may all be very nice, but they are duly executing their routines. They're dumb about and afraid of anything outside the routines, and they don't even know the cumulative effect of each other's routines, and there's nobody at headquarters directing the big routine. They are looking away now. I can feel them looking away the way cowardly waiters do when they know you want them but the food's not ready and they have other things to do. If they looked at me, they would have to face their helplessness.

No good. Morphia, sleep. Please home.

Meg:

School House

In my bed in School House, and, book, between you and me, I am never going back there.

Although I seem to have taken a good portion of the world's medical complex home with me. There is a stainless steel table stocked with fluids and meds. For me. There is a genuine hospital IV wired, probably forever, into the crook of my arm. There is a wheel chair which I don't believe I need just yet, though it sits there, sculpturally suggestive of an electric chair. Much more imposing is the figure of nurse McCarty—Connie—who, all shiny in nursey white, sits like an iceberg in J.'s wing chair, unless of course I tell her I don't need her, which I plan to make the rule. Tomorrow a snappy intercom arrangement will be rigged up between here and the guest room, so Connie and, I understand, two or three others, can periodically mop my brow or prepare my pills or pour more goop into the IV. Poor dear J. had to set all this up, which we can probably ill afford. For the present it all makes the room, the house feel like somewhere else to me, although I'm sure in the days ahead I will find it a godsend. No more hospitals, no more trips, except the last one, and there need be no hurry or flashing lights on that occasion.

Reassuring that there's my morphia capsules on the stainless-steel table, and also, I understand, quite a dose included in my IV drip. So I really am a high-tech de Quincey. Glad, glad, glad to be home. J. has been banished from sleeping in here, not that he would want to, with all this clap-trap and, no doubt, the heavy mist of pathology and rot hovering over the bed.

They haven't said so in plain language, but my stomach-to-bum digestion is probably wrecked, the "interference" with my ileum making continuing peristalsis "unreliable." Juice, water, gruelly samples of baby food for the foreseeable. My fuel, such as it is, is going to come through the IV. What's to fuel? I'm sure folks up at the Kelseys' are exhaling deep, piteous sighs on my behalf. Holistic-ier than thou. Bah, humbug. When their ileums go, they'll get strained pears and yogurt. I have sister morphia.

So, book, this is terminal. What do we think? Probably be easier to think once it doesn't feel so transitional. Might Connie or one of the others reveal unsuspected depths or fascinating secrets? Truth to tell, I'm rather hopefully eyeing the television, now wheeled right up to the foot of the bed. I should in my condition be able to skip right over the reflexive squeamishness and plunge wholeheartedly into the horrors, soaps, talk shows, even the outdoors channel which is always broadcasting from some photogenic 'wild' quarter to show anxious, kitty-faced predators crouching, hiding, then tearing after helpless prey, nearly always some kind of deer and their babies. Just the way it is in vast majestic Nature. But it is actually worse. The subtext screams that the odds are against all of them, even the head lion. Worse than bad odds, it's over. Their futile cycles of predation are just T.V. now, like—exactly like—the gritty police shows. After T.V., only zoos, then only museums.

Oh, book, I am so sick. I am now talking sick, seeing the world sick. I am sure that in a whole other sphere from this sickness and sick room, there are lionhearted, irresistible young Churchills of nature aborning.

Please! J. due at "supper" time. We will dismiss Connie and hunker here in my tent for a spell. Good, good J. There is still J.

* * *

Woke feeling strangely O.K. Impressive, morphia-in-the-drip.

J. touched my cheek before leaving for school. I did not quite come up from my torpor. Connie reincarnated as Gwen. Gwen has lighter hair, same pulled-back do, same resigned heavy no-ankle legs. She reassures me I can hobble my IV thing-y with me into the bathroom. It has friendly little wheels. Not so bad, medical technology.

Arranged rather comfortably, rather regally in bed, free now of Gwen. My head is full of J. This is all very wearing on him, I know. I am aware that I and this other formidable entity, my Care, have become yet another enormity for him to manage. Cruel and wrong, but of course he must do it. I will set myself to this, since I have been discharged from all other earthly duties. I will be easy, I will make this easy for him. I will swallow back bile, if I must, sit up straight, and I will engage that beautiful man in a world beyond Wells and cancer. I will make him laugh somehow.

Read, doze, read, doze, Anthony Powell's *The Kindly Ones*. Good and darkening, like me. J. popped in mid a.m. to sit, see how the arrangement is working. Relieved, I think. Wells roars along. Many big games and matches. I can feel J. steeling himself for everything. Somehow he will summon up the boom-boom attitude required. I am beyond wondering that for boys games have to matter. Go, Wells, go.

Sure of foot, a little stooped I think, and incidentally way too thin, J. plods on uphill, I'm sure he feels, forever. It's the road he knows, the road he chose.

It's also the road we chose. Not merely Wells—in a way, not even Wells. There was plenty of talk and dream, sputter and hope when we decided to marry. Not decided—realized we were going to marry. Never a doubt. Frank and Val, without a lot of thought, put us together that night at the Indian restaurant on Brattle Street and poof! It was all very clear. No more scouting and schemes, wondering if something more might be made out of Philip Lowenthal. All the other men—what am I saying, boys—I knew were lamely hovering around that sure good thing J. already was. I knew he was relieved to find me, somehow fatigued by the wait. The first night he loved me he let me know. Walking me back to my Chauncey Street digs in dewy, chirpy, disorienting first morning, he said to me, "How is it there's nothing wrong with you?" I hadn't brushed my teeth. My stockings were in my bag.

I knew exactly what he meant. Before he said it, I knew. I think we both knew. We didn't decide anything. We converged, irrevocably. Road is the right metaphor. We didn't veer onto it, we found ourselves already, always there, now in step.

Thirty-three years on this road together. The prospects along the wayside are brighter and dimmer, but the road is always the road. We made Brian and dandled him in our arms, hoisted him up over our shoulders, led him by the hand, then, bewildered and grave with hope, let him sprint out ahead, linger furtively behind. Turned off somewhere—do they all? Could he, *could* he be waiting up beyond a bend? Is he forever on some other road, his very own road?

The road, the road. Sometimes sunburnt and laughing we were too full of the sights and sounds, our bodies and glad hearts too full to mind the road. Were we once road weary? Never, never were. Sometimes we sailed that road, and once J., in the days of charts and compasses and tide tables, said to me through the gloom of blue fog and anonymous black water, "We could be anywhere." We were, the *Valmar* a sodden, salt-soaked question mark moving toward a compass point somewhere, we believed, between Freeport and Kittery. Just the road. One time we ascended right out of that fog, so high that everyday atmosphere was fog compared to the light and vivid beauty of those Swiss and Italian lakes. Our road took us there. We arrived on our real legs in our real shoes in a paradise, a myth place that showed itself to us, let us see its paint palette villas, fish shimmering like honey and foil under the piers, stones shimmering like fish, geraniums so red-orange in their painted boxes on the bridges they seemed to make little shouts at the sun. In the shadows and in rosy dusk, we felt the age of the place and all of its hovering souls. Rousseau,

Greeves Passing

Casanova, Hesse. Forgotten rascals in high boots and cod pieces, muslin bloused beauties with baskets on their heads. The doors and window sills cerulean blue, pumpkin orange, forest green. Every tile in its place, every brass hinge richly oiled. In the open market the silver-black flanks of fish, the water-beaded heads of lettuce too alive and beautiful to buy or eat. Carts, donkeys—why, still? Sagging dories and weathered oars. Our road took us there, to Locarno, Lugano, Como. Took us there, and they were waiting for us. Offering us up glasses of wine, baskets of cool plums, steaming trout in buttery sauce. Time slowed, promised, promised to open up to an eternity if we would stop, if we would stay. We sat entranced on terraces and balconies in last light of day, wondering at this. We made love on sun-blown sheets with every window wide open to the rush of breeze and the giddy slip-slop of lake on stone. This place, this clear-at-last Locarno was as real as making love, real as each other.

But it was the road. The road was what we trusted. The road was what we knew. Without even knowing it we were back in the gray world again, even when its sun was shining with all its ordinary might. I wonder now: did we belong there? Is that why we arrived? Or were we just to have glimpsed and felt it, so we'd know?

We kept to our road, the road that passed through Wells and keeps passing through. Like swallows sometimes we swoop aside, J. to his conferences and workshops in Princeton and New York, to Sandwich and Little House and a sniff of the sea, and I, my swallow wings dipping obliquely into the still enchantment of books or even, once, to Kent and Crystal Foote and a tremulous unfurling of body and heart, but our arcs criss-cross the road, define it exactly.

No perspective on our road. We are always just where we have arrived, with no view to any place else. It's not just that I am sick, it's always been that kind of road. We're here, J. and I, only here, this one road just to ourselves. True for me, I know true for J. Surely that is what married means. The only road, the shared only road. This is the deepest, greatest blessing, to have journeyed, to have been one in this way. But is it too cruel finally for the one who is left? Can it be our road without me? Can he travel our road without me, holding the memory of me like a great sack over his shoulder? No, stop, of course not. It is cruel. It's the cruelest fact of all. What—do the two lanes, on that day, narrow to one? Is J. to carry on alone, in his one lane? Is it because I won't see this that I can't see it? Monstrous selfishness in me. But I can't. I can't see J. on that road.

Oh book, where have I come to? Here, I suppose. Right terribly here.

J., beloved J., with every breath I have left I pledge to cherish, celebrate, and, with God's grace, fortify your precious self.

John:

16 December

Mr. and Mrs. Frank Greeve
14 Bingham Drive
Tarrytown, New York

Dear Val and Frank,

Just a note to let you know I am counting the days till you arrive. Some order at last! Some company I can relax in, at last! I am *hiring* two women from the dorm staff to do our house before you arrive. So if not exactly commodious, it will be damned clean.

I've tried to keep you informed about Meg, but be prepared. She looks much more ravaged than when you saw her before Thanksgiving. If it works out, you should see her, but it will hurt. It will also hurt her, for the same reason. All we can do now is love her. That gets through, I think, although the pain now is constant. If she goes before you leave from there, I'll call you right away, as that could entail a change of plans for all of us. It's hard to say much more about that now. Also, no matter how terrible you think I look, don't tell me. I'm getting a complex.

This will be an unusual holiday for us, and I am ashamed of how selfishly I want you here, knowing you will not have the serene break from routine that you enjoy so much and that you deserve. Please tell Hugh that he is not obligated to stay an hour longer than he likes. There is a girl in Boston, isn't there?

Love to all. Drive carefully.

John

John:

17 December

Mr. Jake Levin
R.D. 3
Petersfield, New Hampshire

Dear Jake,

Season's greetings.

I saw your poems in this month's *Poetry*—seemed to be about half of the magazine. Very impressive. I had the impression that they were much airier than anything else of yours I've seen. I remember Ruskin rhapsodizing somewhere about the experience of watching—really watching—clouds as they tuft up, leave misty veils, and by almost imperceptible stages rearrange themselves into new forms. Is that what you're up to? Showing what we commonly perceive as enduring and substantial to be fluid and insubstantial? I hope so, or else I am going to feel really stupid.

By the way, I was glad for your warm letter. Even though people here could not be kinder or more solicitous, they are responding, I suppose quite naturally, to the sad process going on in the sick room; you, on the other hand, are kind enough to respond directly to me. I need that, I won't deny it.

Meg will probably not live another two weeks, and unless she can be made more comfortable, I hope she doesn't. This has been awful, all of it. To see her so physically diminished is painful, but the horror of this thing is to see her so constantly on edge. She gets no rest or relief from pain, except for a brief hour or so after injections. Riding the nausea and pain requires all her energy. Conversation can no longer divert her. I doubt that you have seen

Greeves Passing

Meg cry and probably have a hard time imagining her doing so. She cries much of the day. It's the inability to rest, I think, more than anything else, and the rage at the unfairness of it.

You go through these things, you know, like a zombie. There are openings to visit, and I am there. There is the daily liturgy of school life, and I am there. School teachers, especially headmasters, have to do a lot of acting, but since Thanksgiving the curtain has rarely fallen. It's bad in a way, since I'm supposed to be helping to shape the general experience here—the board is even hounding me to do a jazzy plan for the future. But all I do is preside. Not that anyone is making me. I've been invited to take an indefinite leave, to go south, to do whatever I please—but what would that be? That would be terrifying.

I keep telling myself, as if an external voice, that if I weather this, give Meg my all, keep my hand on the wheel at Wells, do right where I can see it, do not fall too hopelessly behind—then this will show the people here, maybe even the boys, something important. When at some point all of their props are knocked out from under them and they feel like collapsing, they'll recall that it's not supposed to be that way—you're supposed to hang in there the way old Greeve hung in there. I hope this is important, because it's all I'm living for. The voices inside are certainly no help. They cry and give up and assign blame, usually ending up focused murderously on Brian. Interesting that the external voice, the one with no energy, prevails. Maybe it won't prevail, maybe I'll crumple up, but it's still interesting that I want it to prevail—'want' isn't even right; it's just that I know it ought to prevail.

You know, in spite of all our jaded world-weariness, we really don't—at least I don't—think enough about ending up. I'm fifty five and until this fall I never really thought about it at all except as a kind of vague, unemotional tableau of being white haired and more decrepit. Seeing Meg has taught me that it's not going to be that way. It's bound to be something very different, probably something I never imagined. With Meg gone, I will no longer be anxious about being cut down prematurely.

Although, with the event now at hand, I am not ready for Meg and me to be over. That is what I never imagined. I have never gotten used to Meg, never lost interest in her for a second. My intellectual superior, my arbiter, my planner, my renewer. After my first five years with Meg for a confidante, I can honestly say I never again felt inadequate—one down—in the presence of anybody. I probably should have, but such is Meg's solidity. She is such a fact. Marriage is just as substantial as the Northern Lights or Joy or the four-minute mile. Not everybody gets the experience, but it's real, and those who try to subvert it on intellectual grounds or to sully it by their own infidelities can only be those who never had it. Sad for them, but they do more harm than they could ever imagine. Believe me, Jake, this isn't sentimentality setting in (or if it is, it is sentimental recognition, not sentimental distortion). My present circumstances do not lead me very readily into Browning-like sweetness. What a thing, though, to have loved somebody, in no elaborately qualified sense, for thirty-three years. And been loved back.

Nothing goes the way you think. I blink to find myself headmaster of a boys' school in a New England village. I am about to become a "widower." I will, in another deceptive wrinkle of time, blink to find myself *emeritus*, with a Wells rocker—where? In a winterized cottage on the Cape? In a home? Last year I still had a boy's view of the Future. I still thought, against all possible evidence, that an elusive Main Event was ahead. I don't know what I thought it would be. A great book, maybe.

I worry about enduring the school year. The archetypal boy never grows up. He cheats and gets caught, loses himself, finds himself, drops out, drowns, thinks chaotically, thinks brilliantly, keeps graduating and then starting over, teasing me somehow into the game. His energy never flags and he will have no patience when mine does. A soft and pallid Greeve has been imitating himself for months. A thin but insistent voice tells him what sounds to make and where to go.

But his friend Jake knows better.

I'll let you know about Meg.

Love,

John

Brian:

Tangier

A POSSIBLE WHORE

A Story
By
Brian Chasin Greeve

As evening approached, the young man who had been sitting since mid-afternoon at the small window table of Mr. Ghazzanfari's café was increasingly concerned about the dirtiness of his linen suit. The suit had previously been a source of comfort, an imprecise emblem of class or purpose. He had bought it for a few francs at a second hand shop in Marseilles and had been delighted by its near fit and near weightlessness. With repeated wear the knees and elbows had bagged and wrinkled more than he would have hoped, but this was, the young man reasoned, a warm season in a warm place; a wrinkled linen suit would not be unseemly. Not that many travelers wore suits and ties. It was an era of blue jeans or voluminous, elaborately pocketed walking shorts, of tee shirts bearing slogans, of puffily complicated athletic shoes. Men, women, and children alike wore such clothes, at least the Europeans and Americans did, but they were a decided minority in Agadir. In his linen suit, the young man felt appropriate, possibly even impressive, among Mr. Ghazzanfari's customers.

But sitting over a *café crème* and working haltingly over a day-old *Le Monde*, the young man noticed that the cuffs of his jacket were faintly brown. Something priggish and deep within him recoiled at this. The imagined advantage his suit had conferred on him dissolved, and even hours later his mood was permeated by the awareness of his soiled cuffs.

Greeves Passing

The concern, had he been able to consider it objectively, was a veil over a far more pressing agitation. There was a chance, if his friend Oliver Fish followed through in arranging things with Hassan, that he would have a whore, his first, later in the evening.

In addition to undeniable carnal excitement, the young man was, just beneath his surface preoccupation with his cuffs and the not quite coherent sentences of *Le Monde*, almost unbearably apprehensive. A whore. A woman, or a girl, who would exchange intimacies, open the orifices of her body to him for money. The idea of a whore evoked in him stock characters from plays and films, brazen, brightly painted women standing in darkened alleyways in pools of lamplight; back mesh stockings, revealing bustiers; lips bright red, pursed and almost oily with lipstick; a cigarette in hand. Thinking of them as stock characters—like drunks or villains—made whores seem more palatable, safer to the young man.

It was past six, and Oliver Fish was due to come with details of the arrangements. The young man put his paper aside, scanned the street outside the window without interest, and began thinking openly about the evening that lay ahead. Fish said an hour with Hassan's whore would cost one hundred fifteen dirham, an entire night two hundred and fifty dirham. He had forgotten to ask Fish whether he could pay for an hour and decide afterward whether to contract for the rest of the night. He would ask.

Normally at that hour the young man would have considered eating his evening meal, but he had had three strong *café crèmes*, and he could feel his heart beating insistently. He was not hungry.

He decided to order a carafe of red wine, which he would dilute with sparkling water while he waited for Fish. Fish, he knew, might not show up. He was unreliable about time and details. If he had somehow forgotten to talk to Hassan about a whore for his friend, Fish would not be especially bothered. He would apologize, perhaps laugh. The young man felt some unease at this prospect, also relief. He would drink his carafe of wine, pay his bill, and then, before darkness settled on Agadir, take a quick turn through the casbah on his own. He would keep a brisk pace, and he would not give beggars or touts a sideward glance. He would appear to anyone who thought about it a young man on some sort of business, a young man in a linen suit.

The large, shambling figure of Fish appeared before the window. He bent in toward the glass and peered in, shielding his eyes. His face was within inches of the young man's when he recognized him and laughed.

Fish, sun-burnt and grinning, joined the young man at his table. Without meeting Mr. Ghazzanfari's eye, he waved him off. He waited until the proprietor was out of hearing before he said to the young man: "Are you ready for some forbidden pleasures?"

"Tell me the deal, Fish."

"Nothing to it. Hassan's place is in the casbah, not far from here. I'll tell you how to find it. You just knock on his door, ask for Hassan, tell him you are Oliver's friend. He'll know what's up. Tell him you want Farida."

"Tell me more about Farida."

"She's just a girl of Hassan's."

"You don't know her."

"I don't know her, no. I'm not into paying for sex." Fish was grinning so disconcertingly that the young man turned to look out the window. "I've seen Farida, though," Fish continued, "at least I think I have. She looks nice. Young, not fat, not skinny. She looks good."

The young man wanted to ask a dozen questions, a hundred questions about the girl Farida.

"You know this Hassan pretty well?"

"I know him. He's done me a few favors." The young man remembered the small glass vials of hashish oil in Fish's room. Fish drank off the dregs of the young man's *café crème*, then poured wine from the carafe into the cup.

"So he's not going to take me for a ride."

"No. Farida is going to take you for a ride. Hassan will just take your dirham. Have you got it? It's one hundred fifteen."

"Or two fifty for the night."

"Sure, if you've got it."

The young man had five hundred dirham in three different pockets.

Fish reached for the carafe. "You can do a lot better, I mean a lot cheaper, if you're willing to take your chances on the street, but then you really don't know what you are getting. You follow one of those little kids around the bend to meet his sister, and you might meet his brothers instead. Every now and then the Agadir police find a guy in an alley, all cut up with his privates stuffed in his mouth."

"Thanks for that helpful story, Fish."

"I'm just saying, with Hassan, you pay, you get the girl, you go home. He's a known customer."

"Known to you."

"Hey, whatever. I think you're getting the shakes. Fine. Why not. Maybe you should just go up to the Royal Windsor instead, buy some British lady a drink, maybe you'll get lucky."

"Not a bad idea. Cheaper than Hassan."

Fish laughed, and the young man's thoughts turned to the Royal Windsor Hotel. An orchestra played in the lounge after dinner. Tourists drank American cocktails and danced. It seemed at the moment an achingly appealing prospect.

"What time am I expected?" he said to Fish.

"Any time. Why not now?"

In the rosy twilight, the narrow lanes of the casbah seemed less sinister than the young man had imagined, and, as Fish had said, Hassan's was not far from the café.

The appointed doorway was small under a rounded vault. Its snug fit into the whitewashed stonework suggested the entrance to a cave. From within, the young man heard a faint buzzing sound, which closer listening revealed to be the tinnily amplified music of the region, pulsing, frenetic, tuneless to his ear. As he raised his hand to knock, an idea occurred to him which flooded his consciousness with positive resolve. He would ask Hassan if he could take Farida back to his own hotel. The possibility lightened considerably what the young man now realized had been a powerful dread. More even than the hurried, dramatic plunge into sexual intimacy with a stranger, the notion of being led away to an unknown chamber, to an unfamiliar interior from which he was not completely certain he could exit at will—this terrified him.

The young man asked himself: do I have to do this? Am I going through with this for Fish? His thoughts had begun to turn again to the pleasantly commodious and legitimate lounge of the Royal Windsor Hotel, as the door in front of him opened framing a man in an open-necked white shirt.

"Is there something I can do for you?" he said in accentless English.

"Are you Hassan?"

"I am."

"I am a friend of Oliver Fish."

"Yes."

"And he told me I might meet a woman called Farida here."

"You want Farida." To the young man's ears, the words sounded more like a challenge than a question.

"Is she available?" The young man felt his voice quaver and wondered if Hassan could hear it.

Hassan stared hard at the young man in the linen suit.

"You come inside," he said and motioned with his hand.

The young man approached the doorway and said, "What I'd like, if it's possible, is to take Farida to my hotel."

Hassan flashed a look of irritation and said, "We'll talk inside."

Troubled and reluctant, the young man followed Hassan into a dark vestibule where mustard colored walls were illuminated irregularly by a small black and white television set atop a counter.

Hassan stepped behind the counter and eyed the young man.

"So what is it you want."

"I want Farida, and I would like to take her back to my hotel."

Hassan hesitated for a moment, then he said, "Farida stays here. Would you like to see her?"

"Yes."

The young man considered bolting when Hassan retreated behind a curtain into a passage. Annoyed but feeling helpless, the young man felt the imaginary presence of Fish urging him on: Fish, the irrespressible boor, the impresario, the joker.

An Arab girl, followed by Hassan, emerged from behind the curtain. She was tall, nearly as tall as the young man, and she wore a muslin blouse pulled down over the tops of her shoulders. Her hair was shiny, black and long, pulled back behind her ears. Her olive skin was clear but for a regular circle of rouge patted into each cheek. Her lips were painted a burgundy color so dark in the flickering light that they looked black.

"Farida," said Hassan.

"Can she come with me?" asked the young man.

"This is where she works."

Farida inspected the young man with considerable interest. By no means was she flirtatious. She looked him over so directly and so uninhibitedly it could have been taken for defiance.

The young man began in turn to appraise Farida. He tried to picture her naked. She seemed to him merely big, impassive. For a moment he could not imagine becoming sexually aroused.

"What are the terms?" the young man asked.

"One hundred fifty dirham if you visit Farida, three hundred if you stay with us for the night."

Without appetite, his ears ringing, the young man said, "All right."

Greeves Passing

Farida regarded him with widened eyes, but not a smile. She turned to the back passage and held the curtain aside for the young man. As he moved toward her, Hassan said, "One hundred and fifty dirham."

The young man paid without speaking. His heart pounded in his chest. Beyond the curtain the narrow corridor smelled of must, spices, and spoiled food. Still in the passage, Farida took the young man's hand and placed her other hand, tentatively, on his lapel. She said something he could not understand, and when she repeated the words they were clear.

"What would you like?"

"What do you do?" The young man heard himself whispering.

Farida bowed her head. Then she said softly, "I make you happy."

The young man felt a sickening weight in his stomach. He was without desire. He cupped her face in his hands. Her skin was surprisingly dry and cool. She looked up into his eyes, and again the expression showed only interest.

"I'm afraid you can't make me happy tonight."

"Come," said Farida, tightening her grip on his hand and moving down the passage.

More violently than he intended, the young man wrenched his hand free.

"No," he said, still whispering. "I'm not feeling well. Another time. You're a lovely girl."

Farida looked concerned. "Come have some kif."

"Good night," the young man said and turned up the passage toward the vestibule.

Hassan sat at the counter, slumped toward the television. "Is there trouble?"

"No trouble. I'm just feeling a little under the weather—ill." The young man tapped his stomach and smiled uncomfortably. Hassan rose to his feet, looking pained. He opened a drawer and slowly withdrew a metal cash box and set it on the counter top. Farida appeared at the passage entrance, silent and wide-eyed. Hassan glared at her. She returned his look and then withdrew.

"So you are ill," said Hassan, opening the box of dirham notes and coins.

"I'm sorry for the inconvenience," said the young man, leaning his own weight for a moment against the counter. He extended his arms out idly over the counter top, and in the light of the television screen, the darker, slightly oily rims of his jacket cuffs were illuminated plainly. The young man reflexively withdrew his arms from the counter.

Hassan closed the lid of the cash box, then looked at the young man. "You are ill, you should see a doctor," he said and returned the cash box to the drawer.

"Right," the young man said. "Good night then."

In the cooler yet pungent air of the narrow lane outside, the young man made his way toward the deserted square where, early next morning, vendors would raise their cries and hawk their aromatic goods.

He was inexplicably saddened, yet grateful, to be free of Hassan and Farida, the whore. With a stab of irritation it occurred to him that what he dreaded most was his next meeting with Fish. That thought would trouble him for only a few minutes longer, as he did not see Oliver Fish, or anyone else, again.

Meg:

School House

This morning I lighted on a summer night in Dedham when I was seven or eight. School was out for the summer and far from beginning again. Dusk had fallen more quickly than I expected, and I step from behind our garage where I had managed to clear skunk cabbage and burdock and, with such indescribable satisfaction, to dig a hole for something, possibly a grave. Stepping away from my secret, archaic project, I see that darkness has smoked over the back lawn, and fireflies like hovering messengers are glowing and blackening over the dark hedges. Beyond our yard is all the lush business of a summer night, the slosh of bicycle tires over the warm pavement, the sock of a hard ball into an oily leather glove, a little crescendo of laughter from a distant porch, the final squeals of play. Dark now, but with some green still showing with the grays, the street is wonderfully settled, benignly complex. There are secrets everywhere but also a vast encompassing realm where all the secrets are known. And I am alone in shadow at the far end of the dark lawn, rapt, sensing a pattern in all of it and that I am part of it. My first intimation of history.

Me: all alone at the far end of a darkening garden.

* * *

Very uncomfortable since waking. Pressure like a dry ball wedged between my diaphragm and breast bone. Breathing shallow. Same no matter what position I lie in. Can I have grown a great ball in my chest overnight? Please be gas, and pass.

I will rise above this. I will dwell for a time in the dunes, the whole moonscape world of dunes between Truro and Provincetown. I was nine or ten. Two of the very few sentences I can

Greeves Passing

remember from my father: "This is land's end, Meg. This is the end of the world." Dunes at the end of the world. There was one brilliant day near the Race Point light. I slipped away from the family blanket and skittered up over the rise of dunes into a pure arcadia of sand, hillocks of sand, hollows and crags and crevices of sand. No sound but the hissing of beach grass and not another soul. I felt called there, called by the dunes. Knees irradiated where I knelt, I busied myself without a thought, clawing out a trench the length and depth of my body. I lay down into it and managed to cover myself toes to chin, staring up into the chalky light of mid-day. A whooshing in my ears like the sea. If someone had been there to see, there would have been only a little bird-girl's face in the dunes, unremarkable as an abandoned pie. A face in the dunes at the end of the world. No one came to see.

John:

18 December

MEMO
To All Faculty

Let me stress in print what I mentioned briefly in our meeting yesterday: Please be on hand Friday in the dorms until the last student is packed off for home. Phil Upjohn and I have warded off an avalanche of requests from boys and parents for early exits, and we have ruthlessly declined them all, claiming that we are far too committed to our scholastic duties to give up even an hour of precious pedagogy. Hawaii, the Bahamas, St. Moritz, home and hearth can just wait. You can imagine the frauds we will all seem if you yourselves fly the coop early. And again, *use* those final classes—or else those who wish to do so are doomed. Special, warm, seasonal surprises are fine—so are testing and quizzing—but please do not dismiss classes early or altogether.

That said, I hope every one of you has the most renewing, joyful holiday possible. There are no words adequate to express my gratitude for the uncountable kindnesses you have given me since Meg fell ill this fall. And as many of you know, the only thing she has not resigned herself to in her condition is that it has forced her to be separated from all of you.

From both of us, deepest thanks, warmest wishes for the holiday, and our love.

J.O.G.

Meg:

School House

New pitch of wrongness—all one note.

Thought I was through this a.m. in the awful dawn light. Whoever defined life as pulse, as breath? It's neither. It's so much more elemental. It's a hum, a vibration of particles smaller than particles, and when you're finished and all wrong, the hum is grating and somehow off, and because it's off, it chafes and burns in waves, everywhere and nowhere, every cell of the skin tingling with it, skull, throat, pelvis, the arches of my feet. The thing alive in me now is cancer. All I can do is register that. Sour, sulfurous and so wrong.

* * *

Sweet letter from nephew Hugh, wishing me well, of course knowing better.

Every message now is titanic, letters even more so than bedtime visits because letters are disembodied. I see Hugh as physically enormous, energetic and mobile beyond my imagining. What does he picture when he pictures cancerous Aunt Meg in her school house sick bed? Glinting glasses and a bird beak, framed by pillow case. No, that's me picturing. Hugh wouldn't picture me at all, not if he's as whole and well as I think he is. He would avert mind's eye, hug the bright and hopeful shore.

Damn you, Hugh, and your pitch-perfect courtesy and your safe distance. I can hear Val's cooing pleas to weigh in with poor old Auntie Meg.

Not your fault, lovely admirable boy. It's not for you to know that for months I have cast my nets and cast my nets for Brian, for the shambling length of him, for even some good word of him, and he is, I know, beyond lost, gone from me. Hugh's sweet gesture mocks my loss.

Brian is always, presumably, moving about somewhere, distancing himself still further. But that is not how it feels to me. He feels a still and looming presence. He grows and glows before me. I see him in dazzling white places, on white sand, in white cities, in white clothes, under skies scorched white by the sun, there, wispy as gauze but there, and it is I who shrink away from him. That's what dying is—it is shrinking away from Brian.

Give me a day of you. Give me an hour of you. I would without a complaint take any kind of hour. Let me have you home again, dropped in for a night's sleep and change of clothes at Little House. I'll take you slouched over the breakfast table, hair matted and drooped low over your brow. Let me take in with a painter's greed, your denim shirt over pale denim shirt, your jeans broken at the bent knee like some kind of hinge. You could not keep from me my pleasure at your lovely skin, John's boy-face in your bones. You cannot hide your eyes, grey, then blue, pooling with something, quick to disengage. Let me have your voice, that new voice, surprising and deep, never mind the words. I need no words.

When you were thirteen and I would count the ribs on your back and chest, when your legs were stilts, all knee-knob and feet, the walnut of your Adam's apple moved with your talk, and your voice was wondrously like, I used to tease you, waxed paper over a comb. I am vibrating with that voice now. My heart, no something more cavernous than my heart, is opening to that voice and, more, to the deeper cello tone it learned to make when you drawled 'so-o-o-o-o-o,' or 'I don't kno-o-o-o-ow.' I hear it. I feel the tone of it on my skin, *o* sounds, saying 'not now' or 'no.' Be here, sprawl here on this bed. Let me see you, lying back in the cockpit of Valmar, long brown fingers loose over the jib sheet, the blades of your shin, your knees knocked apart. I could look at you, all distraction, the wind in your hair, until the world goes dark.

Once I could tell you, gather your little bird body into me and tell you that you were my good sweet baby. I never stopped needing that. Did I ever tell you, tell J., tell anyone how much I hated losing you to your school clothes, to the gloomy, gangling doubt of being a Young Man, a Wells boy, my lovely stick-bird muffled and armored by his crested blazer and regimental tie. And—crazy boy, crazy world—you knew it. You knew I ached for you beyond all words, and since there was no practical way for it to be otherwise, for you to still be my good sweet baby, you let me know you were forever lost to me. You made those necessary little distances vast. You willed that, did that, maddening boy. You confined yourself in other rooms, rooms where I knew you were. You left the table early, began begging off all former pleasures. You asked your father if you could live in the dorm and let dorm master after dorm master write to us about your puzzling isolation there. I am sure you knew. I felt you knew. I needed the throbbing bass of unknowable music behind your closed door, sniffs and signs of you, the steam of your shower on a mirror, the chalky trail of toothpaste spit into the blue porcelain, something deeper than the scent of you in your damp towels, your socks and tee shirts in the hamper. A phrase, the least phrase from you at the piano and I, from whatever perch in the house, would freeze fast, hold my breath. That was the very promise of heaven for me: you fingering music into the air, the very idea of you making Brian-marked things in the world. Oh, you knew I needed that. Too much, was it? If you gave that up to me, would you disappear? Is offering up to mother the death of a son? Why, please? Why such cruelty. Is holding back the death of a mother? What did I do but love you? I felt you swelling and filling me up and then gave you up. Up and out you went. I was just *friendly*, Brian, I was just nice. You could have been any old way in the world, any old way with me. I would have been thrilled if you had shocked me. I would have worn exasperation like a badge of honor. You stayed quiet. You learned to keep to other rooms, to rise from the piano and walk away without a sound.

I no longer go into your still room hoping to rest my eyes or fingertips on an object you held dear. There are only things you left—the old globe, someone's lacrosse stick, records I'm not sure you liked. In the closet, school blazer, a herringbone jacket, gray flannels, khakis. Not a trace of you.

So why are you here, somehow moving in and out of me with every sick breath? Without moving a fingertip, I am still forever gathering you into me, my good sweet baby, gathering you in, lowering my cheek to meet the warm rosy talc of your baby skull, my fingers moving over the silky milky flesh of your arm, the little cushions of your wrists. Brian, your sweet skull cradled into my neck. I had that. I had you. Be forever there, gathered into me, my good sweet baby.

Brian:

Tangier

How do people write novels? I have spent the last three days working pretty hard on a story which is only a few pages long. The more I work on it, the more I see wrong with it. You end up doubting the choice of every single word, then when you make a change for the better, everything else is out of whack. The only way must be to charge ahead like crazy and save the editing and fixing for later. That of course assumes you've got something pressing to charge ahead and say. In my opinion writers earn their money. One thing is clear now—I've got to read more, and I've got to pay closer attention.

* * *

Life imitated art today, although in a pretty pitiful way. I was sitting in the Belvedere lounge late this afternoon, reading over my poems and my story, and Avery Fish was suddenly at my side. He actually seemed pretty friendly and said nothing about my deserting him last week at the hotel. He got his bag with no problem.

He actually caught me at a crisis point. The old Belvedere is clean and comfortable and quiet, but I've dropped hundreds of dollars here since I checked in. When Avery showed up, I was actually trying to decide whether to have another dinner here or to stir myself to find a cheap café somewhere. I'm down to about $1300.

Avery said I was crazy to be staying here. When I told him my own money problems, he said the answer was to get out of Tangier, and either head south to Agadir (!!) which is cheaper, or move way down the coast to Essaouira, where things are really cheap and where we could freeload a little with some friends of his.

Even though it's totally irrational, I don't want another tourist center. It feels too much like disappearing. Maybe I'm developing claustrophobia, and the ocean's my open door, my escape hatch. Even a road home. Essaouira is right on the shore. Maybe it'll be a quieter, less touristy Tangier. Before I turned in, I asked the hotel manager about Essaouira. He said it was (a) not as prosperous as Tangier, (b) a very interesting city, and (c) worth seeing. That to me was a pretty good review, but he didn't seem very enthusiastic. I asked him if it would be a good place to spend several weeks, and he said it was not a "modern" city.

I'm going to check out the details tomorrow with Avery. I'm trying to convince myself I'm gaining on this sickness, but it's hard to tell when all I do is sleep, eat, haul myself a quarter mile or so to the beach, read, and haul myself back. I can tell it's good to take it easy, but I don't know if I'm any stronger. The beach and the sun tend to make me punchy anyway.

Fact is, I can't afford this hotel, but if I had my energy back, I'd try to get a job here, bussing or bartending or cleaning up. I could also do that in Essaouira, I suppose. Funny name for a place. It has all the vowels. Essaouira. Is-a-where-a. I-swear-a. Is so airy. I's so weary.

Meg:

                          School House

Conference here. Change in the morphia. I keep coming and going. Ice chips no good. Drying up.

* * *

New morphia takes me away, but then I come back. Not much breath for Gwen or even J. Told Gwen today where to put little book when I'm done. Made her walk into the good guest room and promise me she knew the place on the shelf. Very careful about his. She must think I'm mad.

* * *

J. here all afternoon. Darkness falls over us. I fade away and wake to him, each time darker. J. so gray and spent, all bones himself. See what I've done.

* * *

Letters to Brian, J. finished. I watch Connie put them into my jewel box. As if she is slipping me into the dark box to wait.

* * *

This must be the end of you, book. Too sad to bear, but better, don't you think, a period than feeble ellipses.

Clever for the last time. Let the record show that when the body dried up and failed, there was at the end a little rasp of sere cleverness. Which is all cleverness is.

Cleverness, the words themselves are precisely nothing. They are meta-life, instead of life. In the beginning was not the word. The word was always instead. No doubt at all. Consider my credentials.

A baby's new skin, new skull, that is life. A cheek on a cheek. A fingertip tracing the spine's nubs, loving that, loving period.

I wonder—had words failed me, would there only have been fingertips and what, with grace, they found? Love at my fingertips, if only words had failed me.

Fail me now, please. At any rate I am saying good-bye to you. Giving up, failing words. Something tenacious in me doesn't quite want to send you away to the guest room shelf with four or five perfectly clean white pages lying vacant. Do dying thieves itch to pull one more little job?

I release you, waiting pages. Be for some browser white hymns, sighs.

There was John. Brian. Sun on water.

This I know.

PART TWO

John:

        16 January
        Little House

Mr. and Mrs. Frank Greeve
14 Bingham Drive
Tarrytown, New York

I have just given enough thought to answering a thousand and some condolence letters to know that I can't do it. It does nag me, though, that there are so many people I want and need to thank—you two foremost. I can't place a value on the support and love, but I can place a value on the sheer time you have given us and then me since the holidays. That will simply have to stand as a debt. I suspect you were both aware that for a few days after Christmas I seemed to disappear altogether. It is hard to describe that feeling of nothing being substantial, even the loss, even the grief—odd. I remember for some reason the impression that, whereas the day Meg died, a strong drink took me away from the blackening, falling feeling, a few days afterward a drink seemed to pitch me into it. And there you were, a solace beyond alcohol.

Home is indeed a place where, when you have to go there, they have to take you in.

You were both right and not right about my coming here. It is too suffused with Meg for comfort, but that is not the main thing wrong. It's also too insubstantial, too not-enough for what I feel and need right now. It is no company at all, and it shoots me full of the fear that there is no company anywhere. (Pitiful, Greeve, pitiful.) And so I'm taking off. I'd like to pop in on Jake Levin, my poet friend, in New Hampshire, and if he can't manage it, I'll go inn-hopping off the beaten path. It's what I should have done in the first place. I know your place would be easiest, but I have got to toughen up, to practice. I'll drop you cards.

School has begun without me—funny feeling. I'm thoroughly relieved not to be doing it because I can't, but I'm also feeling that August feeling that I couldn't possibly manage a school, even teach a class. It's a funny way for a fifty-five-year-old schoolmaster to feel, but I always feel that way after a lay-off. And if the school manages nicely without me—what then? The hell with it. I shall visit inns and read their books: *Good Morning Miss Dove, A Man Called Peter, Lost Weekend* ,etc.

It feels good to write you—like having you here. Best love to Hugh. Don't tell him his uncle, the Headmaster, is folding up.

Love,

John

John:

> 16 January
> Little House

Mr. Jake Levin
R.D. 3
Petersfield, New Hampshire

Dear Jake,

I won't say things are settled yet, but there is enough regularity in the blur that I feel I can get in touch. Now that it's over it's worse than I thought. You feel prodded by shadows, urged on by something vaguely awful.

Coming here didn't help. The place evokes Meg and then, by a scrap of handwriting or a half-knitted sleeve, documents her finitude. She keeps dying.

What I really would like to do is drive up and see you. Is it possible? I mean now. At any rate, I'm clearing out of here in a few days. I'd clear out immediately, but I accepted a dinner invitation from some nice, retired friends down the lane—how could they ever understand that my presence in their house confirms their luck and fragile safety?

May I come? I'll call Monday a.m. at the college. If you can't do it, leave word. If you can, see you soon.

Best,

John

John:

>18 January
>Little House

Mr. William Truax
President, The Fiduciary Trust Company
P.O. Box 121
New Haven, Connecticut

Dear Bill,

I don't have the fuel yet to acknowledge appropriately the enormous amount of help and love extended to Meg and me over the course of our ordeal, so I won't just yet. I hope you will convey to the board, though, that their efforts and their presence over the holiday period were deeply appreciated.

I am grateful too for this open-ended leave. Wells will certainly be better for it. It's a funny thing, though; it puts me rather on edge.

Between you and me, hiding away out here was not a good idea. The effect is the opposite of relaxing—almost like being hounded by something. I suspect it's truancy guilt of some kind.

Again, deepest thanks. I shall be back in the saddle soon. I'll be in New Hampshire with a friend for a spell, then back down to Wells. Phil Upjohn and Marge Pearse have numbers to call if you need to get in touch.

Warmest regards,

John

Brian:

Essoauira

Maybe a big mistake. I could tell just putting my stuff together and hauling it over to the bus depot I'm not O.K. Brain feels like it's wrapped in gauze, and I'm not quite in my body when I move. Can't blame it on the beach. Waiting for the bus, I sweated through my clothes. Avery showed up about a minute before the bus took off, talking up a storm as usual.

I've never experienced anything like the ride to Essaouira. The bus itself was old and filthy and stank of piss and sweat and rotten flesh. Almost none of the windows opened, and practically everybody on board brought food. A few people carried in goats. My one hope was to sit as still as I could and get my strength back, but that turned out to be impossible. The bus had no shocks. It was like driving along a rocky road on metal wheels. We lurched and banged our way along the coast for three and a half hours, including two long, airless stops. I could barely look out the window at Casablanca. I think everyone was sick, locals and all. Even Avery got quiet after about half an hour, and when we arrived in Essaouira he lost it on the pavement.

I'm sure every tourist who's ever been this way says the same thing—but you have to. One mile west of Tangier, and you felt you were back in biblical times. On the inland side desert and scrub for miles, then a tiny village with five or six buildings of baked earth. Occasionally we'd pass a man in robe and headdress leading a donkey and a cart, shepherds and sheep, a procession of camels. Even with the smell and the battering of the bus, the scene outside was, for the first time since I started traveling, completely alien. Christ, I wish I felt better. This is what I took off to find.

Nothing Avery or the hotel guy said prepared me for Essaouira. The first thing you see is a kind of jarring white resort hotel on a rise overlooking the sea, and for a minute I thought: good, we've just driven through the Holy Land and now we're in Ft. Lauderdale. But beyond the resort is a medieval dream. A walled city with turrets and domes clustered inside like something from a book illustrating the crusades.

The bus entered a gate and clattered and fumed its way up little lanes about six inches wider than the bus. We got out at a market square, less frantic than Tangier, but with identical smells. Avery was sick and had to sit for a while. I was beyond sick.

I made myself a vow on the bus that I was going to go into full-scale convalescence. I was going to rest, read, eat fruit and liquids until I was completely better—no beach outings, no wine lapses, no excursions I didn't want to take. Avery insisted we see his friend, Nigel, first. He suggested we maybe stay a night or two with him, get the lay of the land, maybe get some advice about a doctor for me, then find a good, cheap place to stay. I wasn't up to leaving him and searching out a place to stay on my own, so I went along.

When Avery referred to his "friend" Nigel, I pictured someone like us, approximately our age. Nigel turns out to be in his fifties. Nigel Clough, like Cluff. He's British, a big bear of a man with a bushy beard. Funny manner—low key and friendly, but also suspicious, kind of worried-looking. He was nice enough greeting me, but he had kind of a funny reaction to Avery. He looked like he was holding back, as if expecting something unpleasant was going to be asked of him.

Avery told me Nigel was an antique dealer of some kind in England, and now he lives on a pension which, he said, makes for easy living in Essaouira. Pretty strange living too, in my opinion. You get into Nigel's place by entering a gate that leads *under* a building. You come out onto a bare courtyard, and on the far side of that are Nigel's rooms. The whole thing's below street level, and you feel like you're in a basement or some kind of pit. His place isn't much like a house or an apartment—it's a bunch of rooms connected by doors. There's nothing that looks like a living room or a dining room or a kitchen. There are some benches and chairs, some mattresses covered with carpets, but everything looks pretty temporary and makeshift. When we arrived, Nigel was grilling some lamb on a brazier in the courtyard, and I was surprised, given my lack of appetite lately, how good it smelled—and how good it actually turned out to be.

I guess Nigel's routine is to hold court. Starting around dinner time people started showing up. There were some other older Brits who apparently spend part of their year in Essaouira, some European kids who seemed to be teenagers or early twenties—younger than I am—and six or seven Arab boys. Three of the Europeans turned out to be Danes, and the other one was French. Strange gathering. The common denominator seemed to be that everybody had met Nigel somehow, and he continued to make himself available. Just about everybody brought something with them, some wine, fresh bread, goat cheese, chocolate. One of the Danes was a girl named Marte, blond, tan, athletic looking—very attractive. I don't think she said a word to anyone over the course of the evening. Nevertheless, she had my full attention. Among other things, I'm getting love-starved.

A lot of drinking. That seemed to be the point. But not the ailing Greeve. I told Nigel I was under the weather and needed to turn in. He was very nice about that, and he made up a bed for me and shooed the other people into other rooms and out into the courtyard. He said I should watch my health, and to let him know if I wanted to see a doctor in Essaouira. Tonight for some reason, doing that seems like a good idea. What could I lose?

It's actually feeling good here now. I'm comfortable in this room, it's very cool, and I can hear people laughing and talking out in the courtyard. It's a strange sensation—company. Now I need to sleep.

Greeves Passing

* * *

This is a very easy-going scene. We basically lounge around during the day, maybe go on an errand to the market or to a cafe. Things pick up at night when people come together, play music, and drink a lot. I think it's pretty much a gay group, because Nigel's British friends seem to go off with the Arab boys by the end of the night. Nobody talks about it, at least to me, and even Avery got sort of cute when I asked him what was going on. He said, "Welcome to North Africa." Nigel and his friend Stephen are actually pretty interesting to talk to. Stephen used to arrange bus tours from London to places like Oxford and what he calls "the Shakespeare country." His stories about that are very funny. He kept us going for a couple of hours yesterday—about drivers who would disappear into a pub while the tour was seeing the sights and emerge hours later completely shit-faced, or American women who screamed to stop the bus because their bladders were full. He's a funny, sad little guy, Stephen. You get the impression he's just heard terrible news, but the real problem seems to be his teeth. He has some badly-fitting bridges which he says hurt him constantly. I'm pretty sure he's serious. He said the bridges are typical "National Health" and "you Americans haven't tried that yet." For some reason everything he says cracks me up. I'm fascinated by the stories about his tours, the idea of this old, deadpanned guy just trying to get the customers on and off the buses, but life not cooperating. There could be a story there. The idea of a tired old plodder like Stephen mooning around after Arab boys is funny, but also touching and sad. I've been thinking about something Stephen said about his tours. Several times a week, he said, when the bus got back to London at the end of the day, fewer people got off than got on in the morning. I keep thinking about those lost or dissatisfied tourists making their way around the British Midlands. I wonder how they finally got back. Maybe one or two of them disappeared from the face of the earth.

One bonus I get from hanging around these Brits is the English newspapers, which are terrific. Maybe I'm just starved for newspapers I can read easily, but I really do think they're different and better. The pieces are shorter, livelier, way more opinionated than in the States—the writers are actually pretty mean reviewing books and theatre. But I find myself reading everything, even tearing out bits which give me ideas for stories. If I ever stay anywhere for a while, I'm going to work out a way to order *The Times*, *The Guardian*, and *The Daily Telegraph*. They're worth it for the crossword puzzles alone. Yesterday, I spent, without exaggerating, every waking minute working on an old puzzle from *The Telegraph*. I was obsessed with it. I felt tremendously handicapped not knowing the insider British clues. Bugging Nigel and Stephen about them got to be kind of a joke. But you feel pretty smart when you get those things.

There was another unexpected pay-off from the puzzle. I got two insights. 1) I realized with a jolt that your mind is always working on things, whether you realize it or not. I turned away from the puzzle twice, to eat something in the middle of the afternoon and to catch a little sleep before dinner. Both times I came back to the puzzle knowing for sure things I was clueless about before. The first time it happened I was eating. I was actually in a conversation with Nigel and Avery, and right in the middle of a sentence—my own sentence—I realized that the word for the clue "ordinance" was "assize." I've never used the word "assize" in my life, and I've maybe read it two or three times in history books. I wasn't consciously working on finding it when it surfaced. And when it did, it said: Hey! Here I am! The same thing happened when I took a nap. I thought I'd done all I could do on the puzzle, but when I woke up, it was as if about ten right answers were waiting in line. The point is, they weren't just there—they were pressing for attention. A person, a mind—my mind—was working away at things I wasn't even conscious of doing. Not only that, the other mind/person was smarter than I am, than I am consciously.

Is this what psychology is about? Does everybody else already know this, and I'm just finding out now? It seems amazing to me that for every person there is a pre-person, working deep, working on the big picture, while the person just bumps along trying to get through the day. The pre-person can come forward and join the person for a while, it can work quietly on its own, it can do whatever it wants. But it's smart, its memory is tremendous, and it's obviously in charge. Maybe the job in life is to get to know the pre-person, or just to be the pre-person.

A good question: is my pre-person sick when I'm sick? I have a feeling not, but I'm going to have to work this out. My head is spinning with this stuff, and it's now the middle of the night. Nigel and his boys are still whooping it up. I'm not tired but my body is saying sleep. The second insight was about mother, and I'll get to that.

* * *

I think that every second I was working on the crossword puzzle yesterday, I was somehow aware of my mother's presence. Maybe she's in there with my pre-person. On the surface, it's easy to see why I felt that way. She's probably the best crossword puzzlist in the world. She has a kind of intelligence I'll never have: the calm, careful kind where facts fit, you take time to get things right, and explanations make sense.

What a funny life she's had. She was a student for a long time, then a teacher's wife and an odd-jobber at Wells, then my mother. Today she'd probably be a teacher, maybe a college professor, although she always said all she ever wanted to be was a student.

What a mind. She seems to have read all the novels ever written and all the poetry before World War I. She says that after World War I poetry got very difficult and very personal, and she lost interest in it. She's also crazy about history, especially medieval history. Put all those things together and you've got a mighty good crossword puzzler. She used to rip into the Sunday *New York Times* puzzle the second we got home from chapel. In thirty minutes, with a lot of hmms and ahas, she'd be done. I have never once gotten even most of the way through a Sunday crossword in the *Times*.

She says that everything she really likes—reading, crosswords, theatre, conversation, gardening—is socially useless. It's a joke, but it drives my father crazy. Useless isn't the same as lazy. No one's less lazy than my mother. She's up ahead of everybody, anticipating everything. The faculty—really everybody—is crazy about her, and that's been good for my father. She's an encourager, and she also has a way of making people feel they're smart. So you could never say she's useless. She's just not into action. She doesn't get all fired up to redecorate the house or build something on to the cottage. She just sort of fits in and lives where she is, goes where Dad goes. She can also make me laugh, even when I'm fighting as hard as I can not to.

She's definitely not lazy or useless—although that's not a bad description of me. It's weird to feel her presence like this all of a sudden. I wonder what she'd make of the scene here.

I'm actually starting to feel like a freeloader. Nigel's nice about asking how I'm feeling and leaving me alone, but maybe that's his way of saying enough is enough. I want somebody to tell me a good, cheap place to stay, but I want to keep a distance from this crowd. A lot of the younger folks who pass through Nigel's are looking for a place to camp. That's the last thing I need. I also wouldn't mind a little time off from Avery. He's been pretty helpful to me, but I see a lot more of him every day than I need to. In his own way, he's a pretty secretive guy, too. He'll cut out for three or four hours at a time and never really let you know where he's been. Stephen's all right, I guess. He might have an idea of where I might go.

I think I'll make that soon. New arrival last night from England, a very loud, aggressive guy named Hal Bertram. Very full of himself. He sort of pushes Nigel around, although it's supposed to be all in fun, and Nigel takes it. Avery told me that a few years ago

Hal had a lot of money, importing something, but then he got in big trouble with British customs and then for tax evasion. He did some time in prison.

He took over so fast after he got here, I wonder if he might actually own this place. Avery says no, but it's very odd. Hal's now in charge of the food. He knows some Arabic, and he sends the Arab boys out for things as if they were his staff. They seem to like him, though. They're actually very nice, the Arab boys, although I still don't have a clear take on how they fit into things. They only know a little English, but they've been friendly to me. Their number varies, but I've gotten to know the names of four of them: Yusef, Farouk, Kareem, and Ibrahim. Hal kind of puts them on, and he also tried to put me on a little. He calls me "the invalid."

I also heard him refer to me to Nigel as his "gentle consumptive." He's a definite type, a type I try hard to avoid.

John:

11 February

Mrs. Faye Dougan
1995 Wisconsin Avenue, N.W.
Washington, D.C.

Dear Mrs. Dougan,

I have only the sketchiest idea of what your organization does, but I have been told that you have outreach centers abroad through which you try to locate missing and runaway children. If this is what you do, I would like to apply for your services.

My son, Brian Greeve, age 23, took off on an open-ended trip abroad nearly a year and a half ago. He seemed to tour western Europe from hostel to hostel for a month or so before gravitating to Spain, Portugal, and possibly North Africa. He wrote periodically for several months, asked twice for money. I last heard from him about a year ago. The letter was post marked from Cape St. Vincent, Portugal, which looks on the map to be a coastal village. I have since written to him there several times and received no response. A money order sent there this past September has not been claimed. I have contacted U.S. embassies in Morocco, Spain, and Portugal, but they have found nothing.

Can you help? Do you have finding agents abroad in the countries I have named? If you can help me, I will be glad to pay whatever finding fees are involved. Brian has been no stranger to drugs and their devotees. Centers of that sort of activity may be fruitful places to look.

My son is unaware that his mother became ill and recently died. It is very important that I get in touch with him.

I enclose some photographs for identification purposes. Please do not hesitate to call me if I can provide you with further information that may assist you in finding him.

Yours sincerely,

John Greeve

John:

16 February

REMARKS TO THE SCHOOL

Gentlemen: Not much more than a week ago I stood before you to say a few things by way of getting reacquainted. One of the things I said was that I was glad to be back. Another was that I was concerned about the amount of casual destruction I saw on the campus.

I would like to update those remarks. This morning I am less glad to be back. Apparently a few of you took my statement of concern as a kind of challenge. Since then the following events have occurred: all of the corridor light bulbs on the first floor of Gibbs have been smashed, the pay phone in the commons has been ripped out—the only phone available to underformers for outside calls—and, this one you all, I am certain, have already had a good laugh about: the oldest and most valuable work of art in the school has been permanently damaged.

Let's look for a moment at the last one, the funny one. It must have been hilarious—and daring too—to bash out a great hunk out of the genital area of the statue. Imagine it, the *private parts*! It worked, too. Whoever did this knew his—knew their—school. There has been a lot of laughter and excited comment since Sunday night. And if the deed was meant to say, "Take *that,* school and authority," that worked too. At least it worked with me. I took it, and was alternately dumbfounded, furious, and helpless. It was certainly an effective and dramatic act.

As many of you know, it's right out of the history books, too. Somebody, whether Corinthian trouble makers or Alcibiades and his thuggy friends, hacked off the genitals of Athens' statues

Greeves Passing

of Hermes just as Athens was about to go to war against Sparta. That stunt was effective also—shocking, outrageous and, to the hip and cynical, hilarious. Although you will have to go to the history books to learn how, it also brought down the city of Athens, down from perhaps the height of any city in the western world before or since. It brought down Athens, brought down Alcibiades, brought down his innocent teacher, Socrates, and it brought down the thugs and cynics who started it all.

You know, boys, it means something to strike out at your own symbols.

Statue of a Boy was given to Wells by Thomas E. Wade, member of the first graduating class of the school. The statue has been in the vestibule of Wells House for over seventy years.

Thomas Wade left Wells and made a career as a distinguished journalist before Woodrow Wilson appointed him ambassador to Italy, during which service he purchased the sculpture he would give to us. *Statue of a Boy* is a fifteenth century Roman reproduction in marble of a Hellenistic statue still in Rome. Valued, until Saturday night, at about a quarter of a million dollars, it represents a direct line of western idealism from classical Greece through the Italian renaissance to the twentieth century. The statue is—was—said to represent "the finest human possibilities in the figure of a youth."

So much for human possibilities. The Wells campus, incidentally, is as I reported to you last week: a seedy, sticky mess. And so long as I'm so full of history this morning, I'd like to record a bit of present history. Today, February 16th of this school year, Wells School is a third-line independent school for boys. Good morning.

Brian:

Essaouira

Bad scene yesterday. At least I'm having trouble with it. Slept late, found a cafe for something to eat, then took a long hike all over Essaouira to get my bearings. Actually did some good things: located a post office, an American Express, a bunch of cafes, and I checked out the big resort hotel outside the walls—Hotel des Corsaires. It might not be a bad place to hang out sometimes. They have European papers, a big comfortable lounge, and a pool. The place was practically empty, and I could get an inexpensive room there for 120 dirham ($15).

I was out for longer than I thought and was in kind of a fog as I headed up the stairs and down the hall to my room. When I got there, the door was open a little, which I didn't think much about. I started to go in and then I stopped. Avery and somebody else, Hal Bertram, were inside. It took me a second to recognize Hal. He was standing up, facing toward the window, Avery was sitting down kind of leaning into him, and it took a while for me to realize he was giving Hal sex. I felt like a current of electricity passed through me, and without even thinking, I got out of there. I'm not sure they even saw me.

I wasn't ready for that. I went back to the cafe where I had breakfast and tried to get things in perspective. Two things were screwing me up. The first is I've never seen any gay sex before—in fact, except in movies, I've never looked directly at anybody having sex. I have a feeling you're not meant to. There was also a strong, bad feeling that I had invaded someone's privacy, not that I could have known what would be going on. It's my room, and the door wasn't even closed. One time when I was about fifteen, I was playing tennis with another Wells faculty brat named Greg Lund, and I got thirsty between sets and ran into his parents' apartment to get a glass of water. Their faculty apartment only had one bathroom, and I went straight in. The instant I opened the door, I knew something was off. There was underwear on the floor, the bath tub taps were running, making a lot of noise, and there was hot steam in the air. Kirsty Lund, Greg's older sister, was stretched on her back in the tub. Her arms were up behind her head, and her eyes were closed. I know I just saw her for an instant, but it seemed like an hour, like a movie close-up. I think I could have handled seeing a naked girl in a movie, but seeing a real one, a person I knew, naked and all at once, almost made me sick. The weird thing is I felt guilty. I feel guilty now. I've gone over that scene a thousand times in my head, wondering if she saw me. Her eyes were closed, but she would not have been sleeping in a running bath. If she heard me open the door, or even caught a glimpse of me, closing her eyes might have been the way she handled it. If she shouted or covered up or made a scene, it would have been something we both would have had to deal with. Because we never looked each other in the eye, we had two private dramas (if she saw me come in) instead of one public one.

The scene with Avery and Hal was more upsetting, but less sexy, even though it was sex. I think the reason I didn't get what was going on sooner is that there was nothing very sexual to see. Both of them were dressed. Looking out the window, Hal could have been waiting for a cab or lost in thought. My brain finally had to put two and two together. My pre-person didn't have a clue.

I'm starting to realize I don't have a clue about a lot of things. I didn't know Avery had any kind of relationship with Bertram. In fact, I thought he agreed with me that Bertram was pretty arrogant and obnoxious. Maybe they don't have a relationship— maybe that's just something they do. Cluelessness #2: I didn't know Avery was gay. I had plenty of other hunches about him, for instance that he was druggy (he smokes a lot of kif, disappears for hours at a time), that he isn't too honest with money (lots of little "loans," never picks up a check), that he's a bullshitter about where he's from, where he went to school, who he knows, etc. It never crossed my mind that he was gay. He never talks about sex, and he certainly hasn't shown any interest in me. Maybe he's not gay. Maybe he's the kind of guy who is willing to give Hal what he wants or what he will pay for.

I spent a long time in the cafe before I went back to the room. The door was still open. This time I knocked. They were both still there, lounging on the beds, and very relaxed. The room smelled of kif, but they were drinking red wine from our tooth glasses.

They were very talkative, and Hal was actually pretty nice. They wanted to know where I'd been. Hal told me all about the Hotel des Corsaires and about how Essaouira was originally called Mogador and built up about 250 years ago by a French architect who was down on his luck and got a big commission from a sultan who was actually a kind of gangster. The idea was to open a big-time port for the sultan's schemes. The port never came to much, but the city, being tolerant of everybody and everything, hung in there. It got to be a famous haven for pirates (corsairs), until modern progress replaced that kind of stealing. So the ancient walled city is a fake. But it's still ancient by American standards, and it's a real vision from the pool deck of the Hotel des Corsaires. From the way Hal was talking, I have a feeling they really didn't notice me when I came in the first time.

Before he finally left, Hal got pretty incoherent. He was obsessed by my books—I only have about ten. He kept opening them up randomly and reading. Like an actor playing somebody drunk, he said: "What you educated boys don't realize is that you have choices. Not everybody has choices." He was actually crying.

It is good to have the room to myself for a while. I'm bone tired and even a little hungry, but I can't see a trek back to the cafe. I think I might indulge myself in a small bowl of Avery's kif and call it a night.

* * *

Greeves Passing

Lapse in the journal, a lapse in life. There will be no more compromises, no more slips, no more dope. It's weird what it does. It doesn't make me feel any better, but it sort of coats over the sick feeling and puts it in a compartment. I'm still sick, but I can see it from a distance. I'm like an observer. *Insight*: my pre-person is the observer. But my actual person is still weak and not right. The kif doesn't help. I hate coming off the stuff, even the next day, and wondering whether the stuffed cotton, woozy feeling in my head and guts is the kif or my old crud. I can't be doing myself any good smoking. The stuff goes down like charcoal.

I need to get to work on a cure. This means getting my body dope-free, eating a lot of fruit and drinking a lot of water. I'm also going to stay out of the sun, since maybe that was the whole problem, all that beach time. Worth a try.

I really do think the answer to this sickness is to go after getting well full-time. It's definitely something now—quick sweats, weakness, almost no appetite. It's like mono, and I've got to get rid of it.

Terrible day today, lying in here in the dark, feeling no better than I did when the sun was beating down on me. The picture of Avery and Hal Bertram keeps coming back to me, along with big guilt about my kif binge. No more sun. No drugs. No Hal. And pray for an appetite.

John:

28 February

MEMO
To: Tim Spires, Hallowell House

Tim—

All we need!

Why not give the boy one more chance, alone with you, to say where he got the stuff and who else at Wells was involved. Although it all sounds pretty straightforward to me, please write down a thorough account of how you found him and his explanations for what he did, etc. When you are finished with him, bring him to me.

Extra effort much appreciated.

J.O.G.

John:

28 February

MEMO
To: Phil Upjohn
Director of Studies

Phil—

Tim Spires just walked in on a Hallowell boy, David Wiseman, smoking pot in his room. He's worked him over pretty thoroughly, and in an hour we're going to know about all we're going to know about it. Would you please assemble Student Court and the Faculty Discipline Committee? They ought to meet at their earliest convenience, tonight if possible. I will see to isolating the boy and calling his parents.

Wonderful timing, eh?

J.O.G.

John:

28 February
Midnight

Mr. Jake Levin,
R.D. 3
Petersfield, New Hampshire

Dear Jake,

Good to get your letter. Sorry to have been so long out of touch, but things have been a little crazy here since I got back.

It's a little strange, actually. The problems have been quite ordinary, which is not to say unimportant, school problems, but for some reason they won't be resolved. Even when the right answer is obvious—at least obvious to me—it seems impossible to get a consensus, to act. That of course sounds vague, but I'd have to tell you too much more to make it any less so.

I have spent the earlier part of this evening interviewing a boy who was caught smoking pot in his room, after which I had the unsettling experience of talking to the boy's parents, both on the line at once, two of the most wretched-sounding people I have ever encountered.

I must be losing my heart for this work.

My first annoyance was my realization, when the boy was led into my study, that I didn't know him, that although we are a self-professed intimate community (our catalogue says so), I could not recall ever having laid eyes on this boy before. If I had, I would like to think I would not have allowed him to enroll. The overall impression was somehow unassignably canine. There was a lot of nose and chin and closely set dark eyes. He slouched when he stood, slumped when he sat, avoided looking me in the eye. His attitude may have been surly or it may have been his way of expressing unease. Perhaps it was the pot. He was guileless in a way that made me wish he had guile. Yeah, he said, I was smokin'. Yeah, he said, I know the rules. Yeah, he said, I thought about getting caught. I smoke pot, he said. I like it. Only then did he look directly at me, a look that was not quite defiant, but was at least decidedly sure of itself. When I asked him where he got his pot, he told me: I found it around somewhere. Where? Around somewhere—outside. When I asked if he smoked with anybody else, he said no, never. He lied in the same flat, thick manner in which he told the truth. He was impervious to intimidation, also to instruction, also to inspiration. And the worst of it is that I didn't feel the slightest bit moved to try to intimidate, instruct, or inspire him. Although that is my professional duty. I sent him to the outer office to sit while I went through his personal file. He is a fourth former, entered as a third former. He had C's in his local middle school, where his guidance counselor noted that he was a good citizen who responded well to encouragement. Our admissions officer wrote: "seemed uncomfortable in the interview, parents very aggressive, stressed how many other good schools were on their itinerary." Testing: Top of bottom third independent school norms; derived (Otis) I.Q 118. Grades at Wells 60-70 in all subjects, except Spanish which he fails each term. Activities: went out for third form football, was a back-up lineman, a reluctant practicer, quit mid-season claiming injuries. Discipline: quartered for smoking cigarettes last winter; minor discipline for failing to complete dining hall assignments, Student Court for mauling, with others, a new third former this past fall. Expended to date at Wells: $14,000. Attainments: none.

I called the boy back in and made him sit down and sit up, directly in front of me. I looked dead into his pot-bleary eyes and said: I don't think this is going to sink in, but I'm going to tell you anyway. The reason we have strict rules against pot and other drugs is that they have taken boys we know on a one-way path to poor effort, poor performance, and bad, deep personal problems. This is not something we saw in a magazine. This is what happened to boys we know—to our school. It even happened to a boy in my family. You have not done anything special at Wells. You have been a weak student, and there are signs that you are getting weaker. You participate in very little, and you avoid assigned work. You cut corners. You disregard rules without much thought. You are doing a bad job. You are not growing up, except physically, and you are smoking pot. You like to smoke pot, and you are doing a bad job. Stop doing it. Stop doing it now.

I wished I were his father so I could have slapped him across his doggy face and shaken him till he cried. He waited me out.

They are all waiting me out, Jake.

Good night,

John

John:

29 February

Mr. Dwight Nimroth
Editor, Poetry Magazine
1665 Dearborn Parkway
Chicago, Illinois

Dear Mr. Nimroth,

I have enclosed a poem, "Lesson," for your consideration.

I don't know if you require background information from contributors, but for whatever interest it provides: I am a schoolmaster and have published several poems and some criticism in magazines, newspapers, and literary journals.

My good wishes,

John Oberon Greeve

LESSON

I have held you after class.
I have brought you to this dark place
Of my books and bachelorhood not to bore you
But to tell the truth:

Your work shows ordinary promise;
That is, no special promise;
That is, no promise.
Pressed for information, you volunteer
Fragments of what you have heard us say,
Of what you have, uncomprehending, read.

You stand as noise to an idea,
Unequipped to know the knock of right.
Subtlety, sides of a question surprise you,
Two answers confuse you.
The trickles of your talk
Flow from or into no known stream.

Beginning, even as a bright faced child,
You lacked background.
Unable to assert, you guess.
Yet you are friendly,
You get by.

You may well be loved.
Others, pleased by your shape or smell,
Will touch you and be touched.
Loosed from all certainty, often afraid,
You will assemble and speak out, find all of it familiar,
And sleep.

John:

2 March

REMARKS TO THE SCHOOL

This past fall it was my unpleasant duty to talk to you about some boys who had gotten themselves in trouble with drugs. There were five of them, and as things turned out, all five were dismissed from Wells. We take time to talk about such things in chapel and we make hard decisions about such things for two basic reasons. First, we want to create an environment in which learning and personal development are most likely. The second is that we want to discourage others from following the path of those in trouble.

Apparently the October incident and the October talk were not adequate deterrents. We have lost another boy from Wells, our sixth this year. The boy is a fourth former, David Wiseman. He was caught smoking marijuana in his room by a faculty member who smelled it two corridors away in his own study. The disciplinary proceedings were fairly uncomplicated, as there was not much in dispute. Mr. and Mrs. Wiseman are of course upset and are on their way here to pick up David and his things.

As I said, the disciplinary procedures went without a hitch. However, some troublesome issues linger on. David admits that he likes to smoke pot. I suppose he has smoked on and off since he arrived. His pot comes from somewhere, very possibly from other boys here. He has probably smoked pot with other boys here. To do so he would certainly have had to be deceptive. He certainly must have lied. I am not sure how many of you know David Wiseman, but we are a small school, and certainly a good many of you do. Those of you who know him—perhaps a hundred or so of you—know that he hasn't gone in for much in the way of activities here, perhaps wasn't invited. You know that he has not done well in his studies. You know that he has been in a number of disciplinary scrapes, usually for avoiding things. And you know that he smokes marijuana. You know these things and perhaps find it hard to care about them.

I am starting to think I don't know very much about the drug problem in our school, and as for the caring problem, I haven't a clue about what to do about that one. Maybe together we can work on these things. Otherwise there will soon be another David Wiseman missing from our ranks, and when that stops mattering, Wells ought to shut down and sell its assets.

Good morning.

Brian:

> Essaouira

FLESH

Each of us is a plan for flesh,
A plan we may, within a range, change,
Even, should we choose,
Improve.

Each meal is an offering to Gut—
A gut reaction to Godlessness,
Vegetables, or exclusively "organic"
Stuff, grown far from factories,
Sprouting in natural disarray
And therefore pure,
As if flesh were.

* * *

Richard Hawley

ESSAOUIRA

What a bright blue sun—
Pressing down steam so thin
The white walls waver in the haze.

Clumsy water. Slapping ancient steps
For baked and grinning bathers once.
Polluted now, they say.

No one tells the fish.
They slither into soupy shallows
Where green muck sleeks the stones.

The birds are irritated.
There is no bread here.
In tidy boxes in the squares
Rosy flowers gloat in clumps
Like Swiss children's cheeks.

If only there were bread or wine;
People would die to live here.

* * *

THINKING OF WELLS

In the close spheres of my imagining
They are working out their lives.

As in a faraway stadium
A crowd might roar.

* * *

THE LIGHT OF THE WORLD

Singly, in twos or threes,
Drunks dwell everywhere.
Glowing in stale shirts, baggy pants,
They keep their helpless watch
Over litter and our tireless passing.

If you look (few do), you see
How joy looks boiled,
And these red lamps, these men
Beaming something about a last stand
You would like to forget.

* * *

BROKEN LAWS

As if the strings that held them up
Were snipped,
Minarets drop like trousers to the street.

Crowds of market hagglers
Fall to napping
And dissolve
As donkeys bob like milkweed,
High, high above the rooftops.

* * *

Richard Hawley

MOTHER'S GREAT EXPECTATIONS

That dark food not be caked
Between my nose and lip,
She scrubbed, concerned.

That my letters—tricky coastal maps—
Be rounded out and perch along the paper's lines
Involved a team of teachers.

That, legs of jelly, winded
And falling from the sprinting pack
I finish, I finish.

* * *

VISION OF A GIRL ON THE POOL DECK OF THE HOTEL DES CORSAIRES

In this new panic of right attitudes,
You send out, sexually, a tentative "O.K."
Resolved: to feature body brightly,
Clothes slippery as water,
Nipples ever near.

Tingling as his long looks
Break over you like waves,
You feel it flowing warmly from your core.
Fall back from it, into it,
Creamily as blossoms.

* * *

PRAYER, ESSAOUIRA

Where are you?
My gaze pours over the clean blue harbor,
Rushing past the silken eel grass,
Sweeping off the weathered docks
Through netted rigging of boats becalmed—
Each bow nosing windward
Toward the source—
Where are you?

This sun could cook me
But for a sinless sea-born breeze.
Not a cloud.
The bay expands its mounded belly
To mother Mediterranean sky—
Noon. How brightly
You are saying *soon*!

John:

4 March

Mr. William Truax
President, the Fiduciary Trust company
P.O. Box 121
New Haven, Connecticut

Dear Bill,

I am as impressed with the currency of your information about recent Wells developments as I am disturbed by the substance of your concerns.

I don't like your implication that things are going to smash here because of a "drug mess, a drowning, the St. Ives athletic squabble, worrying admissions picture, and so on." And so on? Those incidents, although genuine concerns, are absolutely typical of what happens in schools, including great schools. A good school isn't good because there are no incidents; it is good because of the way it responds to them. Without distorting the facts, I could make any year at Wells look worse than this one. The flack you've been getting "from a number of alumni" is left over from a flat, half-assed alumni weekend we had earlier this month in the February gloom. I wasn't quite back in the saddle then, and we botched it. See who among your complainants feels that same way after commencement.

Two points of substance before closing: (1) I haven't forgotten "Wells: Ten Years and After." Wish I could. (2) Back to the Stone business, please urge Seymour and others not to back off from the confrontation, not to settle with even a sniff of a payment.

You asked me, with respect to school policy, if it would matter too much if I would curtail the practice of announcing and discussing disciplinary proceedings before the school. Seymour told me in the fall that precedent has been interpreted to be against this practice as defamatory to students and their families. This is bad legal precedent and betokens only poor legal work on behalf of some schools' lawyers. The most positive consequence of any discipline decision in a school is thoroughly processing the trouble through the whole community. You share it. You make it part of the students collective experience. In this way preposterous rumors are squelched, and some actual moral lessons are learned. You tell the students all about what happened and why the deciders decided as they did, because you are neither secretive nor ashamed of what you have done. No good school can do otherwise. This tradition has served us well for decades. Should it buckle for the likes of Mrs. Stone? Don't ask me to practice bad medicine for bad reasons.

Faithfully,

John

John:

4 March

Mr. and Mrs. Frank Greeve
14 Bingham Drive
Tarrytown, New York

Dear Val and Frank,

Thanks very much for your nice offer to have me come down there and relax for a weekend. For what sense it makes, I don't have enough energy to gear up for a weekend of relaxation. Nor, I'm afraid, the time.

If the truth be known, things are not quite going smoothly here. We're getting thrown out of our athletic league for good sportsmanship, we are being taken to court for practicing consistent discipline, and I have just received a long, passionate letter from a man from Jersey Standard who says I need to learn about the real world.

This is a depressing time of year, extra depressing due to school circumstances, extra depressing due to personal circumstances. Everywhere I look I see mess.

I have no business writing in this mood.

Another weekend?

Write and tell me about Hugh, Jill, summer plans.

Love,

John

Brian:

Essaouira

I had to do it. I hauled out the blazer and tie this afternoon and took a stroll through Essaouira. Legs felt pretty shaky, and when the sun hit my eyes it almost knocked me over. But I got around well enough—I think I've got to start some kind of exercise program.

I went out the gate to the Hotel Des Corsaires to get a pot of tea and a paper, and I saw a guy I thought for a minute might be my cousin Hugh. Big, tan horse of a kid wearing tennis whites. He had a perfect bowl of hair just like Hugh's, and he moved just like him. The guy turned out to be German, and up close there wasn't much of a resemblance.

Fat chance Hugh would turn up in Essaouira. My dad wrote me that he's teaching this year at St. Edward's. He'll be great. He's a big, straight-arrow extrovert jock, Yale—the perfect prep school teacher. He was born for it, he'll look great in the catalogue. Probably not a spiffy enough job for Uncle Frank, but my dad must be in ecstasy. He's always been crazy about Hugh. Since we're almost the same age, we were always supposed to be best pals when we were little and staying on the Cape together. Actually, we got along pretty well. He really is a good guy. He was so well-behaved—so predictable—that I was always a little sulkier and creepier with him than I really needed to be. What is that mean-minded stuff in me anyway? I guess I felt that if I was just like Hugh, we would be too good to be true. We'd be a little sickening. Hugh was always nice to me. I can see his big face peering in at us through the screen door at meal times. Life must not have been too interesting at his house. I think maybe, honestly, Dad might have wanted a Hugh, who really was a perfect Wells boy. I think my mother preferred me, creepy or not. Although she liked him well enough, Mother always thought Hugh was funny for some reason. Even when he was serious, he made her laugh.

The brief possibility that he might really be here knocked me off balance. I started feeling totally defensive and worthless, as though, all of a sudden, I was going to have to explain myself and what I was doing. Why is it that when I *know* I'm through playing the measuring up game, I still feel panic attacks about it? It's certainly not Hugh's fault.

I couldn't make myself go inside the Hotel. I wanted a paper and needed the rest, but there was the idea of Hugh. Sometimes it feels like even people's phantoms can get you.

* * *

TO HIS FATHER CHEERING

Unaware of your own old athlete's pacing
Along the sideline, your eyes move
With the ball. Skirmishes
Swell in your chest,
Then break apart into scraps.
Players combine to plays,
Dig in, lunge—almost break
Lung-searingly free—almost
Score.

Across the lime lines, your son
Covers ground, cleats thudding
Over worn green, eyes loveless,
As defenders stream to intersect
His smooth, wide arc.

The force of their quick stampede
Sweeps past your face, tilts
The green turfed plane away—
And the boy has passed you by.
Your voice, with others, rises to him,
Is thrown in his wake.

Feel the good full hurt
Of his loss, your loss,
And what might still be possible:
Across the lime lines, your son.

* * *

Today, without even knowing it, I found myself praying. I haven't prayed since I was at Wells. I didn't even decide to do it—all of a sudden I was praying.

Fact is, I'm scared. I've got a chalky coating on my teeth and tongue, I've been weak and sick and useless for months, and I'm not getting better. It's getting hard to imagine ever being well again, and I'm scared. That's all I know how to say in my prayers: I'm scared, and please help me, please help me.

John:

8 March

Mrs. Faye Dougan
President, PARENTS VIGIL
1995 Wisconsin Avenue, N.W.
Washington, D.C.

Dear Mrs. Dougan,

Your letter was upsetting, but I thank you very much for sending it. In a few weeks you have been able to come up with more than my brother and I did working fairly diligently for a year.

I have contacted the parties you indicated in Washington and I have written the consulate in Tangier. I understand the passport should remain there in case he shows up to claim it. I cannot understand how a lost passport could be kept by the police for so long without somebody trying to get in touch with American authorities, family, etc.

It is hard to feel encouraged by your find. If Brian is alive, I suppose he must, without a passport, be in the vicinity of Tangier. Yet, as you point out, he could not work, bank, or even check into a hotel without a passport. If he is alive, he must be living the most marginal sort of existence, begging even, if that is allowed. I should know more about that possibility before long.

I must also, as you cautioned, be prepared for the possibility that he is dead. If that has happened, why would there be no body? If he was killed by someone and disposed of, why would his passport turn up? I am afraid I find all of the possibilities depressing, as is your disclosure that more than a few European kids pass into North Africa and are not heard from again.

I will, as you counsel, prepare for the worst. I thought I was prepared for the worst, but it keeps worsening.

Again, thank you.

Faithfully,

John Greeve

Brian:

Essaouira

Two days ago I went to see Nigel's Dr. Habib, and it serves me right. Sad-faced guy in a western suit. Except to touch my neck, listen to my chest, and look inside my mouth, he hardly did anything. He wanted to know where I lived and if I had a family. I told him the basics, and he said I should go home. "Go home to your family, rest, and get strong."

For a minute I thought that was going to be it, but he gave me a prescription for penicillin. At least I know one thing about my condition I didn't know before: I'm allergic to penicillin. I've got red, itchy blotches all over my body. When I first saw it, I thought my body had finally delivered the goods—leprosy. I made Avery go over to Dr. Habib's and tell him what I was like. "An allergic reaction" was the diagnosis. So I am to stop taking the penicillin. Thank you, doctor. Thank you, medicine.

I'm weak. I itch, I feel like hell. I look in the mirror like a blotchy faced boozer, and I have $800 to my name.

* * *

Hives are practically gone. This morning it occurred to me that being sick might just be a state of mind. Mind is the headquarters and the organizer. If I can get my mind clear, the crud will lose its support system. I want to do that, to get clear, but it's not going to happen lying around the Pickwick like a slug. I need some normal people, some work to do, a routine. I'm going to rest up one more day, and then I'm going for it.

* * *

Woke up early, washed, put on the blazer and went to the Hotel des Corsaires to ask for a job. The manager there, M. Vadon, is French, with good English. At first he put me off, saying I couldn't work without papers, and for me working papers would be impossible to get. Then he softened up—I think because he knew he could get me to work cheap. I told him I could do anything, even keep the books, which is a preposterous lie. Finally, he said he might be able to find something for me, but the wages would be very low. He couldn't pay me more than he paid the Arabs on his regular staff. I told him I didn't care.

So tomorrow I start as the low man in the dining room. Forty dirham a day, cash. It's pretty pitiful, but if I save it, it'll just about pay for the Pickwick. That's something at least, the first something I've had in months. I might have to spring for some black pants and a pair of shoes, though—dining room policy.

* * *

I think the plan is going to work. I did nearly a full day, from mid-morning through the supper hour. Nonsense work, setting up and cleaning up the dining room. It takes a while to get the routines, to know where to get the right kind of plate, etc., but it's well within my competence. The other bus boys and waiters are Arabs, and Indians, and they're not too wild about my being there. The head waiter, Moukerjee, is very direct with me and stern. He gives me orders in English, but he talks about me in Hindi (I think). He must think I'm an idiot. He doesn't look at me, but the person he's talking to starts looking at me hard, nodding and laughing. It's not bad for your humility, being a minority.

I was tired at times, and I got a few bouts of the sweats, but it was mainly when I was standing around waiting or watching people eat. Doing things is the key. I actually can forget about the crud when I'm doing something. That's what I need to get clear. Maybe doing nothing was at the heart of my problem all along?

***

I can do the job, I think. The only ordeal is standing still and waiting around. That's when I get the sweats. The two other less-than-waiters, Hussein and Said, are getting used to me, and we're getting along. They don't have a lot of English, but they do pretty well. They wanted to know about American music and what I liked. I'm pretty pitiful on the subject, and I think I disappointed them. I told them I liked Ry Cooder, and Said looked confused. Then Hussein brightened up and said, "Yes! Yes! John Cougar! John Cougar!" then something that sounded like "elephant". I'm not the guy to talk to about hot trends in rock 'n roll.

I wrote that Hussein and Said don't have much English. They have a brilliant command of English compared to my Arabic, and I've been here now for weeks. Every place I go, it amazes me—that working class kids in the Netherlands and Portugal and Morocco know enough English to get by pretty well, sometimes other languages too, and a so-called educated preppy person like me can't buy a postcard in anybody else's native language. I was best in France, where a little of my Wells French with Mr. Arliss came back to me, but I'm really pretty pathetic. I focus the full force of my intellect on the front page of *Le Monde*, and I get the gist of the headlines and bits and pieces of information from the articles. I would learn more language watching television, but I can't afford that kind of hotel room. It really bothers me. I think of what I must sound like to a French person or to Hussein and Said when I try an Arabic phrase. I must sound like a mental defective. Still they want to know about the states and American music. I'm a terrible ambassador. We're all terrible ambassadors. I hope I'm not a language idiot forever.

***

A KOAN

A village boy woke up one morning and knew it was time for him to find work. When he told his mother, she said, "My son, you are too young." When he told his father and the other men of the village, they laughed and said, "Go off with the others and play while you still can."

Because it was time for him to work, the boy set about finding something suitable to do. He knew that work must provide something useful, so he decided to work to produce what the village needed most: clear water to drink.

Now the water ran in torrents down from the rocky slopes above the village. The boy's work, he knew, was to capture it and to place it in his hands and on the tables of the people in his village.

He had seen the townspeople carry water in dark wooden buckets, and he had seen them squeeze cool water from pouches made from skins. Since the boy had no axe or blade and therefore no wood to make a bucket, he decided to make a skin pouch for water -- and when he had finished, he would make another. Then another and another! This would be his work.

He needed to find an animal, so that he could cut and squeeze its skin to make a pouch. But all the wild animals, the rabbits and lynxes, weasels and monkeys, ran off at the very sight and sound of the boy. Household animals, the cats and the dogs, did not run off. But the boy could not take their skins without taking their lives, and they were as gentle and familiar as brothers and sisters.

The boy thought long and hard, and then he arose and left the village. He decided he would search the world over for an animal – or a flower or a tree – that would give up its cloak or skin to hold drinking water for his fellow villagers.

Day after day the boy searched for the skin that would enable him to begin his work. Day after day he found only living souls who needed their skin.

Because he searched day after day, and because the search was long and tiring, the boy knew he was working, and at day's end he slept deeply and peacefully. In all the world there was not a happier boy. For there was no one else who worked harder than he did and no one else who would so gladly work forever.

* * *

<u>Novel idea:</u> reconstruct every kind of interpersonal dynamics — power relationships, love relationships, parent-children, etc. — from the standpoint of a waiter. Waiter is completely anonymous, with a crisp, clean, no-emotion voice. Maybe do it all through dialogue. Dialogue and waiting details. <u>The Dining Room</u>. <u>Dining</u>.

Moukerjee says I have to get a pair of black "trousers," also some dark shoes. I don't mind wearing them, but the idea of spending extra energy to go out and find a pair, getting them tailored, going back and getting them sends me into a sweat. I'm still conserving energy. It's a big enough deal to get to the hotel every day. But it's coming, it's coming.

* * *

When you're weak, little things can break you down.

Today I was going along in my little routines, filling up water glasses, laying out plates with little pats of butter, my head totally empty, when I looked up and saw a European family coming into the dining room. A mother and father, two little boys, and a dark-haired girl, maybe 18. The whole family was beautiful, and the girl was a vision. They headed straight for my station, and Moukerjee snapped his fingers at me, as if I might otherwise lounge around and ignore them. I was completely anonymous to them, no eye contact at all, even though I stared hard at the girl. She was really beautiful, clear skin, big dark eyes, and kind of a severe haircut, high up on the back of her elegant little head. They were French.

I would like to know why every time I'm jolted by a new girl, all the old girls rise up to haunt me. All I had to do was look at the French girl, and my head was swimming with Astrid, Deirdre, and everyone else back to the Wells days. For a minute there, I couldn't stand it. I wanted to walk out of the dining room, rip off my pathetic little bus boy tunic and disappear. What the hell am I doing at twenty-three years old bussing tables in North Africa?

The first second I could get away with it, I left my post and headed into the men's room. I had to see myself in the mirror. The news wasn't good. I looked boney and weak. A tall, nothing-looking kid with stringy blond hair and a blond face to match. What's wrong with my face, anyway? Do I have jaundice? I looked like I was made out of a completely different material from the French girl and her family. Maybe I am.

When I went back to the dining room, I got the sweats as bad as I've ever had them. I couldn't even look at her.

* * *

Bad patch—and very stupid two days. I find I'm reasoning at about the level of an eight-year-old. The day after I served the French family, I went home and felt incredibly low. I don't think I slept, and in the middle of the night I thought I was going to crack up. I couldn't think of a single thing I cared about or looked forward to doing the next day, or any day. It felt like the center of my head was about to force itself through my skull and spray out all over the room. The sheets, the pillow, and even the mattress were soaked.

Next day I took my blazer and tie with me to work. I decided that after dinner I was going to hang around in the hotel lounge. I wanted the French family, at least the parents and the girl, to see me there as a customer. That is my level of intelligence now. Fortunately the family sat in Hussein's dinner station, not mine, so I didn't have to torture myself. I barely looked at them. After my shift, I washed my face, combed my hair, and changed into jacket and tie. Then I went into the lounge and ordered a whiskey and soda, which was my next big mistake. I haven't been drinking much of anything, except maybe every few days a glass of wine cut with water. Even that doesn't feel great. I drank the whiskey in a spirit of the hell with it. I expected the worst, but it actually felt pretty good. I still had the no-energy, funny brain-wrapped feeling in my head, but the drink made those things seem very remote. It put them in their fuzzy place, so they didn't bother me so much. I found myself glad I was drinking, and I had a few more, sitting there completely alone, nothing to read, no one to talk to. I liked it. I was starting to see things around me with a sense of humor.

The next day I was very wobbly at work, but also pretty much out of it. Which was fine with me. I went back to the lounge after my shift and decided to hang in there with whiskey and sodas and *Le Monde* until the place closed. I was over my obsession with the French family, but I was into the lounge scene, when Moukerjee came to see me, very uptight, and said I shouldn't be using the hotel as a guest. I told him I was a guest. I actually got pretty defensive (and was pretty shit-faced). I went on about making my own decisions, paying my bill, being dressed properly. Moukerjee was furious. He said I was an employee, not a guest. I told him to get lost, and he said he was going to talk to M. Vadon. I think Vadon must actually have taken my side, because nobody came to bother me in the lounge.

It would have been better if they did. As it is, I got loaded, somehow paid out a lot of money, and woke up sicker than I've ever been in my life. I got Avery to telephone the hotel and to say I would be out ill for at least a day. I don't know who he talked to there, but nobody told him to tell me to forget coming back. But even if they take me on again, I've screwed things up with Moukerjee. I'm failing to measure up to the most pitiful job in the world.

* * *

Health: depressing, terrible. A cough that doesn't bring up anything. Sweats and fever. Lumps in the arm pits. Lousy appetite. Tired all the time.

Assets: A few beat up clothes, one blazer, one tie. Ten books, one back pack, one duffel bag, one polished wooden box, one ivory crucifix, $750 in traveller's checks, and about a hundred dirham.

Accomplishments: none.

Significant relationships: none.

Prospects: regular bus boy work at the Hotel des Corsaires, Essaouira. Happy birthday, Brian.

* * *

Here is the dilemma I face every day. It is the only problem that interests me now:

I feel self-loathing and restless misery if I stay in bed too long and don't get any sun. I have a fantasy that I will bake outdoors in the sunlight and get better. When I do get out into the sun it scorches my skin and makes my eyes and head throb. Indoors, I am certain that sun is the answer. Outdoors, it seems to be trying to kill me.

Dr. Habib gives me a sad look. He tells me to go home.

He thinks that's easy for a rich American. He doesn't know. Home is where the hard is.

***

TRAVELING

These vistas I have lived in—
The Cape, the rocky coast of Maine,
Zermatt beneath the Matterhorn—
Though unsurpassed in postcards'
Still life, they have grown
So strangely still;
Still living this is strange.

(To be continued)

***

Avery's been gone for three days. I haven't seen any sign of him. His things are in the room exactly where he left them. He is frequently out all night, and he never camps here very long, but I at least catch a glimpse of him now and then. There's never been anything like three days.

I'm feeling guilty now that I didn't haul myself over to Nigel's sooner to check. I've been feeling so bone-tired that when I get home from the hotel I just crash. I'm sure he's all right, but three days is strange. I'll try Nigel's in the morning. Even the thought of walking over there is giving me the sweats.

***

Nigel is away, visiting relatives in England. Hal is holding court, and he's got a full house. He said he hasn't seen Avery for days.

He was very cool, a little unpleasant. I don't know why that guy makes my skin crawl. I think it's because he's a fake. I think he made up that ridiculous accent. Maybe I just resent his energy, anybody's energy.

I went through Avery's things this morning. There's not much there except a packet of old letters. Maybe they'll tell me something if I go through them. He also keeps a lot of kif. He left his passport, so he can't be far off. Four days is a long time to be gone. I don't think I've ever gone for longer than 24 hours without seeing him before. Maybe I should check with the Essaouira police. Better yet, I'll ask M. Vadon what he recommends. Old Avery, I hope he didn't get charming and talkative with some real thugs. If he actually is missing, or if he did cut out for somewhere, I'm stuck with the full rent, not that that should be the issue right now. He must be around. His passport is here.

* * *

Bad scene with M. Vadon and Moukerjee. I missed work yesterday, because I was feeling lousy, and I thought I ought to use what energy I had looking for Avery. I took his passport to the police, but we didn't do very well with English or French, and they ended up keeping the passport. And by the way, I can't find MY passport... I hope that doesn't turn out to be a hassle for Avery. I *think* they got the idea that he's missing. I should have gone with Stephen or somebody from Nigel's.

Moukerjee actually managed to make M. Vadon mad about my not showing. Somehow there must have been more customers than usual and they actually needed me. It feels preposterous to get bawled out by somebody when your head is full of pea soup and you couldn't care less. It reminded me of Wells when some dingbat study hall proctor would lose it and you'd just wait him out. It doesn't help that I'm about two feet taller than Moukerjee and he has to talk up to me. He was very worked up. He kept saying to Vadon "He has a jub, but he does not dwit." From his point of view, I probably am a pain in the ass. I'm certainly his least reliable bus boy. But I better get with the program. Vadon said if I miss another day, I'm out.

Then a very creepy thing. I went back to the Pickwick and found Hal in our room. He seemed surprised and flustered. I don't know for sure, but I think he might have been going through Avery's things. Then it dawned on me—he had to have a key. So I asked him, did Avery give him his key. He said no, that the door was open. I never leave the door open. I think the guy's a liar, and he also has a key to my room.

He said he was concerned about Avery being gone and came over to check. I told him I'd let him know when I heard something.

I guess I need a new room.

* * *

Trouble on the streets of Essaouira. I was walking back here from the hotel, and was just about at my door, when a bunch of Arab boys, maybe six or seven, started to give me a bad time. I had seen them coming toward me down the street. They were screwing around, laughing and making a lot of noise. I didn't think anything about it. When I tried to walk past them, one of them kind of butted me with his body. I said something to him in English, maybe "What's up?" Then he kind of pushed me up against the wall, and I started to look around for someone who might help. One of them looked familiar, I think from Nigel's. I looked at him hard, and I think he saw that I recognized him. They were making a lot of noise. The guy who first bumped into me got right into my face saying "English! Hey, English!" and making little kissing and clicking sounds. I started to push my way past him, but they closed in. The sweats were coming on, and the first guy started giving me little slaps on the cheek and touching me up. Things were looking bad, and then a car started moving toward us up the street. There was no way it was going to get by, and I had already decided I was going to do anything I could—even lie down in front of it—to make the driver stop and help. There were two guys in the car, and they looked scared themselves. The driver stopped, looked behind him, as if he might try backing out the way he came. Fortunately he decided not to, and honked the horn a couple of times, then started driving slowly straight into us. There was no room to let the car pass without everybody getting off the street and plastering themselves against the walls, so the whole group, including me, started walking backwards in front of the car. The Arab kids were now very tough, very cool. When we were directly opposite the door of the Pickwick, I made a run for it. I crashed inside and straight up the stairs. As it turned out, they didn't follow me in. If they had, they would have got me, since it took forever to unlock the door to my room in the dark hall. My clothes were soaked through with sweat when I got inside. From my window, I saw that they were still there on the street, sitting back against the wall opposite the Pickwick doorway. I was too whipped to bother about it. I wedged my chair under the door handle and hit the bed. When I woke up, I remembered the boys and checked out the window. The street was empty and dark. The only thing in the room to eat or drink was a half bottle of flat mineral water, which I drank. It seemed a good idea to stay off the streets for a while, and I can't say I was hungry. I'm never hungry now.

* * *

I'm losing my bearings. This morning, by sheer will power, I got up, got clean, made myself eat some couscous and orange squash at a cafe, then headed off to work. It was a windy perfectly clear day, like a cruising day in Maine, and I got as far as the big porch of the hotel, and I stopped. The wind felt like it was blowing right through me, in a great way, like it was cleaning me. The Mediterranean was spread out like a gorgeous mound, and you could see six or seven different shades of blue and green and grey. On the left, empty beach; on the right the palm trees and quayside shops of Essaouira, a nice Essaouira where people fish and make beautiful wooden boxes. Even the hotel's main building, which looks more like a gleaming white courthouse, seems unreal.

Then it hit me. There could not be a more perfect place for me to be. For a person who only likes to think, read, swim in the sea, and see what happens, Essaouira is heaven. But it isn't heaven. I was sick when I got here, and now I'm good and sick. Beautiful things, even insights and humor, don't really register when you're sick. You know what they are—they register in your head—but it doesn't please you. In fact, it hurts. It makes you sad when you know what should create pleasure isn't creating pleasure. That's what stopped me on the porch. I was sick, and the world was going on beautifully without me.

I felt very weird on the porch, and I actually felt myself starting to cry. I couldn't go inside to Moukerjee and the napkins and the silverware. Instead, in a numb kind of way I made my way back inside the walls of Essaouira, walked right through the haggling in the Medina and checked in at the American Express office. I was going home.

Even though it's a down season for tourists, there were lines waiting for both clerks. My idea, although it was pretty fuzzy, was to wire home for money for a plane ticket. I'm down to $440, and that's not going to do it. Even standing in line, listening to people's English, made me feel like I was already on my way, like I was being reeled in. It felt tremendously sad. My head was full of pictures—of being met at the airport, sick, being sized up as sick, of setting up in my old room at Wells, of polite, sick hellos to the old masters when they come over, of being upstairs or off to the side or one closed door away from all the boy business of Wells. My parents' routines, cleaning ladies, school bells going all around me, while I'm—what?—lying around. I could feel and even smell my parents' furniture, the worn oriental rugs, all the clocks ticking and clinking.

I almost lost it. Two heavy black bands from each side of my field of vision started closing in, and I thought I was going to keel over on the floor of the American Express office, so I got out of there. But on the way out, I noticed the bank of telephones on the wall, and I knew that I could shorten the process by just going to a post office and calling overseas to my parents. Why not get it over with, give up, cancel the ocean, the year's distance.

There was a post office just outside the medina, but all the phones were in use. I sat on the floor and leaned back against the wall because I was so whipped. I must have looked like a wino or a bum. A phone opened up, and I went into a little panic, and I could feel the crying coming to the surface again. I went through with it anyway. You can only call out of Morocco by connecting with the central post office in Rabat, and that took a while, since the first operator couldn't understand me. When I told an English speaking operator that I wanted to call the States collect, she took the number and names, and my head started to spin. It would be very early in the morning at Wells, but my mother would be up. I think I realized then that I couldn't do it, no matter what. As it was, the operator told me there would be a delay of two to three hours before she could connect me. Would I still be at that number and did I wish to put the call through.

No. I couldn't do it. I'm so feeble-minded now I can't even remember the prodigal son story, but I'm pretty sure the son had to do something or admit something in order to come back. And he was at least healthy. Can't do it. I don't think I can ever do it.

Then, to complete a great day, I'm dragging my pitiful body up the little lane to the Pickwick so that I can collapse in my bed, and I notice a group of kids walking up ahead of me. They were the guys, at least some of them, from yesterday. Fortunately they didn't see me, and I ducked into a cafe, bought a paper, and waited till they were gone.

I'm probably cooked with M. Vadon and Moukerjee.

John:

12 March

Mr. William Truax
President, the Fiduciary Trust
P.O. Box 121
New Haven, Connecticut

Dear Bill,

Well!

Out to pasture, is it? Why do you say until September? Do you think I'll improve over the interim? Why do you say "rest and refreshment"? If you look closely at the period during which you find me "not myself," you will see that it follows the longest period of "rest and refreshment" I have ever had during a school year. I came back to Wells in February, Bill, because rest and refreshment was about to open its roaring jaws and swallow me up. I *am* myself. The petulant child, the erratic performer up north is I, Greeve. What you are finding fault with is not Greeve redux, but Greeve full throttle, prime Greeve, Greeve as he is.

I hope you know that I am more than able to throw up compelling, unanswerable defenses to all your claims. For one thing, I never pledged, nor would I ever pledge, to refrain from discussing disciplinary actions before the school. Moreover, you never insisted that I do so, you just asked. I'll have to hand it to you though, Truax, you do have your antennae up. The reason I will not throw up my (formidable) defenses is that frankly I did defy you.

I wrestled quite consciously with the issue of discussing the Wiseman boy before the school; it would have been relatively easy not to. At one point I almost phoned you to get an opinion. Then I decided I wouldn't. I knew what you'd say (and see, you've said it), and I knew what I would do. I just went ahead—same sort of jaw I've been giving for twenty years. I fully expected the stink. Just wanted you to know.

The Seven Schools athletic league business is both crucial to the coming year and not important at all. At its nub it's just like the drug discipline/legal business. We are either going to stand by what we always said is important about Wells, or we are going to be convenient. Convenience is easy and safe in these two instances, and evidently this appeals to you and to whomever you are talking to here.

You are right that there is something wrong with the tone of the place. This may be my fault. I'm not sure.

You are also right that I am behind in my board work. Contracts are late, budget is late. "Wells: Ten Years and After" is only embryonic. This is poor form. No excuses.

So out to pasture I go. Who knows about this? Everybody? Let's by all means get together first week in April, in New Haven. The finance committee should meet there too, while we're at it.

By the way, please do not get an outside man to preside during my Rest and Refreshment—unless you really want a new head. It would take him till September to find the Xerox paper. Let Phil Upjohn do it. He's not terribly good "up front," as you business fellows like to say, but he's very savvy about Wells, and the faculty trust him. He can do everything, even the diplomatic stuff, if he knows what's expected.

So it's bugger off, Greeve, is it? I feel like Willy Loman: really liked, really well liked.

Faithfully,

John

John:

14 March

MEMO
All Faculty

Colleagues—

Before we all depart for warmer climes, I want to thank you for your extra effort in bringing this term to a tidy conclusion. As I keep saying, it has not been an easy term. I will not now catalog my woes, except to acknowledge there were woes. You too have had woes.

I hope each of you enjoys the break, enjoyment richly deserved. Contracts will be awaiting you on your return. Sorry for the delay. As I said, woes.

Adios,

J.O.G.

John:

15 March

REMARKS TO THE SCHOOL

It strikes me that the next time you all assemble here many of you will be burnt brown, and all of you will be refreshed. It is easy to forget how important refreshment is: the break in the routine, the sudden change in plans, the surprise. I hope you find it a little refreshing that I am not bawling you out for something this morning. Various people have pointed out to me recently that I seem to be stuck in that groove. My apologies.

This morning I am not going to warn or denounce or complain. Rather, I would like to reflect for a moment in what is an important coming together in this year's religious calendar: Easter and Passover. It's a shame this year that the school's vacation rhythm scatters us all for these sacred holidays. The two events may have more to tell us than all of our other holidays combined.

Friday, April 2 will be both Good Friday and Passover, key moments in Easter and Passover Weeks, respectively. The two events falling on that Friday are not a coincidence; they are, at their heart, the same event. As Western Studies students will no doubt vividly recall, in mid-thirteenth century B.C. a reluctant upper class Hebrew named Moses began a series of demonstrations to convince the Egyptian pharaoh to free the enslaved Hebrews from their bondage and to allow them to seek their ancestral homeland. Pharaoh refused, and in response Moses was able either to visit a series of disasters on Egypt or, as some historians think, convince Pharaoh that a series of natural disasters was brought about by the Hebrews' God. At any rate, boils, locusts, frogs, foul water, and other harassments fell upon Egypt until finally a curse was placed on first born sons. Whether through disease or by the hand of the Angel of Death, Egyptian sons perished. Hebrew sons were saved, they believed, because they had dabbed the lintels of their doorways with the blood of sacrificial lambs. The Angel of Death passed over their households. In a fit of depression, Pharaoh, grieving the loss of his own son, let the Jews go.

You know the rest of the story. The Jews fled in a hurry, narrowly escaping, doubting bitterly that they would survive another generation. Yet through their struggle, they would develop what has been the most enduring religious creed in the western world.

A dozen centuries later another committed Jew, Jesus of Nazareth, would come to Jerusalem, as he and his family had done every year of his life, to celebrate Passover. Like Moses, he came to liberate his fellow Jews from bondage, but not bondage to the state; from, rather, bondage to selfish, shallow living. Like Moses, Jesus had a dramatic effect on people at first, but was doubted and betrayed by them later. Like Moses, Jesus would not live to see the fruits of his labors. In fact, Jesus had so offended the Hebrew establishment during his last Passover week, that, sensing trouble, he was forced to celebrate his Passover meal—his last supper—a day early and in secret.

This was Thursday. He seemed to know that the next day he would be lost to his friends and followers. The Angel of Death would not pass over him, he told them, but he would be the sacrificial lamb whose blood would allow them to live. No one understood any of this, and Jesus was arrested, tried hastily, and killed in the most brutal manner the state could devise.

At this, Jesus' followers scattered or went underground. Three days later, in many different reports, they claim to have seen him again, resurrected and alive. Convinced of this miracle, they spread the word that their leader and teacher had conquered death. This was the message that began the early church.

In a way, the Exodus of Moses and the Resurrection of Jesus are both great triumphs—without them there would be no Judaism or Christianity. Yet they are odd triumphs. Both events required great suffering and the loss of their respective heroes. That suffering and loss are essential to life is still a great mystery; for both Jews and Christians it is the mystery at the very center of life.

At one point during Passover week Jesus tries to explain the mystery to his disciples. These are his words:

> Verily, verily, I say unto you.
> Except a corn of wheat fall into the ground
> And die, it abideth alone; but if it die, it brings forth
> Much fruit. He that loves his life shall lose it;
> And he that hates his life in this world
> Shall keep it until eternal life.

This is what Jews and Christians celebrate in Passover and Easter. Have a joyful holiday.

Good morning.

Brian:

Essaouira

Sacked today. I couldn't handle my responsibilities as bus boy at the Hotel des Corsaires.

Moukerjee didn't even let me get started. He shooed me right out of the dining room and told me to see M. Vadon. Vadon didn't waste any words. He said, "We could not rely on you." I gave a feeble explanation about being so sick, and he said a sick person should not be around diners and food. Which makes excellent sense. I asked him if I could come back when I was better. He said no. I rested for a while on the porch, then went home.

The Arab kid who got into it with me a couple of days ago was hanging around the entrance to the Pickwick when I got back. He was by himself this time, and he didn't try anything. He did say, "Hey, English," when I passed him, and he made some kiss-y sounds. Something's up, not good.

Spent almost the whole afternoon dozing off and reading Avery's letters. They're so old and dried out, they're coming apart at the folds. They're mainly letters from his father. Most of them were written from Buenos Aires to Avery's school in England. They're very formal and distant, some advice, some household news. Strange batch of letters to take with you all over the world. His father has perfect, almost decorative handwriting.

The moral dilemma now is: am I going to help myself to Avery's kif? I can justify it as making amends for his not helping with the rent. I've also sworn off kif, but I can't see that it's going to be a factor in my job performance anymore. I doubt it could make me feel any worse, and, if I play it right, it may make me hungry, which I could use. Fact is there isn't a single thing I can imagine doing instead.

So bring on the Arabian Nights.

* * *

Preposterous two days. Now I remember what I don't like about dope. It's the woozy going in and out of your skin. The buzz isn't really that great, but you get the feeling, mid-buzz, that it's just about to be, so you decide to go for it and smoke a lot.

My time sense is really screwed up when I'm high. I don't know if I'm doing something for a few minutes or two hours. It didn't make me hungry. It didn't make me feel better, and it didn't for a minute make me forget I was sick. No profound visions. Now I'm two days older, and when I turn my head suddenly or look up from the paper in a cafe, it's like the inside of my head is following my vision out through my eye holes. I know this will pass, if I don't smoke any more, but I don't like it much.

Maybe too much of my head has already leaked away. Today I read "The Grand Inquisitor" again in *The Brothers Karamazov*, and it didn't get to me. I remember reading it for the first time at Amherst and thinking it was the saddest and the most powerful thing I had ever read. Today it just seemed like a long lecture. I found myself liking Christ just because I knew he wasn't going to say much. Maybe I'm losing my taste for reading and thinking completely.

I'm sure I'd read better and deeper if I knew more. I hate feeling like I don't have enough background to get what you're supposed to get from literature. Even though I studied *Brothers Karamazov* in a course and took my share of history, I really don't know enough to get what I'm supposed to get. I don't know much about the Inquisition in Spain. I don't know how it was actually set up, especially what was going on in Seville, when the episode takes place. I don't know enough about the history and doctrine of the church to know if the Inquisitor is making terrific points about society, and I don't even know enough about the Bible to know if Jesus's temptations by the devil are being represented accurately. Like a good student, I should go look these things up, but is that what reading is? I want to *know* these things, to know them in deep memory the way my mother and father do. I want to be crossword puzzle smart.

* * *

THE SELF TAUGHT BALLOON

I have a huge, smart head.
Like a dirigible.
(careful, careful—
You'll jar the categories)
Mustn't make me laugh
Or give me a beer
And no rough talk.

Dante Humming,
Newton Ticking,
Little clerks must copy right.

It's huge, just huge.
I'd like to lean it on a tree,
But then I'd spill my metrics
Into sociology.

I always walk on tippy toe.
I know all there is to know

* * *

Today I paid the month's rent, packed all Avery's stuff away into his bag and checked it downstairs at the desk. It felt funny doing that, like saying good-bye to him forever. I have a Buenos Aires address for his father. It's ten years old, but I might write him a note and see what happens. Where could Avery be without a passport or his clothes? I can't stand thinking that he's dead, but I guess it's possible.

I also found a laundry on the other side of the medina, and I've taken practically everything I own there. I haven't had really clean clothes since Señora Carerra did them for us in San Rafael. Meanwhile, I'd like to get a handle on what was going on with the little gang of Arabs who were interested in me last week. If they mean business, I better get out of here.

I keep coming back to why the hell I should be in danger? I have to be the most harmless person in Africa. I don't know what Avery was up to, but I haven't done anything wrong in Essaouira except maybe spread my germs around. Too bad this city can't be what it looks like from the porch of the Hotel des Corsaires: a whitewashed settlement of fishermen and box makers. The city's been built and paid for for two hundred years. It's the sardine capital of the universe. There's plenty to eat, nice weather all year round, plenty of hands to do what needs to be done. Why isn't this the happiest, lovingest, most relaxed city in the world? There isn't even a Dominant Paradigm to overcome. There probably is and I'm too dense to see it.

But people are uptight here. My landlord's depressed, Dr. Habib is depressed, M. Vadon is depressed. Moukerjee is uptight. Those Arab thugs are wired, Hal's wired, Avery was wired. It should be easy to relax and be good to one another any place in the world, but it should be especially easy here. What's wrong with people? It could be done. Why did the sixties people give up?

* * *

Greeves Passing

HIS VOICE IN THE STREETS

The citizens awoke as one
To find their tables set with gifts
Of cakes and cream and dewy fruit.
At midday women at their wash
Disarmed with smiles the garrison
And romped with soldiers round the well.
That evening only finger tips
Tracing the shoulder's cool curve
Could say what lovers have to say,
And those who in the dawning saw
The sun tint each thing peach,
Marveled at such mute concern.

* * *

Hauled my clean clothes back from the laundry today. When I got to the door of the Pickwick, I saw that the Arab group had been following me up the street. Now I'm all dressed up and no place to go. Terrific.

Extremely pissed off and kind of jumpy, I smoked the last of Avery's kif—terrible idea, made me very paranoid, woozy, and the room looks so cock-eyed when I stand up. Jerk!

* * *

I didn't go outside or eat anything all day yesterday because the Arabs were there, and this morning I'm not even hungry. I'm not anything. I can't imagine eating, I can't imagine sex, I can't imagine hiking or swimming or playing tennis or coming up with a new idea. I know I'm sick, but I can't remember what well feels like. I don't believe I'll ever get well.

* * *

This morning I woke up, went out to the lavatory and saw that my urine was black. Nightmare time. No Arabs on the street, but I decided not to risk it and badgered Akbar, the landlord, to let me call a cab from his rooms. I told him I was very ill, and I was so shaky he believed me. I took the cab to Habib, who had a full house ahead of me as usual. By the time he saw me, I was back under control. With lousy French and a few gestures I got across that I had a urine problem—"C'est *noir! Noir!*" Like a man practically dead himself, he got me a glass bowl and told me to go behind a screen and use it. I did, and there it was again, in more light, black. Even he looked concerned when he saw it. "My friend," he said, "That is very bad. You are ill, you really must go home." I asked him if he was going to do anything for me. He said he would prescribe an antibiotic, but that I must go somewhere that had facilities that could take care of me properly. I remembered about my allergic reaction to penicillin, and he said he would prescribe something else.

I got really mad at him then. I was also pretty scared. Was another bottle of pills all he could come up with? What was wrong with my urine? I pointed to my sickening sample in the dish. What was wrong with it? He looked confused. *"Noir!"* I said again. "Pourquoi?"

He said something in French I didn't understand. Then he said it in English: blood.

John:

> 31 March
> Little House

Mr. Clifford Bennett
Trust Department
The Fiduciary Trust Company
New Haven, Connecticut

Dear Cliff,

Thanks for the time on the phone. I've drawn up a fair semblance of what you said would go down in the courts. It's basically very simple. The important thing, I think, is that you and others at Fiduciary are clear of the intent. Here is the gist.

Upon my death I would like my wife's and my share of Little House and the yawl, *Valmar,* which we also owned jointly with my brother Frank, to go to him and his wife. The rest, such as it is, should be divided as follows: one-third to Wells School for whatever purposes its trustees may choose; the other two-thirds I would like you to hold in trust for seven years for my son, Brian, who has been a missing person for some time, but possibly not lost. If after seven years Brian has not claimed his share, then I would like to give it to my nephew, Hugh Greeve, my brother Frank's son.

Enclosed is a more formal statement of the arrangement, witnessed as you stipulated, by Herb Jenkins, proprietor of the East Sandwich Boatyard. Herb is a notary and has also notarized it.

I have also written and sealed a letter to my son which I would like my executors to hold for him until what time, if any, he can be found.

I thank you once again, Cliff, for the impeccable service you have given my family, especially since Meg's passing. You do your work credit.

Sincerely,

John Greeve

* * *

DISPOSITION OF ESTATE

I, John Greeve, being of sound mind and sure judgment, do hereby make on the date indicated below, the following disposition upon my death of my effects and possessions and of all property, revenue, dividends, and interest owned by me or due me.

1. My share of the property of Little House, 9 Ticonsett Lane, East Sandwich, Commonwealth of Massachusetts, shall pass to my brother Francis Greeve, of Tarrytown, New York.

2. My share of the yawl, *Valmar,* shall likewise pass to my brother, Francis Greeve.

3. A partition of one-third of my remaining estate shall in a manner determined and directed by executors appointed by the Fiduciary Trust Company of New Haven, be given over to Wells School, Wells, Connecticut, as a gift. I understand that no special purpose or qualification shall impede the use of this gift by Wells School. Wells School may receive this gift in furniture, library documents, vehicles, or other portable property; or as cash value of such property sold at auction; or as cash and securities from my estate. The determination of the partition, the management of auction or auctions, and the transfer of all cash and securities will be directed by my executors.

4. The remaining share of my estate, in no way including or overlapping the dispositions stated in items one, two and three, shall pass to my son, Brian Greeve, provided he is located and can make a claim to this disposition within seven years from the date of this document.

If after seven years no claim is made by my son on this part of my estate, it shall pass forthwith to my nephew, Hugh Greeve.

This statement is composed in the presence of Herbert Jenkins of East Sandwich, Massachusetts on March 31, ____.

_____

John Oberon Greeve

(Signed)

March 31, ____

_____

(Witnessed) Herbert Paul Jenkins

(Signed)

March 31, ____

_____

(Notarized) Herbert Paul Jenkins

March 31, ____

Brian:

Moved out of the Pickwick today and into a guest cottage at Hotel des Corsaires. It felt like D-Day. The bastard Akbar was put out that I was leaving and almost refused to let me use his phone to call for a car. No help with my bags, just a sullen look. I've never been gladder to leave a place in my life than I was to get out of the Pickwick with its dark hallways and sour stink.

I needed a place where I can get food sent in, where I'm not wondering if those guys are going to crash into my room and finish me off. At first M. Vadon gave me a bad time about checking in, but we could both see the place was practically deserted, and I guess he decided my money was as good as anybody's. My money. I brought about $220 with me. I was actually hoping I could get away with running up a bill while I got my strength back, but Vadon wanted to know how long I planned to stay, and he wanted to be paid in advance. Bastard. The cottages are cheap, but not that cheap. I told him I thought I'd stay for two weeks, and he said that would be two thousand and some dirham—more than all I had. I told him I'd pay him for the first week now and the rest when my father wired me some money from home. "So then you are staying a week," he said. Bastard. By the time I was done talking to him, I was so whipped and spacey, I would have agreed to anything if I could just be in a bed in a room by myself.

The cottage is right off the deck of the pool. It is white stone with a dark blue door, and if I could afford it, I would live in it the rest of my life.

Inside is just as white and blue as the outside. The linen is clean and stiff with starch. There is a tray of mineral water on the bedside table. The room is very pale and bright, even with the shades pulled down. Flashing white light leaks in around the edges of the windows, and the reflections off the pool make wavery lines up the walls. I keep feeling I'm floating up from the bed toward the ceiling. I'm out of it, but no pain.

* * *

TO MY MOTHER AND FATHER

Shortly after I arrived in Europe and started making my way aimlessly around, I made a vow to myself, and because of that vow, I stopped writing home. My vow was that I would not be in touch with you again until I completed a transition I was going through. It's hard to explain. You can probably remember how sour and out of it I was acting the last time we were together. Believe me, that had nothing to do with you or with Aunt Val or Uncle Frank or Hugh or anybody at Wells. It was all me. I was going crazy. Wells felt so small and so familiar that each little routine, each sight of a Wells kid with his jacket and tie and beat up shoes made me want to get out of there as fast as I could.

I knew I was out of that cycle forever, and I wanted to be out of it. But I didn't know what I was supposed to do or where I fit in. You didn't really give me a hard time about that, but I could literally feel you waiting for me to make some kind of productive move. There's nothing unreasonable in a parent doing that. What else could you do? But there's some deep, deep orneriness in me that can't stand anybody wanting anything out of me. Believe me, I'm not proud of that, but it's the way I am. That ornery part—it's like a nerve—is the part of me that's most alive. It's me, actually.

When I got here and started hanging around Amsterdam, I didn't feel much better. I was still pretty defensive and generally not too pleasant. I'd go through long mind games where the western world was a terrible, corrupted place that wasn't worth living in, and then I'd swing back into incredible fits of self-criticism and panic about having no job prospects, about not finishing Amherst, about not knowing enough or how to do anything people valued. I got to the point where I'd hear a good folksinger in a club, and I'd have two days of depression thinking about my lack of musical ability. I'd read a great book and feel stupid for a week. And all the time, and this is *not your fault*—I'd be thinking about you at home at Wells, drinking tea in the living room, wedged in there with all the chairs and sofas and cushions and carpets and pictures and clocks and little statues. I knew you were worried about what would happen to me, and that drove my anxiety out of control.

I finally met some people I liked, a couple with open-ended plans for the summer, and we decided to travel together. That seemed to be the start of something, and I knew it was only going to work if I could somehow chuck my other baggage, so I did. I made a vow that I was going to do my best to forget measuring up to external standards forever. I had standards. I like people. I have an eye for things. I value telling the truth and being told the truth. I also realized I have a huge capacity for loving people, both in the romantic way and in the general way. That and my health and my $3,600 in traveler's checks seemed as if it should have been enough.

I know it was hurtful to you to cut myself off like that, but it felt terrific to make that decision, to start inventing my days and being myself, whatever that would turn out to be. I almost wrote to *tell* you I was going to cut myself off, but that felt too much like asking for permission. I didn't want your permission. But please accept my apologies for any worry and bad feelings I have caused you.

I wish there were wonderful, inspiring results to report from my personal odyssey, but the fact is, I'm in a bad way as I write this. I'm telling you that up front so if you ever read this, you'll understand why I sound this way.

After Amsterdam my friends and I took a ferry over to England, went up north to Scotland (took my last mass on the Isle of Iona). Then down through the south to Cornwall and Land's End. Then all over France, over the Pyrenees into Spain, westward through Spain to Portugal, where we actually lived for a while in a fishing village on the ocean. That was maybe my best time. Beach and thinking during the day, wine and friends at night. No obligations, no schedule, just taking in the colors and the smells and whatever came to mind. One thing that came to mind was starting up a diary, and for the first time I've actually managed to keep it going. Our little household in San Rafael broke up when my friends decided they needed to go back to the States, one to graduate school, the other to paint.

That left me, and I bummed around Portugal and Spain for awhile on my own, but my heart wasn't really in it, and after a week or so I wasn't feeling very well physically -- kind of fluey, no-energy feeling, like mono. I met a guy in southern Spain who told me Morocco was the place to go for the winter, cheap, exotic, etc. I went with him, first to Tangier, then to a city down the Atlantic coast called Essaouira. I was down to about $2,000 by this time, and I needed a place where I could stay put, rest, and try to get rid of my crud.

I haven't gotten rid of it, although I did manage to get rid of my $2,000. Right now, as I write this, I'm really sick. Nothing works, I have no appetite, I'm out of it most of the day, and I'm passing blood. That sounds really terrible, but I'm actually in a way better frame of mind than I was a week ago. I'm light-headed, and my breathing is very shallow and a little panicky, but I feel very light and thin, in a good way. There's no real pain, and I'm staying in a clean, white, beautiful place.

I can imagine you saying, why didn't you let us know? Why didn't you call? And you should know that a couple of weeks ago I actually got in line at the American Express office to wire you, actually tried to put a call through at the post office, but then I chickened out. As bad as I am, the vow still stands. Sick and pitiful as I was, I still felt I knew, or was getting to know, who I was. When I thought clearly about going home and being home, I felt like someone was shutting off my air, and it would last forever. I'm sure that makes no sense.

I'm actually feeling pretty shaky right now, so I'm going to have to get down to the point. What I've learned is that I'm a lot like you, I'm full of you, each of you. I have some of your looks, your mannerisms, even your tastes. I've done some guttery things and stayed in some real holes, but you might be interested to know I keep a jacket and tie, and when I reach my own sleaze limit, I spiff up and go to tea at the poshest hotel in town. I know myself well enough to know that I have to have it both ways.

So you go deep in me, and I really think some of the best things about me are the result of that. But the very fact of knowing that raises the question, what's my part, where do I begin and you leave off? Starting with my Wells years, that became an obsession. Sometimes I hated feeling so anti-you, but anything else felt like I was smothering. That's why I had to keep falling away. You were always fair, always reasonable—personally and publicly. You were so right you were actually wrong. If you really had been selfish, establishment, materialist bastards, it would have been easy for me, I could have kept my distance from that and set up on my new ground. But you weren't like that. You never said, this is it, measure up or get out. You were just nice and concerned. And I never did measure up. I had to reject the whole idea of measuring up in order to stay alive, not that I've done a very good job of staying alive.

Here is something you should know. I haven't been too bad, morally, and that is completely your influence. I've drunk some wine and smoked some dope, but I haven't gotten hooked on anything. I've actually been too sick to be decadent. I've met some people I've cared about, but no real romance and not much sex. I've paid my bills, kept my commitments (not that I've had a lot), and have been straight with people. I've read hard at a few great books, and I think there would have been more of this if I had been feeling better. I actually think I have some kind of brain. I get interested in psychological questions naturally—anything to do with people's motivations fascinate me. If I were the academic type, that's what I would do. I can't compare it to anyone else's, but I think I also have a huge capacity to respond to beautiful things, especially landscapes and buildings. That here-come-the-tears feeling comes up fast and strong whenever I catch sight of the real thing. In fact, I wish you could stand with me on the main porch of this hotel and look out—straight into the Atlantic, empty beach forever to your left, a magical medieval city behind white, white walls to your right. It's the port, the sea, and a kind of heaven all arranged in the same composition. Being able to paint it would be a talent, and I haven't got it, but it's still a great thing to be able to see it and feel it. Not everybody does. What I'm saying is that if you had been in touch with me, even if you had been watching me the whole time over your shoulders, I don't think you'd be too disappointed or ashamed. (*Have* you been watching over my shoulder?)

And please don't misunderstand the things I said first, about you and about Wells. For you, your things, your school routines, your books and your crossword puzzles are right. They are genuinely distinctive. They are admirable. But they're kind of like your clothes, just right for you, but I could never wear them.

Before I came inside to write this, I was out on that porch I described. I was looking out over the Atlantic to the Northwest and feeling I was looking directly at you. In fact, if you happened to be on the dock at Little House and were looking slightly southeast, you were looking right back at me. For some reason, I've never been able to go inland and stay there since I've been traveling, so maybe we're more connected than I thought.

I'm rambling now. I meant to say that none of what I said above is a criticism or a complaint about you or the way you live or the way you were with me. You were good to me—God only knows if you were good for me—and I know that if you could have figured out a way to be even better, you would have done that too.

I haven't been nearly so good in return. But my motive wasn't dislike or disapproval. I needed to stay alive. No great success there either.

So bless you. You are great to each other and with each other. I wish you happiness for as long as you live, and I love you.

* * *

IN THE REALM WHERE TIME GOES ON

Where late afternoon's clear blue
Does not deepen, but opens ever wider,
Where it is eternally not yet time
For another meal, where no stirring
Of sex jumps the pulse, no impulse
Even to browse through papers at hand;

Where John is married to Margaret,
Where seated before a bank of roses, they note
A tabby arching himself, archly.
And the hint of mockery has fallen away
From gallantry, and wit grown loving
Is sooner recalled than spoken.

John:

                        31 March
                        Little House

Dear Brian,

In earlier letters to you, unclaimed and unanswered, I tried to explain how hard it was expressing things to someone who might not be there. In the event that you are there and one day read this, you will know what I mean.

If, when you come home, you will want information, history, Frank and Val will have that. Rely on them for as long as you need. Both of them care about you. I do want you to know, though, that tonight I am fairly clear headed, although not too hot physically. I am steady about your mother's loss this past winter, steady but not "adjusted" to it.

The most recent intelligence I have on you is that your passport was turned over to the police some months ago in Tangier. A lady in an agency told me to expect the worst, which I do.

I am not a desperate man, the way you might think of one in a movie or a Poe story. I feel used up, overcome, gnawed on by irritations which, if I admit them fully to consciousness, will turn out to be the Furies themselves. What I am trying to say, Brian, is that I am not crazy. But I am finished.

This is even harder than I thought. Now my head is full of you, memories of you. Memories of all of us. A pitiful image of you keeps cropping up, like something in Dickens: you return this summer with your knapsack, sunburnt, cheery, perhaps even with a pal or a girl, to surprise Meg and me, maybe even to make some sort of end-of-adolescence, commencement-of-manhood reconciliation, only to find out that your mother and I have, as the Wells boys say, checked out. Just a picture, not what I think will happen, not even necessarily what I want. It's a picture to hurt myself with, because I can't imagine, should that scene ever happen, your being able to handle it. It is a picture of you as me now. Me not you. Every bubble bursts back to me. It should make me sad not to believe in the picture—the part about your coming home gladly to see us—but I don't. I don't think you are alive, Brian. I don't think you are glad or were ever glad in your travels. I think that you are dead and that you died in terror, possibly not in your right mind. I don't think you thought much about your mother and me, which is not to say we weren't crucial anyway. I think your runaways, your school rebellions, your silences, your frightening flights of fantasy when you were little—I think all of them were ways of negating us. Now we are negated, but by our own demons and diseases, not by you. You hurt us, Brian, because you wouldn't let us know how we hurt you. You hurt us, but you didn't kill us. May you live.

Your mother was 34, and I was 33 when we had you. There had been lots of gynecological problems and failures, but then it finally worked. No child was ever more wanted. But we were aware of that, and like intelligent educators steeped in child development, we vowed not to smother you. From the beginning you were given real liberty—and we watched in fear for liberty to fail. Did it? Or was it the watching and assessing and worrying on our parts? Maybe granting liberty negates the liberty. I'm back to "negates." I wish I knew the answers. I was only the father of you, just that once. I was not really very confident about it. I think I was a good teacher (why be modest?). As a teacher and usually as a headmaster, I was very sure, which made me seem even strong at times. But not as a father. As a father, I always felt I was guessing. I felt I was guessing, and I felt you knew I was guessing. I didn't know whether to hit you or hold you, whether to make you turn the light out and go to sleep or to turn up the light so you could see what you were doing. What did I do? I think I generally went on down the hall, thinking about it. Thinking a lot about it. Oh,

Brian! What I wanted was for you to be admirable without ever being told to or told how—to surprise me with your brains and skill and splendid qualities, qualities that would burst forth simply because you were ours and we were good. I wanted you to be happy, one-of-a-kind, passionate, imaginative. I wanted to follow your happiness and be happy about it, like the dads whose hearts thrill in the stands when their sons hit a long ball. Any old kind of long ball would have been fine with me. But you sensed me in the stands. I was not only a dad in the stands but a headmaster in the stands. I don't like to think about that.

I was glad to be head of Wells, Brian. I think I was good at it, and I think people who knew thought I was good at it. I was better than old-fashioned. Like Socrates, but less purely, I had my "little voice" and it told the hard truth. I also had something else that was good for a school—I loved the culture. Not everything, not the whole mess, but the triumphs of its buildings, its pictures, its literature especially, at least the English pockets of it I knew. It is great to love some things like that and stand by them, to be able to pass them on with energy and conviction. What am I talking about? Headmastering. That's what I was. It was good for me, but not for you.

Your mother was headmaster, too, even more so. Her judgment was better, she could take more stress, and she was funnier. Your mother was the greatest talker I have ever known—and that includes some good ones at Cambridge. She was company, Brian. I loved her every minute I knew her, and I love her still. She would say the same, I think. That is rare, Brian, and that is good. It must have been good for you too. It must have been. I don't want to sadden you, but to reassure you, by saying you were obsessively in her thoughts during her illness.

Guilt is inherent to life. If you are alive—may you live—you are feeling guilty. Do not feel excessively so on our account. We lived richly, and, as I say, loved. We didn't collapse because you wandered away from us. Which is not to say, sonny boy, that you don't owe us a few. As the world reckons, we were pretty nice folks, pretty damned nice parents. You got clothed, held, fed, sent-to, given-to, sat up with, nursed, even cultured by some pretty good people. So while a long ball is not really necessary, your very kindest, truest self would be much appreciated.

We are forever in the stands, kid. Sorry. We love and loved you.

Dad.

John:

                                          31 March
                                          Little House

Val and Frank,

Jenkins has mercifully turned on the gas.

This is not a tragedy. I am used up—Meg in December. You were family and I love you for it.

J.

John:

31 March

Mrs. Dorothy Weimer
Editor, the Wells Quarterly
Gibbs House Annex
Wells School
Wells, Connecticut

Dear Dottie,

Enclosed is a submission for the Spring number.

I know we don't print poems as a rule, but since there will be no Headmaster's Letter, maybe you could work it in.

Best to you,

John

A SCHOOL MASTER CONSIDERS SCHOOL

Like the seasons but wordier
History teaching history
A dark road stretching back, back
And I have stepped aside
Just long enough to think about it
And its memory
Is big and drab and urgent
There is something old fashioned about it
Of oak desks and ink wells
Waxed floors and the cane
Of footsteps along cold stone walks
Hurtful days, stained through
With some pulsing infatuation
Days, just days
Fright of first days, waiting days
Proud days, prize days
A sudden recognition
Of cruelty or some small excellence
Days, dressed for school days
Tom Brown's school days
Every school day that ever was
Romeo's, Cicero's,
All Hellas at their little lyres
A bright road opening wide to me
Ghost children chanting something
About verbs
They are cheering in waves
Hymns from voices clear and sad
And gone as bells
Hurrying bells, evening bells
School bells banging me back
To school.

Brian

I may have laughed my last laugh. When I realized I couldn't hold the ledger up and write in bed anymore because the weight of it against my gut hurts too much, I thought: well, book, you've outgrown me.

Fact is, the book's as much me as I am, at least now.

One good thing. I pushed the foot of my bed over, so it's lined up with the window in the door. Even lying down flat I can look over my toes and see the sun on the blue green water in the pool. No deck, no chairs, no building, just flashes of light on aquamarine. It is so beautiful. I like knowing that it's out there, that things like that are true.

AUTHOR'S NOTE

Revisiting previously published work is an emotionally charged business. Doing so with an eye to altering and expanding it is downright perilous. The peril lies in ruining what one has taken great care to get right the first time.

With those considerations firmly in mind, I did revisit two previously published novels, *The Headmaster's Papers* (1983) and *the Headmaster's Wife* (2000) with the clear intention of completing the story—not those two individual stories, but a larger one in which they both participated; thus this "novel-in-fugue."

Writers, even when they are being forthright, are not always clear or accurate about the origins of their characters and their situations. While other writers are certainly entitled to believe they have created their characters, I feel I have discovered mine. Whatever their origin, mine tend to arrive whole and fully formed before I begin transcribing them. This was certainly the case with John Greeve, the narrator of *Headmaster's Papers*. When I wrote the book I was working in a school, a private boys' day school in Cleveland, Ohio, but I was not then, like Greeve, a headmaster. While I liked and admired the man, I was not in age, background, or manner of expression anything like him. Nor was he like my own headmaster, Rowland Paull McKinley, a figure worthy of his own school saga. My school was not in structure or feel like Wells School in the novel, and its faculty and boys were not my colleagues and students in disguise. Before I wrote a word of *Headmaster's Papers* I felt I knew John Greeve as a distinct presence. I knew what was in his closet and in his desk drawers.

When the manuscript was finished and the book published, I felt I had got John Greeve right. A number of readers wrote to me objecting on either emotional or moral grounds to John's seeming failure to thrive at the novel's conclusion. I was interested in these responses but could not imagine Greeve, being who he was, behaving other than he did at novel's end.

For years after its publication I continued to think, even a little obsessively, about the little world described in *Headmaster's Papers*. I did not think about specific incidents that occurred nor even, much, about John Greeve. What I could not stop thinking about was Greeve's wife, Meg, who becomes ill with cancer and dies midway through the school year. Meg was the central, most beloved, most trusted and needed figure in John Greeve's life, and after a suitable period of coming to terms with this realization, I was determined to write her story, which became *The Headmaster's Wife*.

Writing Meg's life in her voice, I felt I was inhabiting her, not fashioning her. I suspect this is what serious actors feel when they lose themselves in the character of a role they are playing. When I was not writing/inhabiting her, when I stepped aside to think about what I was doing, I realized I was a little in love with her—and thus had a vivid intimation of John's love for her.

I had not finished writing *Headmaster's Wife* when it became obvious to me that the great ache, the great void in her life was caused by her emotionally and then literally elusive son Brian who, as a young man, departs the country to travel around Europe, from which he seems to vanish. In my view, Meg's story ends, though sadly, as it inevitably had to.

There was clearly more story, more necessary story, and I began work on Brian immediately on finishing Meg. At this point, some highly distracting personal and professional factors arose that made it impossible to pursue the publication of what I had planned to call *The Journal of Brian Greeve*. Among other things, a number of my other manuscripts were queued up at different points along the publication process. At this point too, my hardback publisher, the late Paul Eriksson, had decided to retire. In the only conversation we had about *The Journal of Brian Greeve* he confided to me that, due to developments in his personal life, he could not bear to think about lost children, much less publish a book about one.

At this point in my life there were enough other matters to attend to and enough other books in the works that I was more than happy to let Brian's story simmer for a while. At length, however, it was clear to me: that neither John nor Meg nor Brian can be fully conveyed apart from the others. Although I did not know it earlier, their combined stories were The Story all along, and thus the production of *Greeves Passing*.

Even after so much time in their company, I cannot reliably account for why the Greeves came to bear on my life as they have. What I have to say about them I have written, to which I can add only that I miss all three of them.

        R.A.H.
        Ripton, Vermont
        September 1, 2014